Michael's
THE · NEW GUIDE

TURKEY

THE NEW GUIDE
Michael's
TURKEY

Managing Editor
Michael Shichor

Series Editor
Amir Shichor

INBAL TRAVEL INFORMATION LTD.

Inbal Travel Information Ltd.
P.O.Box 1870 Ramat Gan 52117
Israel

Intl. ISBN 965-288-117-1

Text: Menachem (Chemi) Shkolnik
Graphic design: Michel Opatowski
Cover design: Bill Stone
Photography: Sharon Bentov
Photo editor: Claudio Nutkiewicz
Editorial: Sharona Johan, Or Rinat, Lisa Stone
D.T.P.: Michael Michelson
Printed by Havatzelet Press Ltd.

**Sales in the UK
and Europe:**
Kuperard (London) Ltd.
9 Hampstead West
224 Iverson Road
London NW6 2HL

**Distribution in the UK
and Europe:**
Bailey Distribution Ltd.
Learoyd Road
New Romney
Kent TN28 8X

U.K. ISBN 1-85733-114-1

CONTENTS

TABLE OF MAPS

Preface

There are few countries which have undergone as many changes as Turkey. Turkey is the historical bridge between east and west, Europe and Asia. Almost every nation that has set foot in this diverse land has left its mark – from the Accadians and Assyrians, the Hittites and Greeks, to Alexander the Great and the Romans, as well as the Byzantines and Ottomans. Present day Turkey is, to a large extent, the outcome of a man of vision and strength: Atatürk, who strove to westernize Turkey with a strong European influence.

Turkey's historical and cultural wealth includes a wide range of mosques, churches, ancient cities and historical and archeological sites. But that is not all; Turkey has also been blessed with a beautiful and richly varied landscape – lovely beaches on the Mediterranean and Aegean coasts, large flat plains and mountain ranges that slope down to the sea.

Turkey caters to the needs and tastes of any tourist. In the West, one can find fascinating sites alongside holiday resorts set on beautiful shores. Those in search of adventure can head for the exotic East, a region that is as yet unknown to the western tourist. No one can afford to give İstanbul a miss – the city in which past and present live comfortably side by side.

The sheer size of Turkey and its numerous sites, make it necessary to plan your trip carefully and in as much detail as possible. Whatever information you need for making your arrangements can be found in our guide. In addition to an introduction that discusses the country's history and culture, you will find here many suggestions, recommendations and instructions, as well as routes and ideas that will help you enjoy what this wonderful country has to offer.

Chemi Shkolnik, a seasoned traveler who spent some years touring Asia, Europe and America, devoted many months to acquaint himself with Turkey, and he has collated here a great deal of data from his own experiences and from those of others who have fallen under Turkey's spell.

I am convinced that your travels in Turkey will turn into a fascinating journey, fondly remembered years from now. Touring Turkey is a different and enriching experience that is not easily forgotten.

Michael Shichor

Using this Guide

In order to reap maximum benefit from the information in this guide, we advise the traveler to carefully read the following passage. The facts contained in this book were compiled to help the tourist find his or her way around and to ensure that he enjoys his stay to the upmost.

The Introduction provides details which will help you make the early decisions and arrangements for your trip. We suggest that you carefully review the material, so that you will be more organized and set for your visit. Upon arrival in Turkey, you will feel more familiar and comfortable with the country.

The suggested routes are arranged according to geographical areas, a system that allows for an efficient division of time and ensures a thorough knowledge of each region. More so, this guide will direct you to unexpected places that you may not have heard of and did not plan to visit.

The chapters on main cities include maps and indexes of sites that will help you find your way. On reaching each city, the guide will direct you to recommended accommodation and restaurants.

The rich collection of maps covers the tour routes and special attractions in great detail. Especially prepared for this book, they will certainly add to the efficiency and pleasure of your exploration of Turkey.

The Turkish language is probably unlike any language you are familiar with. For your convenience, therefore, we have added a short dictionary containing some basic words; these may help you while traveling around the country.

To further facilitate the use of this guide, we have included a detailed index. It includes all the major sites mentioned throughout the book. Consult the index to find something by name and it will refer you to the place where it is mentioned in greatest detail.

During your visit you will see and experience many things – we have therefore left several blank pages at the back of the guide. These are for you, to jot down those special experiences from people and places, feelings and significant happenings along the way.

Because times and cities are dynamic, an important rule of thumb when traveling, and especially when visiting a country like Turkey, should be to consult local sources of information. Tourists are liable to encounter certain inaccuracies in this guide, and for this we apologize.

In this guide we have tried to present updated information in a way which allows for an easy, safe and economical visit. For this purpose, we have included a short questionnaire and will be most grateful for those who will take the time to complete it and send it to us.

Have a pleasant and exciting trip – Bon Voyage!

PART ONE:

GETTING TO KNOW TURKEY

History

At a glance, Turkey's cultural development can confuse the tourist who is not a historian. Throughout history, Turkey has acted as a bridge between Asia in the East and Europe in the West. New forces rose from within, strengthened their reign and then fell in favour of newer forces, all leaving their mark on the fabric of history.

Initial evidence

Cave drawings, primitive utensils and a Neanderthal skull discovered in Karain, near Antalya on the Mediterranean shore, suggest that the area was home to a ten thousand-year old civilization during the paleolithic age. This (and other evidence) tells of an agricultural society that hunted, using tools of stone and bone. Other discoveries from the neolithic period, uncovered in excavations carried out in Hacılar, bear witness to the fact that this was a society that dwelled in both villages and fortressed towns. Stone utensils disappeared with the advent of clay and bronze. It has also transpired that this civilization led a highly developed cultural life, one that included fertility and hunting rites.

The third millennium BC saw the Hattians develop trading ties with the neighbouring Accadian kings. Rich in natural resources, the land attracted Assyrian traders who settled in the Cappadocia region. Early Accadian parchments first mention Turkey as a Hattian kingdom. Other evidence points to trade relations between Troy and the states of the Aegean shores. An impressive exhibition of relics from this period can be found at the Museum of Anatolian Cultures in Ankara.

The great conquests

The Hittites (1750-1180 BC), Indian-African tribes that arrived from Asia in the third millennium BC, conquered Anatolia (the Asian part of Turkey) and established one of the three greatest forces of the ancient world. The Hittites made their capital in Hattuşaş, (to the east of present-day Ankara), building an impressive fortress in its center. In addition to fortifications, the Hittite age excelled in the construction of large palaces and temples. The empire finally fell in 1180 BC, defeated by the Trakyan tribes who came from West Bosphorus. It was at this time too that Troy fell, thereby clearing the path for Greek settlement along the coasts of the Aegean and Black seas.

Following the fall of Hattuşaş, Asia was left without a major governing force. Therefore, independent city-states were formed by emigrants from Greece, who defended themselves against the attacks of nomadic tribes. The Greek towns were built mainly along the Aegean shore by migrating tribes who were united through various charters and treaties. To the east, the kingdom of Urartu grew and strengthened, while in the north, along the Black Sea, Milettian colonies were established. The center and west of Anatolia saw the rise of the Phrygian kingdom that reached its pinnacle in the eight century BC under the reign of Midas, "the king with the golden touch". The Assyrian kingdom took advantage of the vacuum created by the absence of a central governing

An exhibit at the Archeological Museum in İstanbul

force, and spread into Asia Minor; an expansion which was finally completed with the fall of Carchemish. 1180-546 BC.

The Persians – Cyrus the Great, King of Persia, conquered Asia Minor in 546 BC, including the Greek settlements on the Aegean coast, among them Smyrna (today İzmir) and Ephesus, in which a highly developed Greek culture had flowered under Persian rule.

These Greek coastal settlements united with Athens in a revolt against Persia, but were defeated in 449 BC. The two great wars waged by the Persians against Athens ended in Persian defeat, due to the latter's brilliant military strategy. The ground had now been laid for Alexander the Great to make his grand entrance into the world arena.

The Hellenistic period

Few monarchs have fired the imagination as did Alexander the Great. Philip II, the Macedonian king and Alexander's father, was determinated to liberate the Greek settlements on the Aegean coast from Persian rule, but was murdered in 336 BC before achieving his goal. Alexander, then barely twenty years of age, ascended the throne and set out to fulfil his father's dream. He moved his forces to Asia Minor over the Dardanelles. The decisive battle against the Persians took place in 334 BC on the shores of the Garnikus River. The Persians were defeated, and the road to Asia lay open to Alexander. The young king's troops swept through Asia Minor and the Middle East, reaching India to the East and Egypt to the South.

Alexander died at the age of 33, and with him perished his dream of

The statue of snake-haired Medusa at Didim

building an empire that would combine western (Greek) and eastern (Mesopotamian) cultures. The Hellenistic rulers who inherited his kingdom – though not his wisdom – divided the land between them. Among them were Lysimachus, King of Trakya, and Seleucus, who, after Lysimachus' death, took control over most of Anatolia in the third century BC.

These and other warrior-kings reigned over independent states that were heavily influenced by Hellenistic culture and habits and spent much of their time – and money – waging wars with one another.

The Galatian kingdom spread across cental Anatolia, and while the Trapezos kingdom (today Trabzon) established itself on the shores of the Black Sea, the Bithynians built the city of Pursa (today Bursa) as their capital. Of these kingdoms, the strongest was Pergamon, ally of Rome. To this day, the remains of the Pergamonian capital, Pergamon (today Bergama), comprise one of

the more important and impressive excavation sites in Turkey.

Asia and the Eastern Roman Empire

Atalus III, the Pergamanian king, died in 133 BC. With no heir to the throne, the kingdom was annexed to Rome. The new lords established an Asian-Roman province, of which Ephesus and Pergamon were its important cities. Always looking to expand, the Romans completed their Anatolian conquest under the great warrior Pompeius. Later, Trajan and Hadrian used Asia Minor as a bridge between continents during their eastern wars.

Saint Paul brought Christianity to Anatolia, and small Christian communities quickly sprouted throughout the Roman Empire. In the year 324 AD, Constantine defeated his rivals and became the sole monarch over the central empire. As if to reconfirm the victory of Christianity, the famous Council took place that very year in Nycaea (today's İznik), in order to solve worldwide theological disputes over the Holy Trinity and the status of the Holy father and his son Jesus.

In 330 a new city was built on the ruins of the Hellenistic city Byzantine and was named Constantinople, after the king, laying the foundations for the thousand-year Christian Byzantine Empire which was to follow.

The Byzantine Empire

The Byzantine Empire was founded on the ruins of the Roman one. Their legacy included military and managerial expertise, combined with a highly-developed Greco-Roman culture. In the fifth century, the Byzantine fortifications stood their ground against the invasion of the Barbar tribes, attempting to topple the Roman Empire. The Byzantine Empire successfully retained its independence.

In the sixth century, Emperor Justinian and Empress Theodora expanded the borders of the empire and conquered Italy, Southern Spain, and territories in North-Africa. Justinian

established his empire by developing codes of law, systems of civil government and adopting Christianity. To glorify the new faith, he had a cathedral built in Constantinople. The Aya Sofia Cathedral was innovative in both architectural concepts and building methods of the time.

Despite disputes and frequent changes of dynasties, the Byzantine Empire developed as an empire that combined Roman military tradition and orthodox Christianity with a Hellenistic lifestyle. It succeeded in defending itself against its Persian (6th century), Arab (7th century) Bulgarian (9th century) and other enemies.

A new force to be contended with appeared on the horizon in the eleventh century. They were nomadic Asiatic tribes, known by their Chinese name Tuo Kwui, who had fled from the Mongolians into Central Anatolia. During their journey across Asia, the Tuo Kwui adopted the Islamic faith and took on the name Turks. Many of them joined the Seljuk tribe, and together met the Byzantine forces at the decisive battle of Manzikert – and

An archeological find with an inscription at Efes

Many sultans are buried in this cemetery near the Köprülü Mosque at İstanbul

won. The new Seljuk kingdom quickly took root in Anatolia and made Bakonia its capital. Smaller Turkish tribes, such as the Orthokidic and the Saltucian tribes, carved out small kingdoms for themselves and established local governments.

The rising power of the European states and their Crusader forces, manifested itself in the fourth crusade. On their way to Jerusalem they attacked Constantinople from land and from sea, and finally conquered the city in 1204. Its Byzantine rulers fled east to Trabzon on the shore of the Black Sea, and in 1261, the Byzantines took advantage of the crusaders' weakness, reconquering the lands they had lost. However, the new Byzantine Empire never succeeded in regaining its past glory.

The Ottoman Period (1452-1922)

The Turkish tribes, cruel and determined warriors, came together under the leadership of Osman I. The Ottoman lineage began establishing itself in the 13th century, until it finally captured the throne from the Byzantines in the 15th century.

Bursa fell in 1326. Thrace, the European Turkey, was conquered in 1362. The Mongols defeated the Ottomans in 1402. After their leader's death, however, the Mongolian reign deteriorated and the Ottoman dynasty regained power.

The Ottoman expansion continued almost uninterrupted, despite counter attacks. In 1452 Mehmet the Conqueror entered the gates of Constantinople, changed the name of the city to İstanbul and thereby effectuated the end of the Byzantine Empire and the Islamic Ottoman Empire.

The Ottoman Empire expanded quickly. Sulayman the Magnificent rebuilt İstanbul and Jerusalem. In 1517 the Ottomans conquered the Holy Land and in 1529 they reached the outskirts of Vienna. Europe in its entirety shuddered at the thought of the Turks. The conquered Christians were forced to submit to a child tax. Children, taken from their families, were converted to Islam in the service of the Sultan. Some were enlisted in the elite corp. of *Janissaries*; the rest disappeared into the civil service.

The empire reached its peak quickly but did not succeed in sustaining its control. In 1565 Sulayman the Magnificent was defeated in Malta, and from then on began a slow process of decline, that lasted for centuries. There are several reasons for this decline. Many historians believe that the Ottomans stagnated and lost the initiative and military mobility essential to an empire. While Europe was slowly coming out of the dark ages and developing systems of thought, industry and military strategy, tradition settled into the Ottoman court of the 16th century. The *Janissaries*, the elite corps, were the central force of the empire and the Sultanate lost all real influence outside of Turkey.

The decline of the empire was hastened forward by such events as the peace treaties signed by Turkey in the 18th and 19th centuries with Russian and the European powers.

Atatürk sitting proudly on his horse

Due to its military inferiority, Turkey was forced to give up land. The few attempts to halt the disintegration – such as the creation of a parliament in 1877, and the revolt of the Young Turks in 1908 – did not succeed in arresting the process.

Kemal Atatürk and the Establishment of the Turkish Republic

The Ottoman Empire was finally brought to its knees with the start of World War I. The Sultanate lost its grip on power, while ineffective politicians allied Turkey with Germany. Most of the battles ended in dismal Turkish defeat. Between 1915-1916, the Turks turned their frustrated fury on the Armenian people. An estimated number of one million Armenians were murdered by the Turkish forces or died seeking refuge in neighboring countries.

Turkey surrendered. The final territories, among them the Holy Land, were taken from Turkey at the end of the War. East Turkey was returned to the Armenians, Thrace to the Greeks and South East Turkey to the French. All this strengthened the sense of embitterment that had been brewing in the Turkish people. Resentment in the army was clearly apparent. The Sèvres treaty in which Turkey formally surrendered and the Greek invasion of İzmir under the auspices of the Allies in May 1919, were the last straw: the revolt began. In June of that year, Mustafa Kemal, who led the Turkish forces in the famous battle of Gallipoli, drew a private declaration of independence and gathered round him, in the east of the country, those forces opposing the Treaty of Sèvres. The government in Istanbul resigned and Kemal's supporters won the parliamentary elections. The allies, however, refused to permit the opening of Parliament. But Kemal was not daunted and established in Ankara what he called "the great National Assembly", the Turkish parliament's name to this day.

The Sultan's government sentenced Kemal to death as a traitor, and instructed the Turkish forces to oppose Kemal's forces. The Greeks conquered Bursa, and Kemal continued strengthening his forces with units deserting the Sultan, as well as enthusiastic civilians. In August 1921 the Greeks attacked Ankara, but were defeated by Kemal in a fierce conflict that lasted three weeks. In the summer of 1922, Kemal went on the attack, regained İzmir, driving out the Greeks. The last Sultan fled, thereby bringing down the final curtain on the Ottoman Empire.

With the onset of peace, Kemal began to wage a different war. Turkey was declared a republic, Ankara its capital and he its president. He then set out to bring the twentieth century to Turkey. His fiercest opponent, he knew, was the social and political strength of Islam. But in 1924 he dismantled Turkey's central religious institution, thereby separating religion and state. A civil code of law was enforced instead of the Islamic one. In addition, religious schools were abolished and a national education system was established.

But Kemal was not yet satisfied. He was determined to change the daily life of all Turks. The turban and fez (men's' head-dress) and the *yashmack* (women's' veil) were put away in favour of European dress, the Arabic alphabet was exchanged for the Latin one and women gradually gained greater equality, including the right to vote. In 1935 the Turks were ordered to choose surnames for themselves, as is

Atatürk's Mausoleum

common in the western world. For himself, Kemal chose the name Atatürk, meaning the father of the Turks.

Atatürk learned from the mistakes of the Ottomans and looked to strengthen ties with neighbouring countries rather than oppose them. Before his death, he ensured that Turkey was well out of World War II. Any attempt to seek separation from the united Turkey was quickly crushed, particularly that of the Armenians and Kurds in the east. But otherwise, within Turkey, he used neither secret police nor terror tactics. In his private life, Atatürk was a solitary and fastidious man.

In November 1938, he died at the age of 57 from a liver ailment. Before his death, he ensured Turkey's neutrality, that eventually kept it out of World War II. The adulation and honour bestowed on him by his people is in evidence to this day.

Turkey today

On the death of Atatürk in 1938,

restored to the people.

The ANAP (Homeland) Party won the 1983 and 1987 elections; Turgut Özal served as prime minister and later as president. In 1993, with President Özal's demise, Demirel became president, while Mrs. Tansu Çiller replaced him as prime minister, the first woman in Turkey to fill this post.

During the Gulf War (Jan.-Feb. '91), Turkey was a passive ally and enabled American Forces to enter her territory. Many planes took off for sorties and bombardments from Turkey's military airports. At the end of the war, when Iraq began massacring the Kurds, more than 100,000 refugees came to East Turkey.

General Inönü, Atatürk's close supporter, became President. Inönü's foreign policy was similar to that of his predecessor, while in internal affairs he proved himself a multiparty moderate democratic leader, and allowed Turkey to have free multi-party elections.

In 1950 the Democratic Party won the elections, and introduced changes in government that were greeted with enthusiasm. However, due to inadequacies in leadership, these changes ultimately led to political instability. The army, viewing itself the protector of the Turkish Republic, intervened and deposed the government three times – in 1960, 1971 and 1980. After these military coups, power was

In order to solve the water problems in East Turkey, Turkey proposed certain projects to construct dams on the Euphrates and the Tigres. Some of these projects have already materialized, but a dispute arose between Syria, (which uses water from the river extensively) and Turkey and between Iraq, for which these rivers act as a life-line. Hence the fate of these important national projects is uncertain.

The square in front of the University of İstanbul

Dates for Reference

BC

Paleolithic Period (pre-7000 BC) – rock drawings at Karain, concentrations of stone and bone implements throughout Anatolia.
Neolithic Period (7000-5500) – Beginnings of agriculture in Anatolia.
Chalcolithic Period (5500-3000) – Appearance of pottery and copper tools in Hacilar and Chatal Höyük.
Early Bronze Age (3000-2000) – Beginnings of colonization of Troy. Building of fortified cities. Period of ancient Hittite culture.

2000 –	Establishment of Assyrian trading colonies.
1900 –	The Hittites build Hattuşaş.
1180 –	Fall of Troy.
1200 –	Fall of Hattuşaş and the Hittite kingdom.
1100 –	Beginning of Greek migration to the Aegean coast.
1000-900 –	Rise of Orerto culture in eastern Anatolia.
667 –	Establishment of Byzantine Empire.
650 –	Beginnings of settlement of the Black Sea coast by Miletan colonies.
546 –	Conquest of Greek cities by Cyrus, king of Persia.
334 –	Anatolia conquered by Alexander the Great.
323 –	Death of Alexander the Great.
261 –	Rise of Pergamum.
133 –	Death of Atallus III king of Pergamum, who bequeathed the realm to Rome.
130 –	Rome establishes Provincial Asia.

AD

40 –	Paul begins spreading the Gospel in Anatolia.
330 –	Constantinople made capital of Byzantium, the Eastern Roman Empire.
527-565 –	Byzantium at its zenith, under the rule of Justinian.
663 –	Arab invasion of Asia Minor.
1071 –	Seljuk victory over Byzantium opens Anatolia to the Turkish tribes. The Seljuks become the major power in Anatolia up to 1283.
1204 –	Conquest of Byzantium by Latin-Christian armies in the Fourth Crusade.
1261 –	Byzantine Emperor Michael recaptures Constantinople from the Crusaders.
1299 –	Birth of Osman, founder of the Ottoman dynasty.
1363 –	Bursa becomes the new Ottoman capital.
1402 –	Mongolian warlord, Tamerlane, defeats the Ottoman Sultan Beyazıt I.
1453 –	Seige and capture of Constantinople by Mehmet II (the Conqueror), name of city changed to İstanbul and made capital of the Ottoman Empire.
1520-1566 –	The Golden Age of the Ottoman Empire, under the rule of Sulayman the Magnificent.
1876 –	Abdül Hamid announces the Constitution and convenes the National Assembly.
1908 –	Young Turks revolution.

INTRODUCTION

1914 –	Turkey enters World War I, allied to Germany.
1919 –	Atatürk musters forces to oppose the Sultan and his oppressive rule.
1921-1923 –	Turkish War of Independence.
1923 –	Treaty of Lausanne. Proclamation of the Turkish Republic, with Atatürk as its president.
1938 –	Death of Atatürk.
1950 –	Democratic government is elected and the People's Party, founded by Atatürk, is ousted by the Democratic Party which forms the government.
1960,1971, 1980 –	Seizure of power by the military to protect democracy in the face of political instability.
1983 –	*ANAP* Party headed by Turgut Özal wins the general elections.
1987 –	*ANAP* Party re-elected.
1991 –	The Gulf War – The Proper Way party under the leadership of Süleyman Demirel win the elections.
1993 –	Demirel elected President; Tansu Çiller becomes Prime Minister.

Geography and Climate

Turkey lies in west Asia between latitudes 36° and 42°; its total area is about 302,200 miles (767,000 sq./km), of which 97% is in Asia and 3% is in Europe. Its length, at the longest point, is 970 miles (1,565 km), its breadth 400 miles (650km). It is bounded on the east by Armenia, Georgia and Iran, on the southeast by Iraq and Syria, and on the northwest by Greece and Bulgaria.

The country is surrounded by sea on three sides: the Black Sea and the Sea of Marmara to the north, the Aegean to the west and the Mediterranean to the south. Its position as a land link between Asia and Europe has given it great strategic importance. The Central Anatolian Plateau is surrounded by high Taurus moun-

tains to the south, rising to a height of 16,400ft. (5,000m), and to the east and north the Pontic mountains. This fact determines the division of Turkey into seven geographical and climatic regions.

The Marmara Region: This region includes eastern Thrace from Edirne to İstanbul, the peninsula of Gelibolu, and the Southern Shores of the Sea of Marmara. The land is very rich and known for its low green hills and its fruit and olive orchards. The average air temperature is 15°C and it is the most humid region of all Turkey. The major cities are İstanbul, Edirne, Bursa, Çanakkale.

Central Anatolia: Turkey's central plateau lies at an average height of about 2,950ft. (900m) above sea level. The arid plateau is surrounded by high mountain ranges which block the passage of rain clouds. The plateau's northern incline causes the rivers to flow towards the Black Sea. A large part of the run-off does not get as far as the sea but forms salt lakes on the plateau, the largest of which is the Tuz Gölü – a very large salt lake. The climate is dry with cold, snowy winters and hot dry summers. Central Anatolia's main towns are Ankara and Konya.

The Aegean Region is a western-sloping plateau extending from Anatolia to the Aegean coast. Above the plateau rises the Ulu Dağ Mountain, 8,167ft. (2,490m). The rivers, including the Büyük Menderes, flow westward into the Aegean Sea. The region is character-ized by a temperate Mediterranean climate with some summer rain. The major cities are İzmir and Aydın.

The Mediterranean Region: The Taurus Range in this region is a high chain of mountains to the south of Anatolia, creating a massive wall which descends steeply to the

Mediterranean from a height of 9,840ft (3,000m). The rivers are short and flow from the mountains to the Mediterranean. The Seyhan and Ceyhan rivers form a fertile delta where the town of Adana is situated. The coastal strip is long and narrow, with a typically temperate Mediterranean climate. The Taurus range is cold and sparsely populated. Antalya and Adana are the two main towns.

The Black Sea Region: The Pontic Mountains along the Black Sea rise to a height of 6,560ft. (2,000m). The eastern range is higher, rising to 13,120ft. (4,000m) joining the Armenian mountains in southeast Turkey and the Caucasus to the northeast. Due to geological faults between the mountain slopes and the Black Sea, the land is not suitable for settlement and cultivation. Settlement is possible in the silt fans spread out in the estuaries of rivers flowing down from Anatolia to the Black Sea. The Kızılırmak – the country's longest river – flows for 805 miles (1,300km) from the Anatolian plateau to the Black Sea. Temperatures in the Pontic mountains are low, rising with the descent to the Black Sea. Northern winds from Russia cause high precipitation, up to an annual 2,000mm. The main towns are Trabzon and Samsun.

Eastern Anatolia: The meeting between the Pontic Mountains in the north and the Taurus range to the south creates the mountainous zone of Eastern Anatolia, forming the country's eastern region. Seismic activity at the convergence of the two ranges has caused pronounced folding, to the extent of faulting. Lava eruptions from the faults has formed a basalt and volcanic mountain landscape, the rugged terrain characteristic of eastern Turkey. At its highest point it rises to 16,400ft. (5,000m) on Ağrı Dağı (Mt. Ararat). Petrified lava has formed a drainage barrier to the run-off, creating freshwater lakes on the mountain tops. The Tigris and the Euphrates drain the Eastern Anatolian mountains on their way to Southeast Anatolia.

Eastern Anatolia has an extreme, mountain climate. Hills and valleys

The rocky landscape of Cappadocia

are covered in snow throughout the cold winter and summer temperatures may reach over 40°C. These inhospitable conditions make for a sparse population. Erzurum and Diyarbakır are the major towns.

Southeast Anatolia: This region is dry and hot. The land is comprised of rolling steppes with rock outcrops. The rivers Tigris and Euphratus continue to drain the land on their way to Syria, Iraq and the Persian Gulf.

Flora and Fauna

Geographical and climatic conditions are conductive to the development of the rich natural vegetation in most of the country. The Aegean and Mediterranean regions are covered with Mediterranean woodlands, dominated by conifers and oaks. Anatolia has a semi-desert landscape characterised by low scrub such as aromatic wormwood. The higher areas are characterized by conifers, especially various species of fir trees and cedars.

The forests in Turkey have been greatly damaged due to the extensive use of trees for construction and fire wood. Even today villagers still cut down trees in the forests. The government endeavours to preserve nature reserves such as Yedi Göller, Uludağ and Sümela, and to protect its natural rich forestry. Just as the utility of the forest mutilated the plant-life, hunting has greatly harmed the wild-life. Turkey's wild-life was once rich and varied, but today due to the popular sport of hunting, agricultural development and the use of pest-control substances in the fields, it's hard to spot animals during a visit to this country. Turkey's wild-life can be found on the walls of restaurants and shops. Amongst the skins and stuffed animals one can see deer, wolves and foxes. Bears are scarce in Turkey and live in the heart of the forest. It is especially distressing to see bears, caught by gypsies when cubs, and trained to perform at markets and tourist-centers.

There are many species of seagulls near the Aegean shore. The white stork builds its large nests in protruding places. The migration route of storks and other birds passes over the Bosphorus and on Spring days one can see huge flocks of birds on their way to Africa. At Kuscenneti

near Bursa there's a beautiful nature reserve for birds, near Bursa called "Bird's Paradise". At the great salt lake in Tuz Gölü one can see settlements of nesting flamingoes.

Population

The population of Turkey is growing rapidly. From 12 million inhabitants with the declaration of the Republic in 1923, the population has grown to 57 million. The most populated city, Istanbul, has around 7.5 million inhabitants. Other densely inhabited cities are: Ankara (3.2 million), İzmir (2.7 million), Adana (2 million) and Bursa (1.6 million). Turkey is still a predominantly agricultural country with most of its population in rural areas, but for some time there has been a marked migration from village to town, and farming is gradually being abandoned in favor of industry and commerce.

The Turkish nation is comprised of Asiatic tribes which have blended with Arabs, Greeks and Persians. Turkish history, a series of invasions and conquests, has left its mark on the present Turkish nation. The largest of the country's minorities is the Kurds in the southeast, after which come the Arabs, Greeks and Armenians. Because of ethnic friction the authorities tend to minimize the size of minorities, claiming that in total they form only one tenth of the total population.

Religion – though 99% of the population is Moslem, following Atatürk's reformation measures, Turkey became a secular state.

Political System

Turkey is a democratic and secular republic. It is a member of NATO and an associate member of the European Common Market.

The structure of Turkish government institutions today is based on the 1982 Constitution, with a series of amendments introduced in 1987.

The National Assembly, which has 450 members, is the legislative arm. It is elected in regional elections for a five-year period. The National Assembly elects the president of the republic, who has to win a two-thirds majority of the total votes in one of the first two rounds of votes, or a simple majority in the third round, in order to be elected.

National Assembly

The Turkish National Assembly was first set up on April 23, 1920, by Mustafa Kemal Atatürk. The 1961 constitution split it into two houses – the Legislative House and the Senate.

The constitution of 1982 reunited the National Assembly into one House with 450 seats. Its powers include passing laws, supervision of Ministers' Council, consolidating the budget and ratification of international agreements.

Parliamentary decisions are only reached when there is an absolute majority pertained by those present, the minimum forum being a quarter of the members of the House.

Executive Branch

This consists of the president and the Council of Ministers (the government).

The President – The president of the republic has wide powers of authority, both in foreign and domestic affairs. The president is head of state and is elected by parliament for seven years. He is responsible for implementation of the constitution and the functioning of other state institutions.

The president is entitled to convene a meeting of the National Assembly or the government whenever he sees fit. He can be removed from office by a three-quarters' majority of the members of parliament.

Three bodies operate under the president's aegis:

The National Advisory Council – responsible for supervision of the law and the functioning of the institutions of authority. The Council has nine members appointed by the president.

The Presidential Council – a body set up under the 1982 Constitution. Its members are appointed every six years. Their function is to examine parliamentary legislation before endorsement by the president. The

Military at Konya – arm in arm

Council is an advisory body to the president on questions of legislation, and examines questions of internal and external security.

The Council for National Security – chaired by the president and is made up of the prime minister, the chief of staff and ministers of defence, foreign and internal affairs, and commanders-in-chief of the land, sea and air forces and security forces. The Council puts forward its stand on questions of national security to the Ministerial Council.

Ministerial Council (the government) – this is headed by the prime minister who is appointed by the president, and is responsible for the appointments of the ministers in his government. The prime minister must be a member of parliament, whereas for other ministers this is not necessary. Traditionally, the president appoints the leader of the victorious party in the parliamentary elections.

The government must obtain a vote of confidence from parliament after presentation. The parliament can bring down the government by a no-confidence vote. The president, too, can declare new elections under certain circumstances.

Political parties

Following the September 1980 military coup, the political leadership of all parties which had previously held power were removed for a period of five to ten years. The 1982 constitution enabled the re-establishment of the parties, and the displaced politicians were not permitted to participate in the renascent political life.

This restriction was relaxed on the eve of the 1987 elections, and today everyone over the age of 19, excluding civil servants and the military, can belong to a party.

The ruling party in Turkey is The Proper Way party led by former Prime Minister Süleyman Demirel.

The second largest party is The Social Democratic Party headed by Murat Karayalgin İnönü (son of a former prime minister).

The third largest party is ANAP (Homeland). A party in favor of private enterprise and non-interference of the government in trade and industry. In the 1987 elections ANAP won an absolute majority in parliament.

The other parties, including the left-wing parties of former Prime Minister Bülent Ecevit did not exceed the minimum percentage, about 10% of the electorate, and are not represented in parliament. The Social Democratic Party and The Proper Way form a ruling coalition in parliament.

Sheep-tending near the ancient port city of Patara

Economy

Although Turkey is changing from an agricultural to an industrial society, agriculture is still the main branch of the economy. The major crops vary according to geographic region: wheat and cereals in Anatolia, cotton in the Aegean region, high grade tobacco on the Black Sea Coast, rice in the rainy Pontic region; on the mountain slopes peasants grow deciduous fruit trees, especially nut and fig. Livestock farming is mainly based on sheep raised for wool and mutton. On the edges of the Anatolian plateau goat-raising is also common, especially the Angora goat with its high-grade wool.

Industrial enterprise centers mainly on processing agricultural produce and exploitation of natural resources. İzmir is famous as a center for processing agricultural produce. Turkey has coal, chrome, lead, zinc, sulphur and salt. Iron and coal ores have made it possible to set up a large steel industry along the Black Sea coast. Turkey also has textile and wool industries. Some oil is found near the Iraqi border. Electricity is produced by dams built on the country's large rivers. The tourist industry is growing rapidly and brings in significant foreign currency revenue.

One of the major projects aimed at helping economic growth in Turkey is GAP in South-East Anatolia, a project that combines the building of dams, hydroelectric-electric power stations and irrigation systems on the Euphrates and Tigris rivers. This project will have a great effect on the agriculture, transport, education, culture and tourism of Turkey. Construction of the dam at Atatora, one of the dams in the project has already been completed and is one of the largest in the world.

In recent years the tourist trade has grown rapidly in Turkey. A combination of interesting historical sites and a fully developed foundation for tourism (which include sport centres and vacation facilities) makes Turkey a first-class tourist attraction.

Rapid industrialization has its price: an external debt of over $30 billion, and an annual inflation rate which since the early '80's, has never been lower than 60%, in spite of all the government's efforts. Raising the standard of living and improving the economic situation are at the center of government planning. These efforts also determine Turkey's foreign policy, which favors widespread ties with countries such as Iran, Syria and Israel, despite the great socio-political gap between these countries and Turkey.

Language

The Turkish language is an Asiatic dialect. The language does not belong to Semitic or Indo-European groups. Linguists have given up on the question of whether the language belongs to the Altaic group, to which Finish and Hungarian belong, or whether it belongs to a branch of the Turkish family of languages, an independent group of languages, which also includes Mongolian.

As part of Atatürk's policy of becoming European, the Turks use a Latin alphabet. The most common foreign language is German, perhaps because of the large number of Turks who work in West Germany, and the number of German tourists.

The following are the rules of Turkish pronunciation which should make it easier to pronounce names and words that appear in the book:

Letter Pronunciation

Letter	Pronunciation	Example
c	dj	*Caddesi*
ç	tch	*Çanakkale*
e	always pronounced (even at the end of the word)	*Postane*
ğ	not pronounced	*Dağ*
ı	as in "uh"	*Sıcak*
j	as in "vision"	*Jandarma*
k	as in English	*Küçük*
ş	sh	*Beş*
ü	as in German ü	*Güle Güle*
ö	as in "urgent"	*Ördek*

Architecture

The vicissitudes of history have left an amazingly varied architectural heritage in Turkey. Almost every period and every regime has left its imprint on the landscape. The traveler to Turkey is exposed to styles of the different cultures. The Museum of Anatolian Cultures in Ankara has a collection of many exhibits exemplifying this assortment of styles. This museum is perhaps the most suitable for explaining the chronological order of building styles to the visitor.

In the first division four main architectural periods can be seen: Hittite, Greco-Roman, Byzantine and Ottoman-Turkish.

The **Hittite Period** is characterized by thick fortified walls, temples and huge palaces and open-mouthed lions. In contrast to the monumental architecture, the gold and silver ornaments are designed with great delicacy and skill. In Boğazkale (Hatttuşaş) the wonders of Hittite architecture may be seen.

During the **Greco-Roman Period**

open amphitheaters abounded; the amphitheater at Miletos could accommodate 25,000 spectators. Symmetrical building dominates, with rows of columns supporting the roof, in many temples. The most common columns are simple Doric columns, Ionic columns recognized by the ram horn design on their entablature (top) and Corinthian columns with their elaborate carvings at the capital and base (for example, the columns of Hadrian's arch in Antalya). The chief building material in this period is marble, which the builders also used to clad brick structures held by cement. Roman influence is seen in the heated baths and the aqueducts.

During the **Byzantine Period**, Greek temples were replaced by large Byzantine churches, where the emphasis was on the depth of the space, and large supporting arches were built to emphasize man's insignificance next to the greatness of God. The Ayasofia Church is a wonderful example of this building.

The **Ottoman-Turkish Period** – The Seljuks were the first to embell-ish Moslem religious institutions and schools. Seljuk architecture is easily recognized by the pyramid-shaped stonework carved above a gateway. This architecture has oriental motifs reminiscent of Persian art. A typical example of Ottoman architecture are the many mosques with high pointed towers, tiled with decorated ceramic tiles common in Turkey. The style, which flourished under the architect Sinan, is called Turkish, for this was the first style developed in Turkey that was not imported from abroad. A wonderful example of the Ottoman style is the Sultanahmet, the Blue Mosque in İstanbul.

Custom and Tradition in the Face of Change

The social revolution started by Atatürk is not yet over. The great Turkish leader tried, through a series of decisions and laws, to transport Turkish society from the Middle Ages to the twentieth century. The

Strolling amongst column fragments – remains from the Greek port city in Priene

In contrast to this freedom, Turkey has a popular Islamic movement which preaches the return to the old religious values in the fundamentalist style. In 1979, this movement held a large demonstration against the regime, resulting in public disturbances and provoking military intervention to restore order.

As visitors and bystanders, one should appreciate the real difficulty of this rapid cultural transition which took about 400 years in Europe. The Turks expect tourists not to interfere in their affairs and it is important to avoid taking a stand in the social conflicts which one may confront during a visit. This attitude will be recognized with the warmest gratitude and hospitality of the oriental traditions, and with every possible show of friendship.

transition from a rigid, rural, patriarchal Moslem society to an enlightened democratic and industrial society is still in progress. The status of women in Turkey is a good example of the problematics involved in the Turkish social transition. In the villages, a woman is regarded as a slave in the possession of the man. Women cover their head and their mouth, which are considered unclean. A woman's voice is also considered unclean, and she is therefore forbidden to address men outside the family. Most women marry before the age of 15. In the large urban centers, on the other hand, women are free from traditional restrictions and may be seen in modern dress in the streets and shopping centers.

Another example of reformation can be seen in the attitude towards religion. Islam forbids drinking alcohol, eating pork and idol-worshipping; but Turkey defines itself as a secular state and in the urban centers, Turkish Moslems may be seen drinking wine and eating on Ramadan in public places.

Music, Contests and Folk Dancing

Various streams of folk entertainment and culture developed under the encouragement of the Sultans, who were lovers of folk culture and traditions. Various streams can be discerned in traditional music, martial music originating from central Asia and performed to this day by military bands like the *Janissaries* Orchestra (*Mehte Takımı*) at the İstanbul Military Museum; mystical-religious music performed on various flutes by the dancing dervishes (*mevleviler*) centered at Konya; and popular music with a moral like the ballads of the troubadours, still performed at fairs and in villages by traveling musicians (*aşıklar*).

Every region in Turkey has its own traditional dances. The dancers wear impressive colorful costumes. Along the Black Sea coast the *horon* is danced – men attired in black and silver join hands and move to the notes of the Turkish violin, the *kemençe*. Another impressive dance performed by men is the shield and sword dance *(kılıç kalkan)*, symbolizing the defeat of Bursa by the Ottomans. The dance is performed to the clang of swords and shields without any other music, in Ottoman battle uniforms. These dances can be seen in and around Bursa.

Another dance based on percussion rhythms is the spoon dance *(kaşık oyunu)* performed to the sound of clapping of wooden spoons held by the dancers. This dance can be seen in the region between Konya and Silifke. In the Aegean region one finds the *zeybek* dance in which the colorfully costumed dancers re-enact national scenes and symbols of heroism and sacrifice.

In the folk contests and fairs one sees various forms of traditional Turkish entertainment. The shadow theater of Karagöz was a popular form of entertainment before the advent of cinema and television in Turkey. The Karagöz began at Bursa in the 14th century, with characters such as Karagöz the Clown and his friend, Hacivat. The Karagöz theater still performs in towns and villages in the Bursa area and in the Bursa market the shadow puppets can be bought (see "Bursa").

Among the popular sport contests is the *yağli güreş* – oil wrestling. The matches are held in summer at Kırkpınar near Edirne. Wrestlers smeared with oil try to bring each other down without losing their balance. Another interesting folklore contest is camel battles *(deve güreşi)*, which can be seen in the Aegean region in the middle of January, in the village of Selçuk, for example. In this contest, camels "fight" until one proves its superiority. The loser is quickly removed

from the arena to save it from being injured by the victor.

In eastern Turkey the game of throwing a wooden javelin (*cirit oyunu*) is popular. Two mounted teams try to gain points and win the contest by hurling javelins at the opposing side. Traditionally, this game is a version of ancient bloody contests using metal javelins and swords, a kind of mounted duel.

Folk Story-Tellers

Turkey's most famous story-teller is Nasreddin Hoca, a humourist who lived in the 13th century and whose fables are known throughout the whole of Turkey. Yunus Emre, a poet and philosopher, is one of Turkey's treasures; he too lived in the 13th century and wrote about love, friendship, brotherhood and justice. Another great poet is Köroglu, from the 15th century, known for his courage and senti-mental prose.

Turkish Baths

One of the traditional Turkish plea-sures is a visit to the *hamam* (Turkish baths). The pleasure is twofold – physical and visual. The bath house originated because most of the houses in town had no wash-rooms; the *hamam* is a relic of the

At the Turkish Baths in Bursa

Roman bath houses that were built in almost every city.

The *hamam* is not a health club, as in the western world. The attendant *(tellak)* gives the bather two towels and a pair of wooden sandals as he enters the dressing cubicle. Wrapped in the towels and wearing the wooden sandals, the bathers enter the halls of the *hamam*. Inside there are several rooms, each kept at a different temperature. Most *hamams* have outstanding marble-floored halls, sitting and resting slabs and enormous washbowls. After you have "sweated it out" in one of the heated rooms, the attendant reappears and pours a bucket of warm water over you. He then scrubs you with a coarse washcloth, removing all the city grime and dust from your weary limbs. The massage that follows the bathing is a brief pressure and flexing massage, unlike western massage. In the cooling-off room, you can relax and order a hot or cold drink.

Bathing at the *hamam* is a personal affair. Undue exposure of intimate parts of the body is met with disparaging remarks by the local bathers. Separation between the sexes is absolute and men and women naturally have separate entrances and separate rooms or separate days.

The Café Culture
Even the smallest hamlet in Turkey has at least one café (*kahve*), where the male population meet daily (no women are allowed in!), to drink coffee, exchange views, play a daily game of backgammon and light up their water-pipes.

The "third eye" – good luck charms for the superstitious

PART TWO: SETTING OUT

Why Turkey?

Turkey's mild climate, spectacular beaches and a wide range of other attractions, together with its convenient "cost of touring", have contributed to a very rapid growth in European tourism; Turkey today replaces its traditional rival, Greece, as the prime tourist attraction along the Eastern Mediterranean coast.

Many of Turkey's visitors arrive in İstanbul. This beautiful oriental metropolis combines a rich cultural and historical heritage with the effervescent bustle of a commercial city and market. Any visitor will enjoy the abundance of tourist attractions in this city. Western Turkey offers the tourist both well-preserved ancient cities and modern beach resorts. The efficient tourist services in this region have made it a popular touring and vacation center for Europeans.

Tourism in the Anatolian plateau is centered around Ankara, the capital of Turkey, famous for its museums, and the fantastic Göreme Valley in the Cappadocia region. Eastern Turkey is a backpacker's paradise: spectacular natural scenery, picturesque villages and rock-bottom prices. The tourist services in Eastern Turkey are extremely basic; the hotels are modest and the roads rocky. Near the eastern borders are some sensitive areas where entry is forbidden without a special permit from the army. Based on the present tourist conditions in Turkey, it seems that the more adventurous visitor will be attracted to the east, while the more conventional guest will plan a trip to the classic sights in Western and Central Turkey.

For the Woman Traveling Alone – Women traveling on their own in Turkey are likely to be harassed, as in most Mediterranean countries. In İstanbul and the western part of the country, a woman can travel alone safely, while it is not recommended that she tour the eastern part of the country on her own. A wedding ring may ward off some of the problems and problem-makers, as will dressing modestly. Women are advised not to walk unescorted late at night anywhere in Turkey. Two women traveling together needn't expect much trouble.

How to Travel

In response to the growing number of tourists in Turkey, a wide choice of organized vacations and tours are now offered. Planning your trip in advance will guarantee a minimum of difficulties and problems. It is important to remember that few Turks speak English, and sometimes a visit to this country involves language and communication difficulties.

Organized vacations fall into two main categories: **vacation**

packages, which include flights and accommodation at the desired vacation spot, usually on the coast, and **guided group tours**, with the route and schedule set in advance. The price of such tours usually includes the flight, hotels, transportation, guides and entrance fees to sights visited.

Another way is to plan your own, individual tour. This allows you to tailor the schedule and destinations to your own needs, and you are more likely to make contact with local residents, but it also leaves you solely responsible for the entire task of organizing. Because of the richness of these places, visitors to the classic sights in İstanbul and western Turkey who want to fully understand what they are seeing will probably need a knowledgeable guide. It is possible to obtain such assistance from local guides, who stand at the entrance to the central sights such as Efes, Pergamon, and others, or through local travel agents for the smaller sights.

Luxury tourism in Turkey is restricted to İstanbul, which offers a number of exclusive hotels and entertainment centers. First-class tourists and business people coming to Turkey in the tourist season should reserve their flights and hotel rooms well in advance, although there is a large number of reasonable and fairly high-priced hotels in İstanbul and Western Turkey.

Backpacking in Turkey is still very enjoyable and very inexpensive. The rugged landscape of Eastern Anatolia, the Taurus canyons and the other fantastic natural sights await those who are willing to wander off the main roads and sleep in simple lodging. For those who want to climb mountaintops and to visit remote villages, the natural and the human landscape in Turkey provides a sense of pioneering and a retreat from the modern world.

Those who choose this type of visit require more patience and tolerance than money. The lengthy time spent traveling and the simplicity of the accommodations may make the trip difficult, and you should prepare yourself emotionally for such an experience.

In recent years Turkey has become a popular destination, much in demand for those seeking sun and beaches in the summer and skiing in the winter. Vacations and package deals are offered at prices that are relatively very low for a similar vacation in Europe.

One can find endless opportunities to "rough it" along the enchanting coastline of Turkey on hired boats and yachts of all sizes and prices. There are also organized "flotilla tours", led by expert local guides. Among the most popular routes are:

İzmir-Kuşadasi – Homer's Odyssey.

Kuşadasi-Bodrum – St. John's Journey.

Bodrum-Marmaris – Leisure and snorkelling.

Marmaris-Fethiye – In the steps of St. Paul.

Here is a list of some leading Marinas:

Ataköy, İstanbul, Tel. (212)560-4270, fax 562-7270. Levent, İzmir, Tel. (232)422-7794. Kuşadasi Turban, Tel. (256)256-1752.

How Much will it Cost

Turkey has been and still is an inexpensive country for the western tourist. A vacation in Turkey is less expensive than one in any other European location and will cost less than one on a similar level in most tourist centers of the world. Getting to Turkey is easy and inexpensive, whether by air, sea or land.

The young traveler or economy tourist will find that $70 is enough for a week of modest touring. $120 will buy relative comfort.

Well-to-do tourists will need no more than $60 a day for a couple. This is ample for a room in a moderately-priced, clean hotel, plenty of food and transportation within Turkey.

Luxury tourism is not inexpensive in Turkey. A room in an exclusive hotel costs about $170 per night. Such hotels can be found in İstanbul and Ankara. Renting a car is a more expensive pleasure than in western

An array of fish afloat on the Bosphorus at İstanbul

Europe, and it should be arranged in advance, as demand exceeds supply.

Companies arrange vacation packages to the south of Turkey. In season, the price comes to $700-950 including airfare and a week's accommodation at a hotel.

How Long to Stay

Three weeks of intensive touring are enough in most parts of the country. Because of Turkey's size, its spectacular sites and its low prices, we recommend dividing the trip into two: A two to three week visit to İstanbul and Western Turkey will acquaint you with the country, its residents and its past. You should devote at least two weeks for a fascinating visit to Eastern Turkey; a month in this area will also seem short.

A visit to the Anatolian plateau can be combined with the western or the eastern tour. Travelers with plenty of time on their hands can add a visit to the less frequented areas, such as the Black Sea or the Iskenderun Bay near the Syrian border.

When to Come

The tourist season in Turkey lasts from April to late October. In the spring and fall the weather is very pleasant in the Aegean and Mediterranean regions, as in most eastern Mediterranean countries. The only good time weather-wise to visit the Black Sea and Eastern Turkey is between May and September. In the Anatolian plateau, the temperature drops considerably on summer nights, and you should plan accordingly. The average temperature in Turkey is 30°C in July and August and about 20°C in the spring and fall. The warmest region is the Mediterranean coast and the coldest is the eastern region, where temperatures sometimes fall far below 0°C.

When planning your trip you should

also take the religious and national festivals and holidays into account.

Official Holidays

January 1 – New Year's Day.

April 23 – National Independence and Children's Day.

May 19 – Atatürk's Commemoration and Youth and Sports Day.

August 30 – Victory Day.

October 29 – Republic Day.

Festivals and Fairs
January
Camel Wrestling Festival – Selçuk

March
International Film Festival – İstanbul

April
In late April the Gunpowder (*mesir*) Festival is held in Manisa near İzmir. A special drink that contains gunpowder is prepared. It is said that those who drink it gain good health, youth and virility.

The international Children's Day is held in Ankara on the 23rd.

April-May
Ephesus International Festival of Culture and Tourism – Selçuk

International Arts Festival – Ankara

May
International Nysa Culture and Art Festival – Sultanhisar

Yunus Emre Culture and Art Week – Eskişehir

The amphitheater at Aspendos

Aksu Culture and Art Festival – Giresun

International Music and Folklore Festival – Silifke

May-June
International Asia-Europe Biennial – Ankara

June
International Offshore Races in İstanbul and İzmir

Foça Music, Folklore and Water Sports Festival – Foça (near Izmir)

Marmaris Festival of Music and Folk Dancing – Marmaris

Kafkasör Culture and Art Festival – Artvin

International Bursa Festival – Bursa

Safranbolu Architectural Treasures and Folklore Week – Safranbolu

June-July
Çeşme Sea and Music Festival – Çeşme

İstanbul International Art and Culture Festival – İstanbul

Traditional Kirkpinar Wrestling – Edirne

INTRODUCTION

International Culture and Art Festival – İstanbul

Ihlara Tourism and Art Week – Aksaray

July
International Folk Dance Festival – Samsun

Ceramic Festival – Kütahya

Nasreddin Hoca Festival – Akşehir

Hittite Festival – Çorum

August
Troy Festival – Çanakkale

Mengen Chefs Festival – Bolu

August-September
İzmir International Fair – İzmir

September
Javelin Games – Konya

Kemer Carnival – Kemer

Folklore Week – Safranbolu

International Grape Harvest Festival – Ürgüp

Yağci Bedir Carpet Festival – Sindirgi Balikesir

September-October
International Akdeniz Song Contest – Antalya

Culture and Art Festival – Diyarbakır

Mersin Art and Culture Festival – Mersin

October
Ahi Brotherhood Cultural Week – Kirsehir

December
Mevlana Commemoration Ceremony – Konya

Ramazan Bayramı: The ninth month of the Moslem year falls in different seasons, because of the lunar calender. Life throughout Turkey changes with the beginning of Ramadan, commemorating the revelation of the Koran to Muhammad. The Ramadan fast requires Moslems to refrain from putting anything – even a cigarette – in their mouths, during the hours of daylight. During this holy month in towns and villages around the country, drummers walk through the streets waking the fasters, so that they can eat before sunrise. At nightfall a cannon shot declares the end of the fast, and the eating continues well into the night. Work hours are shortened and many restaurants outside of tourist areas are liable to be closed until dark.

Kurban Bayramı (the Festival of the Sacrifice) is the most important religious holiday of the year in Turkey.

It commemorates the sparing of Isaac from Abraham's slaughtering knife on Mount Moriah. During the holiday, lambs are sacrificed and used for the traditional holiday meal. The most important act in this tradition is to give a sizeable portion of the meat to the needy and to donate the skin to a charity organization. Holiday customs include exchange of greeting cards and visits to relatives. The holiday lasts four days, and the streets are crowded with people who are on vacation. It may be hard to find a hotel room or a seat on a bus at this time. The banks are closed for a week, with the exception of a few branches in the larger cities, which are open to serve tourists.

Getting There

By air
The Turkish airline *(THY)* has regular flights from Europe to İstanbul, Ankara, Izmir, Antalya and Dalaman. Pan American and European airlines fly between İstanbul and North America. Singapore Airlines operates direct flights from Turkey to the Far East and Australia. In the tourist season, inexpensive charter flights from European cities such as London and Munich reach several destinations in Turkey, such as Antalya. Students and youth are sometimes eligible for discounts on most flights, so it is worth organizing the appropriate documents before starting out. İstanbul Airlines operates low fare charter flights.

By sea
Passenger and vehicle ferries connect the cities of the Turkish coast with Italian ports. In the summer, ferries sail from Venice and Brindisi to İzmir. The trip from Venice takes about three days, and two days from Brindisi. From the Greek islands there are daily ferries from Rhodes to Marmaris and from Samos to Kuşadası. Boats between Lesbos and Ayvalık, Chios and Çeşme and Kos and Bodrum leave most days of the week during the tourist season. When the season ends, they sail less frequently, and in

Fish on display at the Golden Horn Bay

some cases the service is discontinued.

It is important to note that the Greeks are liable to make it difficult for travelers. At one time, visitors who left the Greek islands were not allowed to return; this regulation has since been cancelled, but you should check on any recent developments.

Regular daily ferries join Southern Turkey with Northern Cyprus (the Turkish Zone).

By land

By bus: Spacious buses depart for İstanbul from Paris, Geneva, Munich and other European cities. The trip from central Europe by bus takes about 60 hours. The bus ride from Athens takes 20 hours. The most inexpensive way is to take a local Greek bus to the border, cross into Turkey on foot, and go on from there by Turkish transportation to Edirne and İstanbul. Those taking a bus from Europe should check the route and make sure to have visas for all countries which require one; otherwise, you may be taken off the bus at the border. The seats on the bus are numbered and free seats should be kept vacant for additional passengers.

By train: Train lovers will be happy to know that the Orient Express has been reinstated and again travels from Europe to İstanbul. But the price is fit for a Sultan. Other trains, less fancy and much less expensive, link central Europe with Turkey. The İstanbul Express travels from Munich to İstanbul in 35 hours. The most unusual way to travel to İstanbul is by train from Athens. The trip of 868 miles (1,400km) takes 36 hours or more (less than 24m.p.h./40k.p.h.!). According to the Ottoman train schedule, the same trip at the beginning of the century took only 30 hours! Like bus passengers, anyone traveling on the train must prepare visas for the countries the train passes through, otherwise one will not be allowed to continue the journey.

By car: You can drive to Turkey through Yugoslavia, Greece and Bulgaria. Those who travel through Bulgaria need a transit visa for 48

The Emir Sultan Mosque at Bursa

hours, in which time they must travel across the country. This visa should be obtained in advance from your local Bulgarian consulate rather than counting on assistance from the Bulgarian border police.

At the Turkish border, the car is registered on the passport of the driver, who must take it out of Turkey upon leaving the country. You may not bring a car belonging to someone else, or a rented car, into Turkey. The driver must hold an international driver's license and car insurance. Third-party insurance can be purchased inexpensively after crossing the border – pray you will have no need to use it.

cover the traveler's health expenses and loss of belongings. You should note the limitations of the insurance and make sure that the coverage also applies to damages incurred due to cancellation of the trip (financial losses due to cancelling flights, hotels, etc.).

Documents and Customs

Citizens of the United Kingdom, the United States, Australia, Canada, and most of the countries in Western and Central Europe do not need an entry visa unless they plan to stay for more than 90 days.

The bearer of an international student card or youth card is entitled to discounts on flights within Turkey, at museums and at other sites.

Customs regulations are similar to those elsewhere: you are allowed to bring into Turkey 400 cigarettes, 5 liters of alcoholic beverage, etc. There is no restriction on foreign or local currency, but large sums should be declared.

Insurance

You should not set out on your journey without suitable insurance. Most policies are sold by travel agents and insurance agents and

Currency and Exchange

The US dollar and the German mark are the most familiar foreign currencies in Turkey. You can exchange money in the bank. Keep the receipts; you may be required to present them upon leaving the country. Because the exchange rate fluctuates daily, you should not change the entire sum you plan to use on the trip at one time.

Credit cards are accepted in the large tourist centers, but in remote areas they are not recognized at all. The most widely accepted cards are *Visa* and *American Express*.

Travelers' checks from *American Express* and *Thomas Cook* are welcomed in the large tourist centers, in good hotels, in car rental agencies and the like. It is best to have travelers' checks in US dollars or German marks. To

A hotel in Göreme Village

change travelers' checks in the bank you must present your passport. Transferring money to Turkey is time consuming because of the bureaucracy.

The black market is restricted and exchanging money there is considered a serious offense. Outside of the tourist centers only Turkish currency is accepted, and when you change currency in the bank you must be prepared to patiently fill out a multitude of forms. At any rate, don't worry about getting stuck without any local currency. In response to the flood of tourism, the Turks have opened exchange offices (or stands) at every tourist spot, in addition to restaurants and souvenir shops.

Health

The health services in Turkey are fairly good in main cities and major tourist centers. The western tourist in urgent need of hospitalization will find the American hospital in İstanbul the most comfortable. There are many doctors in the big cities; most of them know some foreign language from their studies abroad.

For less serious problems, you can turn to a pharmacy, (*eczane* in Turkish). Most pharmacists do not speak a foreign language, but by gesturing you can probably get what you need. Most of the medicines are manufactured in Turkey, but it is best to take along medicines you are familiar with, especially in the case of allergy medicines and medication that you take on a regular basis.

Most of the expensive restaurants in Turkey are clean, and the food is tasty. However, before going into an inexpensive restaurant, you should check its appearance. If you are not sure how clean it is, look for another place to eat. It is all right to drink tap water, but most tourists prefer mineral water and soft drinks. It is perfectly safe to drink tea and coffee but milk and dairy products tend to go sour quickly.

There is no need for any special inoculations before entering Turkey.

What to Take Along

You don't need any special equipment for touring Turkey. Backpackers should use a backpack with an inner-metal frame that gives some back support. Those planning long hikes should also take a sleeping-bag and a small set of cooking equipment.

Clothing: The Turkish people are very careful about their dress; it is rare to see Turkish people dressed sloppily. Nice-looking sportswear will probably be appropriate for all your needs.

Photography

The nature and history of Turkey provide a wealth of spectacular shots for the amateur and professional photographer alike. However, photography is not allowed in train stations, airports, army bases and closed border areas. Occasionally one is allowed to take pictures in mosques and national memorials. At some sites, an admission fee is charged for taking a camera in, but you can check it in at the entrance. Turkey is a paradise for photographers, but permission should be requested before photographing people, especially peasants and women. In most parts of the country it is easy to find major brands of film, but it is very expensive and therefore recommended to bring your own.

PART THREE: EASING THE SHOCK – WHERE HAVE WE LANDED?

Getting Around in Turkey

By air: Turkish Airlines *(THY)* operate flights from İstanbul to 15 major cities throughout the country. The flights are not expensive, and the destinations include Van in the east, Ankara in the Anatolian plateau, Kayseri in the Cappadocia region, Antalya on the Mediterranean coast, and more. Students with the appropriate student card are eligible for discounts on flights within Turkey.

By sea: The Turkish ship company operates routes on the Black Sea, the Aegean Sea and the Mediterranean Sea. The Black Sea ferry sails once a week from İstanbul to Trabzon via Samsun. The ferry between İstanbul and İzmir is particularly popular, and you should reserve seats in advance.

In the tourist season the company offers a 10-day trip from İstanbul to the Mediterranean beaches, such as Alanya and Antalya. Short ferry trips can be taken from İstanbul, the Marmara Sea and İzmir. The trip along the Bosphorus Strait from İstanbul gives the tourist an excellent view of the strait separating Asia and Europe.

One of the more popular trips is Mavi Yolculuk (The Blue Journey) – a yacht trip on the Aegean seashore. These sailing trips are generally organized by travel agents, but one can independently organize a group of 8-12 people and rent a yacht. The yachts leave Kuşadası, Bodrum Datça Marmaris, Fethiye, Kaş, Kemer and Anatolia. The price is $250-600 per person for a week and includes the rent of the yacht, the crew, food, gas, port-tax, water and ice. April-October are the favoured sailing months.

By bus: A fleet of modern, spacious buses links the different parts of the

country. The service is efficient, and the fares are relatively low. A large number of bus companies compete for passengers. Tickets, are sold in special offices, not on the bus itself; the seats are numbered. In big cities, where the bus station, the *otogar*, is far from the center of town, the ticket also includes transportation from your hotel or the ticket office to the bus.

When the bus starts traveling, a boy walks through the bus and sprinkles fragrant rose water on the passengers' hands. During the ride, he distributes bottles of water from a cooler on the floor of the bus. The bottles look like they have been filled and closed in a factory, but actually, the boy fills them at roadstops and replaces the cork. Every four hours, the bus-stops at a roadside restaurant for a short refreshment break. Smoking is allowed on buses and may present a problem for those who suffer from being in a closed smoky vehicle, especially as one cannot open any windows.

The efficient bus network is complimented by the *dolmuşes*, minibuses used for short trips. The driver calls out his destination, and collects passengers for all stations on the way. A ride on a *dolmuş* is liable to be over crowded with passengers and live chickens. The *dolmuş* stations are usually located next to the bus stations.

Trains: The train service in Turkey is efficient, but only on a few routes exist. The fast and efficient lines run between İstanbul and İzmir, and these include trains with comfortable sleeping cars. In contrast to the buses, most of the trains do not keep to their schedules, but visitors who have time to spare may find a special charm in a trip on a Turkish train, stopping at picturesque

villages and towns. The long journey from İstanbul to Van takes between three and four days. This trip is described in great detail in Paul Theroux's book, *The Great Railway Bazaar.*

Taxis: These are easy to find in the big cities. The price is half of that for a similar trip in Europe. The drivers operate a meter for every trip; if there is no meter, ask the driver to show you the price list (*tariff* in Turkish) and set the price before he starts out.

Car rental: The major international car rental companies, such as *Hertz*, *Avis* and *Budget*, have offices in Turkey's major cities. You can rent a car from their offices in İstanbul, Ankara, İzmir, Bursa and at sea resorts on the Mediterranean and Aegean coasts. The prices for car rental may be as high as $350 a week (not including gasoline). In the major cities there are also small local agencies, which take less money for renting cars – around $250 a week. But their reliability is somewhat questionable.

An interesting alternative is to **hitchhike**. Because traveling by bus and by *dolmuş* is very efficient and extremely inexpensive, there are few hitchhikers. In areas where there is not much public transportation, such

as the eastern part of the country, and on short trips from the main road to a remote sight, you have excellent chances of getting a ride. The drivers are friendly and usually speak no foreign language. Your best chance for getting a ride is on a loaded truck on its way to the border. A woman traveling alone is unadvised to hitchhike.

Driving: The Turkish roads present no special problem for the driver. Most of the roads in the western part of the country are reasonable, they are signposted, and there is no problem in finding gas stations. The roads in Anatolia and in the east are much worse, and sometimes fairly good dirt roads or roughly paved tracks go on for many miles.

Drivers, on the other hand, should be especially cautious. Cars that fail to stop at a red light in the city are common; and as for the attitude toward pedestrians, a cab driver in İstanbul explained succinctly, "Even if one person is hurt, we have another 5 million like him in this city..." Pedestrians, beware!

On the inter-city roads drivers know no fear in over-taking. Avoid traveling in the dark. The maximum speed permitted on inter-city roads in 100 km per hour, but Turkish drivers ignore this law...

Accommodation

The first hotel in Turkey was the *Hotel Angleterre* in İstanbul, opened due to pressure from the British Embassy in 1841, (the embassy staff grew tired of hosting the businessmen who came from England and spread out their bedding in the embassy). The Egyptian owner of the hotel generally dictated his guests' schedule, and even told them which newspaper to read...

In 1892, a major event took place in the Turkish hotel industry. The *Pera Palace Hotel* opened in İstanbul with great splendor and accommodated the nobility of Europe. The passengers of the Orient Express were brought here from the Sirkeci station in rickshaws. To this day the hotel still operates, and it is worth a visit to this living museum of the grandeur of the past.

The hotel industry in Turkey has developed considerably since then. Today the tourist may choose from a large number of hotels of different grades. The hotels are government-supervised and are graded with the customary star system. HL signifies a luxury hotel; H1 also a 5-star hotel, and H2, H3 and H4 are moderate standard (H4 is equivalent to 1 star). M1 is a high-standard motel; M2, a lower-standard motel; the pensions are graded similarly: P1 and P2.

Luxury hotels can be found in İstanbul, Ankara, Anatolia, İzmir and at all the new major seaside resorts of the Turkish Riviera; they are not expensive by western standards: about $250 to $350 for a double room. The number of good hotels at the 4-star level is greater, and the price for a double room is about half as much as in a 5-star hotel. Tourists who want to stay at a 4 or 5-star hotel during the tourist season should reserve their accommodation in advance, as finding a room during the peak season may be difficult.

There are a large number of moderate hotels to choose from. A double room in a 2- to 3-star hotel costs about $35 to $60. In most Turkish cities you can get a clean room with an adjacent bathroom for less than $40. For backpackers and travelers on a low budget, there are pensions and inexpensive hostels. The rooms are simple, modest and clean, a paradise for backpackers. Because of the low prices of the inexpensive hotels and pensions, few travelers stay at hostels, where you can get a room for the night for next to nothing.

A double room in a pension or a simple hotel costs between $7 and $20. At the inexpensive hotels, you should ask to see your room before you register. The rooms vary in size, furnishing, and proximity to the noisy road. Most of the hotels are clean.

Throughout Turkey one can find guest-houses at reasonable prices and with a "homey" atmosphere. It's worthwhile booking up through the tourist-agencies.

In the resorts along the coast western investors have set up tourist centers devoid of the special Turkish touch. These concrete monsters, which include hotels and large shopping centers, lack the unique character of Turkey.

Camping in Turkey is becoming increasingly popular and scores of sites are available throughout the country. A detailed Camping Map and list of sites is available at most tourist information centres abroad.

For official help and information contact: Grençlik Ve Spor Grenel Müdürlüğü, Grençlik Hizmetler; Dairesi, Rüzgarlı Sok. No. 10, Ulus, Ankara, Tel. 310-0219, 310-2232/36.

Turkish Cuisine

The splendid past has left its mark on Turkish cuisine. The country's history has had a marvelous effect

on Turkish cooking. The empire that brought paprika to Hungary and coffee to Europe takes credit for a long list of delicacies, which make a visit to Turkey a true gastronomic experience.

According to the experts, there is no better food between Paris and China, though Turkish food does not possess the delicacy of French cuisine, nor the imagination of Chinese cooking. Turkish food is made of the most simple ingredients, but a great deal of work and skill turn these basic foods into an excellent meal, reflecting the simple grilled food of the Norman tribes, and the splendor of the cuisine of the Sultan's court.

You'll find restaurants on every corner, and they can be divided into a few types: the respectable *restoran*, with white tablecloths and personal service; the *lokanta*, where the atmosphere may be less luxurious but the food is as excellent; self-service restaurants (*hazır yemek*), with a large steam table in the middle, where the waiter stands waiting for you to indicate what you want; the small restaurants, called *kebapçi* or *köfteci*, which offer grilled beef or lamb, salad, bread and a glass of *ayran*, the local yogurt drink.

Hors d'œuvres: The meal begins with a selection of salads (*meze*), in oriental style, with a wide variety on small plates. The selection varies from one restaurant to another and you should find out what the specialties are. Among the most outstanding are eggplant salad (*patlıcan salatası*), stuffed grape leaves (*dolma*), snails stuffed with rice and nuts (*midye dolması*), red caviar spread (*tarama*), and marinated sheep's brain (*beyin salatası*). You shouldn't order the main course of the meal together with the salads, as everything will come at the same time and the hot food will get cold.

Soup: The Balkan *Çorbası* serves as a second course or first course in the winter. You should try the "wedding soup" (*düğün çorbası*), containing large pieces of mutton. Other excellent soups include the hearty red lentil soup (*kırmızı mercimek çorbası*), and carrot soup (*havuç çorbası*).

Shopping at Marmaris

Meat: The word *kebab* is a general term for Turkish cuisine, and refers more to the method of preparation than to a specific dish. The famous shish-kebab (*şış kebap*), based on pieces of mutton, small onions and tomatoes, is not the only kebab, and the others are also worth a try. Meat patties (*köfte kebap*) are excellent, and melt in your mouth. *Çöp kebab* is made of small pieces of mutton on skewers. Adana-style kebab is much spicier than the regular type.

Other methods for preparing meat are as steak (*bonfile*), wrapped around a spit (*döner kebab*) and in marvelous meat and vegetable dishes, cooked and served in a burning ceramic pot called *güveç*. Still other vegetable and meat dishes are cooked in a heavy black metal pot, the Turkish version of the Chinese wok. These dishes are called *sote*. For chicken lovers the Turks have a special dish – the Circassian chicken (*çerkez tavuğu*): chicken pieces seasoned with garlic and paprika, an ancient recipe brought to Turkey from the Caucasian mountains.

Fish: Turkey is surrounded by water on three sides, and therefore there is an extremely rich selection of fish in most of its regional cuisines: there is calamari (*kalamar*), tuna (*palamut*), smoked tuna (*lakerda*), swordfish on a skewer (*kılıç şiş*), and a special delicacy made of mackerel stuffed with pine nuts (*uskumru dolması*). These dishes are popular throughout the country, but especially, of course, in the coastal regions.

Side dishes: The Turks devote a lot of attention and care in preparing their rice, *pilav*. Mothers used to test their prospective daughters-in-law by the way they prepared rice, for which the Turks have many methods. Rice and pine nuts (*iç pilav*) is served in many restaurants.

The delicious Turkish pizza (*pideci*) is served in special restaurants (*pide salonu*). Another side dish is cabbage stuffed with ground mutton (*etli lahana dolması*).

Ekmek, fresh bread, is offered in abundance: sometimes a virtual mountain of bread is set down next to the table in large plastic buckets.

For vegetarians: Turkish cooking clearly leans toward meat dishes. Vegetarians will enjoy Turkish bourekas (*su böregi*), yogurt (*ayran*) and a special dish of tomatoes and eggs (*menemen*). Excellent nuts and dried fruit are available in special stores (*kuru yemiş*). With the exception of local yogurt, dairy products are not very popular in Turkey. There are few types of cheese and they are not particularly good.

Desserts: Desserts in Turkey range from the sweet to the very sweet. Most popular is *baklava*. In the summer, a dessert of seasonal fruit is recommended, such as melon

Street stalls on the road at Kemer

(*kavun*) or watermelon (*karpuz*). In the tea houses, restaurants and just about everywhere, the sweet, strong Turkish tea, *çay*, is served in little glass cups.

Restaurants are open from early in the morning until late at night. Restaurants in Turkey – even the best of them – are relatively inexpensive. The price of a meal for two in a fine restaurant is only about $60, and you can get a good, varied meal in a perfectly good restaurant for just a few dollars, from $5 in a small restaurant to $12 for a meal in a central location. The price usually includes a service charge. You do not have to leave a tip but if you enjoy the meal, it is customary to leave 10% for the waiter.

Despite the Moslem prohibition against drinking alcohol, you can find beer, wine and Turkish-made alcoholic beverages in restaurants and coffee houses. The most popular of the alcoholic drinks is *raki*, an aniseed flavored drink from the same family as Greek *uzo*, Arab *arak* and French *pastisse*. *Raki* drinking is a ritual, and it is always served with appetizers. At the end of the meal tea or coffee is served. Tap and mineral water is available throughout Turkey, but it is unadvisable to drink the tap water.

Shopping

The bazaars of Turkey offer all the charm of the Orient. Small stores and crowded stands are arranged on the colorful streets. The merchants are friendly, offering you a cup of *çay* (tea), making the bargaining somewhat like a street theater. The special atmosphere and the low prices make any visit to the Turkish marketplace un unforgettable experience.

There are no inexpensive electric appliances in Turkey, but there are crafts in great abundance. The most outstanding are the carpets. The closure of the Persian and Afghanistani markets to the West has drawn greater attention to Turkish carpets. The carpets are woven in a variety of patterns, in different colors and sizes. The price of a carpet is based on a number of factors, such as the number of knots, and only an expert can really estimate its value. It seems that the only measure of the quality of a carpet is the merchant's final price. You should be careful of poor quality carpets that look like they come from the Sultan's palace, for which the merchant goes down to a tenth of his initial quote. Try to befriend one of the carpet merchants; he will certainly be happy to reveal a little of his knowledge.

In addition to the carpets there are *kilim* – woven fabric in different patterns. The largest selection of carpet and *kilim* stores is, naturally, at the large bazaar in İstanbul; here you can find almost anything, but the prices are fairly high. You will find better prices in the cities in central Anatolia, such as Konya and Kayseri.

Besides carpets, the country offers many leather goods, particularly coats and belts. The leather coats are inexpensive compared to the West; but the quality is usually not very high and the styles are fairly conventional. The *Modes* factory near Istiklâl Boulevard in İstanbul, opposite the *Derya* restaurant, is popular with tourists. You should check the leather coats closely while you are still in the store. The most fancy and exquisite leather goods are available in the Derimod Shop in Osmanbey. Visitors who stay about a week in İstanbul can have a leather suit or coat tailor made.

Other impressive hand-made goods include oriental brass implements, oriental-style jewellry, ceramic tiles, and hand-painted porcelain plates. Antiques, including carpets, should be purchased with caution. You may only buy in a certified shop, and will need a license to take the item out of the country. The buying, selling or exporting of antiques without permission is considered a serious offense and is punishable by imprisonment.

Turkey exports many textile products to Western Europe and the United States, and export surpluses reach the local markets. Most of the clothes wear out quickly, but their low price may compensate for this. Bargaining is accepted practice in the Turkish markets, where the merchants set a higher price for western tourists. It is acceptable to offer 60% of the price suggested by the merchant, and to close the deal after some negotiating. There are, of course, countless exceptions.

In the large market in İstanbul you can see all the goods the country has to offer. In different regions you can find the products characteristic of the locality. Experience shows that it is worth buying what you want wherever you find it, as hand-made items differ from region to region. You can usually come to an agreement with the merchant.

Vacations

Yachting
All entry ports in Turkey permit yachts to anchor in their harbour. The marinas in Kuşadasi, Bodrum, Kemer and Antalya are run by the Turkish Tourist Bank and are open throughout the year, as is the marina in the holiday village Altin Yunus in

Çeşme. At the marinas, one can purchase all necessary equipment, stock-up on food and gas and hook-up to electricity and water. One can obtain more information about anchoring possibilities at the local tourist offices or at the Turban Turism A.S. situated in the above mentioned cities (main office: Ankara/Kızıl 32, Karanfil Sokak Tel. 117-4192, fax 118-5469.

Weather forecasts are broadcasted every day on channels 16 and 67 VHF at the following times: 9am, 12pm, 3pm, 6pm and 9pm. Each forecast is broadcasted twice, with an interval of 5 minutes. between each report. For further information contact: Çevre Bakanliği, Devlet Meteorologi Gn. Md., Kalaba 06120, Ankara Tel. 359-7545, fax 359-3430.

The coast of Turkey has many inlets especially between İzmir and Antalya, therefore anchoring is very convenient. The depth of the water is 1-12 m. Yachting in Turkey is a most pleasurable experience, but one must follow certain rules: Avoid sailing in a zig-zag between Turkey and Greece; fly the Turkish courtesy flag from 8am until sunset; and don't pick up antiques from the beaches.

One can also rent yachts in Turkey. A leading yacht agency is Yeşil Marmaris Tel. 2290 (Marmaris), 528-5510 (İstanbul). The agency rents out yachts, crews and equipment, advises and helps plan routes.

Skiing
In recent years skiing locations have opened in Turkey. They are usually situated on afforested mountains of average height. There are skiing locations in Anatolia, Ankara and near Bursa (for details see city and surrounding area routes). The best season for skiing is between Jan.-March.

Mountain Climbing
The best time for mountain climbing is between June-Sept. Some mountains, such as Mt. Süphan can be climbed only in July and August. Other mountains

worth climbing are the Kaçkar mountains located between Riza and Hopa, Mt. Ararat (Ağri Daği), Büyük Ağri Cilo-Sat. A permit from the appropriate authorities is required. Other information is available at the foreign office in Ankara, Tel. 117-2790. Before setting out it is advisable to inform the mountain climbers' club in Turkey of the destination and the planned dates. The club will inform the authorities of that particular area so they can be of assistance when and it it becomes necessary.

Mind your Manners

The Turks maintain clear, set rules of behavior. There is a developed set of greetings for each and every occasion. The Turks do not expect the tourist to master Turkish nor their rules of etiquette, but you must observe some basic manners.

Throughout Turkey you should be sure to maintain respect for the country, the religion and the family. It is illegal to offend the honor of Atatürk, the Turkish people and the Republic. In case of a misunderstanding, apologize immediately and stop the debate. The apology is generally accepted willingly and solves the problem. Dress modestly when visiting mosques. Women must enter with their head and shoulders covered. It is best to avoid visiting mosques on Friday and during prayer hours. Photographing with a flash and any other disturbance to the worshippers is considered rude. Men should not address Turkish women directly; it is permissible to answer them politely if they address you. Turkish women do not go out alone at night, and a woman touring alone who does so will be considered unrespectable and can expect to be propositioned accordingly.

General Information

Keeping In Touch

There is a post office in every city. It is marked with a yellow sign with the letters PTT (post, telephone, telegraph) in black. In small towns there is one PTT office. In İstanbul there is such an office in every quarter.

Public telephones are located in the PTT office and outside of it. The telephones are operated with a special token (*jeton*). For calls within the country, or collect calls, use the red phone and small or medium-sized tokens. For international calls, you need medium or large tokens (*büyük jeton*), dial 99 – country code – city code and then the number . In addition to these, there are also a few new telephones that do not take tokens, but a magnetic card. You put the card, which is worth several dozen tokens, through a slot, and at the end of the conversation the appropriate number of meter units are recorded. There is almost no queue for these phones, and you can purchase the card at PTT offices.

Phone connections with Europe are good and can be made within a few minutes.

There are yellow mailboxes in the PTT post offices and in tourist centers. You can also buy stamps and aerogrammes in hotels and at kiosks.

It is best to send packages from a small town and not from the central parcel post office in Karaköy, İstanbul. The bureaucracy in Karaköy is overwhelming, and the customs inspections are exhausting. In small towns, package sending is handled with efficiency and speed. The tourist can receive mail through the poste restante. In İstanbul you can get mail at the PTT branch in the Eminönü quarter, near the Sirkeci train station. You can also receive mail at the *American Express* offices in the country.

Changing Money

The Turkish currency is the Turkish *lira*. The rate of exchange in the banks changes daily, and therefore you shouldn't change a large amount at once. Save the receipts of your exchange transactions; you may have to show them upon leaving the country. The black market is not developed. Private currency exchange is considered a serious offense in Turkey. In many shops you can pay in dollars, German marks, and the like, and ask for a better rate for the foreign currency. In rural areas, only the Turkish *lira* is accepted, and the local residents are often reluctant to accept or change foreign currency.

Business Hours

Banks are open Monday through Friday, 8:30am-noon and 1:30-5pm. On Saturday and Sunday the banks are closed.

Stores are open from 9am-7pm, except for an afternoon break from 1-2pm in İstanbul. Most stores, including the large bazaars, are open Monday through Saturday and closed on Sunday.

Post Offices are open from 8am-midnight, with no break. Government offices are closed on Saturday and Sunday. In the summer, government offices close during the hot afternoon hours. Although the large majority of Turks are Moslems, Friday is generally a regular working day, and Sunday is the day of rest.

Tourist Information Offices

Here are a few international Turkish Offices:

United Kingdom: 170-173 Piccadilly, London WV1 9DD, Tel. 071-734-8681.

U.S.A.: 821 United Nations Plaza, New York, NY 10017, Tel. 212-687-2194.

1717 Massachussets Ave. N.W., Suite 306, Washington D.C. 20036, Tel. 202-429-9844.

The Turkish effort to develop tourism is also expressed in a network of tourist information offices. Municipal and national information offices are located in every city, and they offer booklets and maps. In many cases the employees at these centers speak no other language than Turkish. The information offices are marked with signs showing the ancient Hittite sun. At the airport in İstanbul there is an efficient information office, where the tourist can get helpful assistance.

Now for a word of warning. During

the last two years, Turkey has been revolutionising its telephone (and fax) network. Even after the standardization of phone numbers (a 3-digit area code + a 7-digit local number) there are still frequent changes. It is simply a must to enquire on arrival, at the airport information office, whether an updated list of numbers (Tourist Offices, railway stations, car-hire agencies, Red Cross, hospitals etc.) is available.

Useful Phone Numbers

Fire – 110

Emergency – 112

International Operator – 115

Telephone Information – 118

Postal Code Information – 119

Police – 155

Rural Police – 156

Measurements, Electricity, Time

Turkey uses the metric system. The electric current is 220 volts. The outlets are round, so appliances with a square plug require an adaptor. Temperatures are measured in Celsius.

The Turkish clock is two hours ahead of Greenwich Mean Time.

For Further reading

Reference
Turkey, Geoffrey Lewis

Archeology
Ancient Civilizations and Ruins of Turkey, Ekrem Akungal

History
The Emergence of Modern Turkey, Bernard Lewis

Literature
Gallipoli, Alan Morhead
The Mask of Demetrius, Eric Embler
The Great Railway Bazaar, Paul Theroux
Travels with My Aunt, Graham Greene
Murder on the Orient Express, Agatha Christie
Innocents Abroad, Mark Twain

Movies
Gallipoli
Yol
The Herd

A Recommended Tour

A visit to Turkey should be divided into two – a tour of the western part of the country, and a tour of the east.

Western Turkey: First we will become acquainted with the European part of Turkey, the area around İstanbul, around the Marmara Sea and Thrace. The tour then takes us to Ankara, and after a short sojourn in the capital city, we continue south to the Anatolian plateau, and to one of the highlights of the tour – the Cappadocia region and the Göreme Valley. This area is so special that even visitors to Eastern Turkey insist on stopping here on their way east or before returning to İstanbul and home.

Those continuing on a western tour head southeast from Cappadocia, to the Dervish city, Konya. From here there are a few options for continuing to the Mediterranean: those who want to lengthen their trip along the coast turn southeast toward Silifke and from there west. Another possibility is to go west from Konya to Beyşehir and south through the Taurus mountains to Alanya and Antalya on the coast. You can also reach Antalya by another nice route, from Beyşehir west over Lake Eğridir and the charming town of the same name, Isparta and the Taurus ridge. From Isparta you can continue west toward Pamukkale and Kuşadası, skipping over the entire Mediterranean coast area and most of the Aegean coast.

Cover the Mediterranean coast from the east, from Adana westward to Marmaris, and from there continue along the Aegean coast, via Kuşadası and Efes, with a sidetrack to Pamukkale, to the Marmara Sea and back to İstanbul.

Eastern Turkey: The recommended tour route of Eastern Turkey is to fly from İstanbul to Erzurum, one of the central eastern cities, and start the tour of the east from there. Land travelers can reach Cappadocia, and from there turn east to Sivas and Erzurum.

From Erzurum we continue to Kars – a straight route or through the Kaçkar mountains. From Kars we turn to the Doğubayazıt and Mount Ararat and on to Lake Van. The route from Van goes west, to Diyarbakır, one of the major cities in the region, which is mainly Kurdish. From here there are two possibilities: toward Mount Nemrut and the wonderful temple at its peak, and from there to Cappadocia and the west; or to southeast Turkey – Mardin, Urfa, Gaziantep, and the Iskenderun Bay.

The **Black Sea** region can be included in the tour of Eastern Turkey: from Ankara go northeast toward Samsun on the coast, and from there travel east along the coast, via Trabzon, to the Kaçkar mountains.

The lovely shores of Kekova, on the Mediterranean Coast

TURKEY

TURKEY

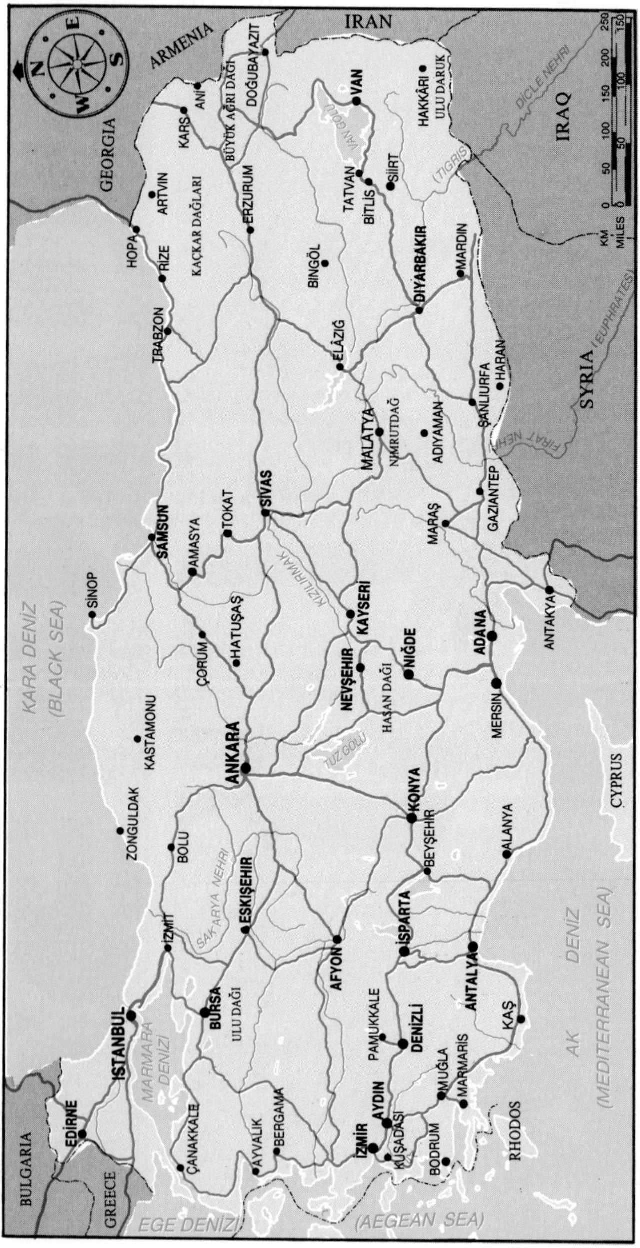

IRAN
ARMENIA
GEORGIA
IRAQ
SYRIA
BULGARIA
GREECE
CYPRUS
RHODOS
KARA DENİZ
(BLACK SEA)
AK DENİZ
(MEDITERRANEAN SEA)
EGE DENİZİ
(AEGEAN SEA)
MARMARA DENİZİ
VAN GÖLÜ
TUZ GÖLÜ
KIZILIRMAK
SAKARYA NEHRİ
DİCLE NEHRİ
(TIGRIS)
FIRAT NEHRİ
(EUPHRATES)
İSTANBUL
EDİRNE
ÇANAKKALE
AYVALIK
BERGAMA
İZMİR
KUŞADASI
AYDIN
BODRUM
MUĞLA
MARMARİS
DENİZLİ
PAMUKKALE
BURSA
ULU DAĞI
İZMİT
ESKİŞEHİR
AFYON
ISPARTA
ANTALYA
KAŞ
BEYŞEHİR
ALANYA
KONYA
ZONGULDAK
BOLU
ANKARA
KASTAMONU
ÇORUM
HATUŞAŞ
SİNOP
SAMSUN
AMASYA
TOKAT
SİVAS
NEVŞEHİR
HAŞAN DAĞI
NİĞDE
KAYSERİ
ADANA
MERSİN
ANTAKYA
MARAŞ
GAZİANTEP
MALATYA
NIMRUTDAĞ
ADIYAMAN
ŞANLIURFA
HARAN
ELÂZIĞ
BİNGÖL
DİYARBAKIR
MARDİN
TRABZON
RİZE
HOPA
ARTVİN
KAÇKAR DAĞLARI
ERZURUM
KARS
ANİ
BÜYÜK AĞRI DAĞI
DOĞUBAYAZIT
TATVAN
BİTLİS
SİİRT
VAN
HAKKÂRİ
ULU DARUK
N
E
S
W
KM 0 50 100 150 200 250
MILES 0 50 100 150

İSTANBUL

History of the City

The fascinating story of İstanbul begins in the period when the Hellenistic culture began to flourish, and the *polis* (the Greek city-states) were established, one after another, along the Mediterranean coasts. Byzas, a Greek from the region of Corinthia, set out in search of a new city-state. Legend tells us that on his way he went through Delphi and asked the oracle where he should establish his land. The oracle gave the cryptic reply "opposite the land of the blind," adding no further explanation. Byzas and his subjects set sail in 667 BC. As in all legends, there was also a sudden storm, which swept our heroes to the refuge of a protected and quiet natural bay. When they looked around, they saw the small village on the Asian side of the straits (today Kadiköy). Byzas remembered the oracle and understood that the inhabitants on the Asian side were blind in that they did not see the convenient bay, the Golden Horn Bay. At the edge of the bay, where the Topkapı Palace is located now, Byzas established his city-state and called it Byzantium.

There is an important historic fact in this legend: the Golden Horn is an ideal basin in the Bosphorus Strait. The strait separates Asia from Europe, and was once a major channel of sea transportation, connecting the Mediterranean with the Black Sea, and offering those who controlled it a prominent strategic, military and economic advantage.

Byzantium existed for 850 years until the late second century AD, when it was conquered by the Roman Septimus Severus, who renamed it Augusta Antonia. The city was almost completely destroyed in battle, and was rebuilt by the Romans. The wars between the Roman emperors further influenced the fate of the city. In 330 AD, Constantine the Great took the city from the Emperor Licinius and, as was the custom, he changed its name to the New Rome, and later to Constantinople, under which name it remained as the capital of the Byzantine Empire for the next 1,123 years.

The Byzantine Empire, enjoyed a period of prosperity and Constantinople became a center of wealth and power in this section of the eastern Roman Empire. Ayasofia, the largest church in the world at the time, was built between the imperial palaces and the opulent Hippodrome. Streets, houses and water and sewage systems were built in the Greco-Roman tradition, making the city one of the most advanced of its day and a center of western culture. The military power of the Byzantine Emper-

The Blue Mosque at night

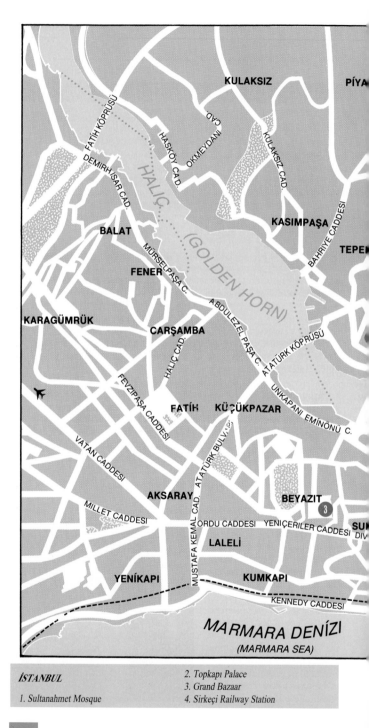

İSTANBUL

1. Sultanahmet Mosque

2. Topkapı Palace
3. Grand Bazaar
4. Sirkeçi Railway Station

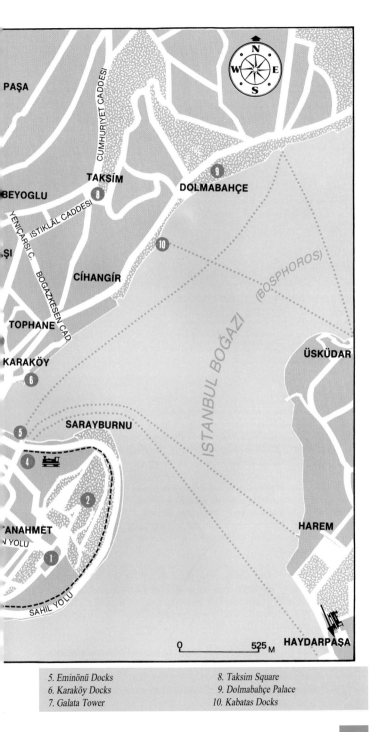

PAŞA

BEYOGLU

TAKSÍM

DOLMABAHÇE

CUMHURÍYET CADDESÍ

YENÍÇARSI C.

ISTIKLÂL CADDESÍ

ŞI

BOGAZKESEN CAD.

CÍHANGÍR

TOPHANE

KARAKÖY

ÜSKÜDAR

SARAYBURNU

ISTANBUL BOĞAZI

(BOSPHOROS)

ANAHMET

N YOLU

SAHIL YOLU

HAREM

HAYDARPAŞA

0   525 M

5. Eminönü Docks
6. Karaköy Docks
7. Galata Tower

8. Taksim Square
9. Dolmabahçe Palace
10. Kabatas Docks

TURKEY

The Bosphorus Bridge above the calm blue waters

ors enabled them to ward off many attempted invasions, and with the exception of a short period of Latin rule in the thirteenth century, when the city was occupied during the Fourth Crusade, the tradition of the Byzantine-Christian rule continued until the Ottoman era.

In 1453, Mehmet the Conqueror rode his horse into the Ayasofia Church, the symbol of the Byzantine Empire, heralding a new great era in the history of the city. Ayasofia became a mosque, and the name of the city was changed to İstanbul. The Ottomans were merciful to the residents (by standards of the time), and allowed them to stay in the city. The Sultans concentrated on building the city and its walls, as if trying to eclipse the achievements of previous rulers. In the sixteenth century, Sulayman the Magnificent erected many buildings in Istanbul, including Süleymaniye, the largest mosque in the city. In the early seventeenth century, Ahmetı added the Sultanahmet mosque, the marvellous "Blue Mosque." Despite the decline of the empire, the last Sultans continued to construct opulent edifices, such as the white Dolmabahçe Palace, which was erected in the nineteenth century, when the empire was already nearing its end.

After the First World War, the republic under Kemal Atatürk was concerned about the position of the large city. Kemal Atatürk strove to end the Turkish people's glorification of the imperial past, and he also wanted to move the capital from the Greek border and the sea, because of the city's vulnerability to surprise military attacks.

Thus Atatürk moved the capital to Ankara in Anatolia and from there he undertook to lead Turkey into a new, modern era. The glory of Istanbul has declined slightly since the establishment of the republic, but there is no doubt that this is still the largest and most exciting of Turkey's cities, a living museum of the magnificent imperial past.

The Layout of the City

İstanbul is located on the Bosphorus, the strait that divides Asia and Europe, and that connects the Marmara Sea with the Black Sea. It straddles two continents; its eastern section is in Asia, and its western, in Europe.

The Golden Horn Bay (Haliç) divides the European side into two – the old city and the new city. The old city is the site of historic Byzantium, Constantinople and İstanbul. In the center of the old city is the Sultanahmet district. The central road in the old city is Divan Yolu, which connects the Sultanahmet district to the Beyazit district, Lâleli and Aksaray, west of Sultanahmet. The large covered Bazaar (Kapalıçarsı) is also located on Divan Yolu. The Eminönü and Sirkeci quarters are located in the old city along the coast of the Golden Horn Bay.

The Galata and Atatürk bridges connect the old city with the new. Galata bridge (which was destroyed by fire in 1992 and later renovated) connects the Eminönü quarter with Karaköy, where the international harbor is located. The new city encompasses ancient cities, such as Galata and Pera, which expanded and became part of modern İstanbul. Here you will find the lovely Galata Tower and the modern Taksim Square, the area of the luxury hotels. The main street in the new city, also known as Beyoğlu, is Istiklâl Cad., which connects the Tünel (subway) Square, Taksim Square and the

A view from the Galata Tower

prestigious Cumhuriyet Cad. in the Taksim quarter. This street is closed to all vehicles except the tram. The foreign embassies and consulates and offices of the international airlines are located in the new city.

The Asian side: Across the Bosphorus Strait, on the Asian side, are the Üsküdar and Kadiköy suburbs, with the Haydarpaşa train station lying between them. The ferries to Kadiköy and Haydarpaşa leave the Karaköy and Eminönü platforms from the European side.

Climate

The climate in İstanbul is very pleasant for visiting at the beginning of the summer in April and May. The hot season continues from June to late September, but there are summer rains. During this period, the temperatures drop in the evening due to the cool wind from the Black Sea. The coldest month in the year is January. The average temperature reaches 7°C, and snow sometimes falls on the nearby hills.

How to Get There

By air: The Atatürk International Airport is some 15 miles (25km) from the center of the city. The most comfortable way to get to the center of town is by taxi, which costs between $7 and $10, depending on your destination. The bus to the city leaves the airport from the domestic flights terminal. The bus stops at Aksaray in the old city and continues to the Turkish Airlines city terminal, between Galata Tower and the US consulate. Buses leave every half hour from 5:30-9am, and from 2pm-midnight; from 9am-2pm, they run once an hour. An internal bus runs every 10 minutes between the international terminal and the domestic flights terminal. The ride to the center of town takes about 40 minutes and costs about $1.

By sea: Most international sea carriers to Turkey reach Karaköy,

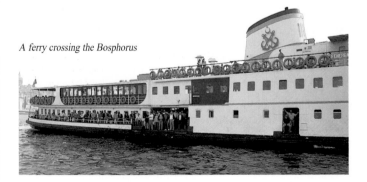
A ferry crossing the Bosphorus

near the site of the Galata Bridge. From the port you can catch a bus, *dolmuş* or taxi to any spot in the city.

By train: The train from Europe takes you to the Sirkeci station near Topkapı Palace. From the train station it is possible either to walk to the Sultanahmet district or take public transportation to your destination.

Trains from Anatolia reach Haydarpaşa station, on the Asian side of İstanbul. From here there is an excellent ferry service to the port of Karaköy. The ferry schedule in Karaköy coordinates with that of the major trains; the trip is pleasant and quite convenient. A taxi is much more expensive.

By bus: Buses from Europe arrive at the Topkapı station. The name of the station has already confused many a tourist, who got off here expecting to find themselves in the center of the old city, near Topkapı Palace. The station is located outside of the walls of the old city, far from the center. The best way to get to the city from the Topkapı station is by taxi.

Bus or *dolmuş* passengers must change at the Aksaray station. Some companies include a minibus service to the center of the city in the price of the ticket; one is advised to check which company provides this useful service before purchasing a ticket. Buses from Anatolia also stop at the Harem station, on the Asian side of the Bosphorus. Only residents of Üsküdar and Kadiköy get off at this stop; the rest go on to Topkapı station.

By car: The E5 road goes from Europe to the Atatürk airport. From the airport you can continue toward the city on the same road. Past the airport, there is a turn off to the road crossing the Bosphorus Strait and

continuing to Anatolia, for those who do not wish to enter İstanbul. If you continue along the road, rather than taking the turn off, you will reach Aksaray and the Sultanahmet district. A prettier route is via the Marmara Sea coast. Get off the highway near the airport and continue by following the signs to Ataköy or Yeşilköy. The road winds along the coast alongside the old city walls, giving you get a fantastic view of the strait.

Area codes: 212, 216

Tourist Services

There are tourist information offices at the Atatürk Airport in İstanbul, Tel. 573-7399, and at the Karaköy International Port, tel. 249-5776. In the Taksim district there is an information center in the lobby of the *Hilton Hotel*, Tel. 233-0592. Visitors to the Sultanahmet district can find assistance at an information point located at the western end of the Hippodrome, Tel. 518-1802. The employees in these offices speak several foreign languages and they distribute a selection of booklets and maps.

Car Rental
Avis and *Hertz* have several branches throughout the city and at the international airport.

Avis
Divan Hotel: Tel. 231-4100.
Hilton Hotel: Tel. 241-4650.
Taksim quarter: Tel. 141-2917,
Yedikuyular Cad. 4/A.
Atatürk airport: Tel. 573-6445
(24 hours a day).

Hertz
Sheraton Hotel: Tel. 231-2121.
The new city: 241-6996,
Cumhuriyet Cad. 295.
Atatürk airport: Tel. 663-6300
(24 hours a day).

Accommodation

During the tourist season it is best to reserve a room in advance for at least your first few days in İstanbul. The traveler, arriving in İstanbul in the middle of the night in July and August without hotel reservations, is liable to have difficulty in finding accommodation, and is advised to reach the inexpensive hotels in the Sultanahmet district by the morning or early afternoon, so as to find a room. Off-season it is not difficult to find accommodation of any standard, in the city. Out of season, many hotels offer discounts or are willing to bargain, reducing rates by 10 to 20 percent.

Generally, the hotels in the new city, and in the Taksim district in particular, are of a high standard. The closer you get to Taksim Square, the more expensive the hotels are. The least expensive are the simple hotels in the old city, particularly in the Sultanahmet District. There are only a few exceptions to this generalization. Tourists with a limited budget should head for the old city. Those with a moderate or generous budget will find what they are looking for in the prestigious Taksim District.

Deluxe Hotels
(5 stars and higher; HL according to the Turkish system):

There are four luxury hotels in the Taksim district in the new city of İstanbul. All of which possess the cosmopolitan atmosphere expected of this type of accommodation.

Marmara İstanbul Hotel: the tallest building in the city, and the view

from the top floors is breathtaking, Tel. 251-4696, fax 244-0509.

Sheraton Hotel: 80174 Taksim Park, one of the largest hotels in the city, with 424 rooms, Tel. 231-2121, fax 231-2180.

İstanbul Hilton: Cumhuriyet Cad., Harbiye, is considered one of the finest *Hiltons* in the world. It is excellently located – overlooking the Bosphorus. A visit to the rooftop restaurant is a special experience because of the view; recommended to those staying at other hotels, as well. Tel. 231-4650, fax 240-4165.

Divan Hotel: 2 Cumhuriyet Cad. Offers more reasonable prices than the other three. You will find a calmer ambience here, Tel. 231-4100, fax 248-8527.

There are also some exclusive hotels located outside the city center, including:

Tarabya: In the quarter of the same name on Kefelikoy Cad., Tel. 262-0710, fax 262-2260.

Çinar: Tel. 573-2910, in the Yeşilköy District, near the airport.

Expensive Hotels
(4 stars; H1 by the Turkish system):

At this standard there are two hotels that preserve an atmosphere of the glorious empire of the past.

Pera Palas: 89 Meşrutiyet Cad., near the US consulate, Tel. 251-4560, fax 251-4089. Established at the turn of the century. The hotel was opened to accommodate the passengers of the Orient Express, and among its guests were the Who's Who of Europe of the time, including King Boris of Bulgaria and Agatha Christie, author of *Murder on the Orient Express*. The

hotel, which opened in 1892, has been renovated a few times, but has nevertheless preserved its original charm.

Yeşil Ev: ("The Green Residence") located in the Sultanahmet District between the Ayasofia Church and the Blue Mosque. The hotel opened in 1984, in one of the largest and most beautiful nineteenth-century buildings in İstanbul. It has a charming garden, a perfect place for a rest and a light meal after visiting the Sultanahmet District and for those staying in the new city. Has only 20 rooms, Tel. 528-6764.

The Turkish hotel chains have built more modern expensive hotels:

Pullman Etap: Mesrutiyet Cad., Tel. 251-4646, fax 249-8033.
Dedeman Hotel: 50 Yildiz Posta Cad., in the center of the new city, Tel. 274-8810.

Turban Carlton: On the shore of the Bosphorus, far from the city center is another prestigious place to stay, Tel. 242-2464.

Zürich: 37 Harikazadeler Sok. A

most outstanding hotel, if this hotel is full, you can look for other hotels of the same standard along the street, Tel. 512-2350, fax 526-9731.

Moderately Priced Hotels

(2-3 stars; H2-H3 by the Turkish system):

Of the wide selection of hotels at this standard we recommend:

Dilson: on Siraselviler Cad., in the central Taksim district, Tel. 252-9600.

Keban: next door to the Dilson, Tel. 251-5320.

Bale: on Refik Saydam Cad., near the British Consulate, Tel. 253-0700, fax 250-1692.

In Lâleli, in the old city of İstanbul, there are several moderately priced hotels.

Büyük Keban: Gençtürk Cad. 47 in Aksaray. 132 rooms, and there are good chances you will find a vacant one, Tel. 512-0020.

Elit: Yerebatan Cad., Salkim Söğüt Sok. 14, Tel. 512-7566. Centrally located.

Inexpensive Hotels

(1 star; H4, M1, M2, P):

İstanbul is a paradise for the low-budget traveler. A selection of hotels await the adventurous and lively visitor to this city. Most backpackers turn to the Sultanahmet District. The busy streets in the district are full of inexpensive hotels, offering a bed in a large room or a small double room at low prices. This district is particularly suitable for young tourists who want to be near the action. The hotels in this area are crowded, noisy, and generally lack privacy. You will find two pleasant hotels here:

Yücelt Hostel: opposite the Ayasofia Church, which despite its name is not associated with any hostel organization.

Büyük Ayasofia: near the *Yücelt Hostel*. The rooms in this old establishment are not particularly attractive, but its location and the verandas over the courtyard of the Ayasofia Church give it a special charm. Tel. 516-9446.

A good alternative to the bustling Sultanahmet District is the selection of inexpensive hotels in Aksaray and Lâleli. In Lâleli, west of İstanbul University, there are several hotels on the small street, Harikazadeler Sok., among them *Ayda*, at number 11, and *Oran*, at number 40. In the Taksim District, the *Inka* Hotel, opposite the US Consulate, has 42 rooms at reasonable prices. There are also hostels in the student dormitories in the universities, which house tourists during the vacation months. Details are available at the tourist information offices. A large youth hostel is located at 63 Cerrahpaşa Cad., in Aksaray.

What and Where to Eat

The wealth of restaurants in İstanbul makes a visit to the city a gastronomic experience. The selection of restaurants covers the entire spectrum, from small alcoves, where they prepare kebab and other meat on the grill, to exclusive restaurants with uniformed waiters and muted background music. The golden rule is to follow your eyes and your nose. Do not hesitate to enter an unfamiliar restaurant; on the contrary, the tourist is likely to discover new culinary treasures. It seems that every tourist has a restaurant from among the endless selection, which he or she recommends to friends planning a trip to Turkey.

There are several famous restaurants in İstanbul that enjoy a reputation of over a hundred years. The well-known *Abdullah* Restaurant has moved from its location of the last century in the center of town to the Emirgân Quarter, Koru Cad.11, Emirgân, Tel. 277-5721. The restaurant serves excellent sea food. High quality Turkish and international food can also be found at the *Dört Mevsim* ("Four Seasons") Restaurant in the center of the new city, Istiklâl Cad. 509, Tel. 245-8941.

All the luxury hotels have good restaurants. The restaurant in the *Divan Hotel* (Tel. 231-4100) and the *Revan* Restaurant in the *Sheraton* are particularly recommended. A feast in the atmosphere of the turn

Savour some delicious slices of the Turkish delicacy – döner kebab

of the century can be enjoyed in the *Pera Palas Hotel*. The restaurant on the roof of the *Hilton* offers a remarkable view in addition to excellent food. Reservations should be made in advance for the exclusive restaurants.

Other good restaurants include *Haçibaba*: 49 Istiklâl Cad., Tel. 244-1886; *Ziya*: Mim Kemal Oke Cad., 21, Nişantaşı, Tel. 261-6005, specializing in Turkish dishes; and the well-known *Liman*, Yolcu-Salonu Üıstü, Karaköy. Open noon-4pm, for lunch only.

The Kerran Saray restaurant-night club has an inviting atmosphere, delicious food and an oriental show every night at 9pm, 30 Cumhuriyet Cad., Tel. 247-1630.

A well-known restaurant in the old city is the *Pandaley*, at the entrance to the spice market, which is also open only for lunch. In the Sultanahmet region is the famous *Pudding Shop*. This is where the

Old İstanbul – a view from the Golden Horn Bay

colorful groups of hippies stopped on their way to India and Nepal in the late 1960s on the *Magic Bus* from Europe.

A large number of restaurants specializing in sea food can be found in the Kumkapı Region of the old city, between Sultanahmet and Lâleli, opposite the Beyazıt Mosque. It is worth wandering through the charming alleyways and trying one of the small restaurants.

Getting Around

By car: Try to avoid the crowded areas of Sirkeci and Karaköy. The narrow streets of the old city make the flow of traffic very difficult. There are few gas stations in the city, and it is best not to wait until your tank is almost empty.

By train: A few electric train lines run from the Sirkeci Station, serving the residents of İstanbul. The major lines go to Florya and Ataköy, on the Marmara coast.

By subway: İstanbul's subway, *tünel*, deserves an entry in the *Guinness Book of Records* rather than in tourist guides: this is the shortest subway in the world 765 yards (700m) between Karaköy and the southern end of Istiklâl Street. The train was built by French engi-

neers in the last century, so that the wealthy residents of the city and European merchants could travel comfortably between the commercial area in the Galata District and their homes in Pera. The trip is inexpensive and requires a token, which can be purchased at the entrance.

By ferry: This is the recommended means of transportation in İstanbul. The trip by ferry costs the same as by bus, and it is generally faster and more interesting. The dozens of ferries and the many platforms may confuse the passenger; before boarding make sure that you are getting on the right ferry.

Platform Details

Destination	Station of Departure	Platform Number
Kadiköy	Eminönü	1
Üsküdar	Eminönü	2
Bosphorus Strait	Eminönü	3
Bosphorus Strait	Eminönü	4
Princes' Isles, Yalova (ferries)	Sirkeci	5
Kadıköy	Karaköy	7
Haydarpaşa (train station)	Kadıköy	8
Princes' Isles, (Yalova ferries)	Kabataş (near Dolmabahçe)	B
Princes' Isles, (Yalova)	Bostanci (Asia)	5

One of the finest experiences of a visit to İstanbul is a night trip on the ferry by the light of the city – destination unimportant. This is a "must".

Sites to See

İstanbul is absolutely overflowing with historic sites, which reflect the power and wealth of the ancient empire. A walk through the streets and alleyways of the city presents the tourists with the remnants of a splendid past: palaces, mosques, churches and bridges, some of which have become museums, some still in daily use. The peak, undoubtedly, is in the Sultanahmet district in the old city. Standing on Divan Yolu you will be overwhelmed by the enormous plaza and the ornate buildings, giving you a sense of the greatness of the past.

Topkapı Palace
(Open: July-Aug. 9:30am-7pm; Sept-June 9:30am-5pm; closed Tues.)

Topkapı Palace is spread over a large area and comprises many sights and exhibits. Many visitors combine a tour of the palace with a visit to the nearby Ayasofia Church and the Sultanahmet Mosque, but this is not recommended as it is too exhausting. A visit to the palace will take the entire morning, and afterwards you will certainly want to rest. Mozart's opera, *Seragalio*, is presented annually in the palace, during the International İstanbul Festival.

Topkapı Palace was built by Mehmet the Conqueror. It was constructed between 1459 and 1465 on the ruins of ancient Byzantium, and served as the court of the Sultanate and the center of rule of the Ottoman Empire until 1853. In its days of glory, the palace housed over 5,000 people. Over the years, the Sultans continued to build and renovate the palace to suit their changing needs. It is not a single building but rather a royal village, with many buildings serving a variety of purposes.

In the courtyard of the Topkapı Palace

The main entrance to the palace is through the **Imperial Gate** and the **Court of the Janissaries**. The *Janissaries* were the elite soldiers of the kingdom, who served as the Sultan's personal guard. The origin of the *Janissaries* is in the *devşirme*, the child tax demanded from the conquered Christians. These highly acclaimed Turkish soldiers were mainly Christian children from the

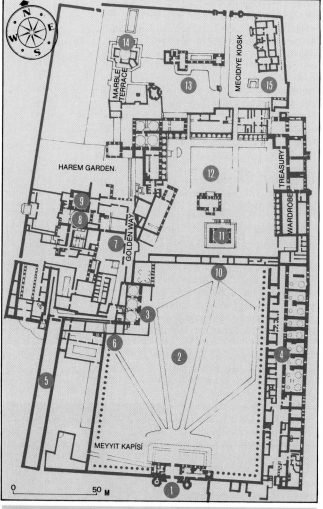

TOPKAPI PALACE

1. Gate of Salutations
2. Courtyard of the Divan
3. Divan
4. Palace Kitchens
5. Royal Stables
6. Entrance to the Harem
7. Courtyard of the Valide Sultan
8. Hall of the Emperor
9. Salon of Murat III
10. Gate of Felicity
11. Audience Chamber
12. The Third Courtyard
13. The Fourth Courtyard
14. Kiosks
15. Restaurant

Balkan states who were taken from their families, converted to Islam and trained for war at an early age. As the Sultanate weakened, the status of the *Janissaries* increased. This is the courtyard where the *Janissaries* received their food in large rice bowls. When they were not pleased with the Sultan, they would turn their rice bowls over, drum on them with large spoons and rise against the ruler. This cost quite a few Sultans their heads.

The Courtyard of the *Janissaries* served as a utility area for the palace, housing a bakery, a coin mint and various storage rooms. There are three museums here – the Archeological Museum, the Museum of the Ancient Orient and the Museum of Tiles. We recommend that you visit these separately and not as a part of your tour of Topkapı Palace. Though seemingly less convenient, it is better to devote all your energy to the palace and to come back on another day.

An impressive exhibit at the Archeological Museum

The Archeological Museum contains precious ancient items, including the splendid Alexander sarcophagus, decorated with the image of Alexander the Great. Another outstanding item is a statue of Bes from Cyprus. On the second floor, you will find the Siloah inscription. If the second floor is closed, you can ask the museum management for assistance; they are likely to comply with your request if you present a convincing explanation for your desire to see the inscription such as for studies, research, etc.

The Museum of the Ancient Orient (Eski Şark Eseleri Müzesi) contains an exhibit of the cultures of the ancient Orient, including important historic relics such as the Treaty of Kadesh, the oldest peace treaty known in history, from the year 1269 BC. This treaty was made between Ramses II, King of Egypt and the Hittite Kingdom. Other outstanding exhibits include colored tiles from Babylonia depicting lions, which date back to the period of Nebuchadnezzar II, and ceramic plaques inscribed with the Laws of Hammurabi in cuneiform.

Çinili Kösk (Tiled Pavilion) is housed in a decorated kiosk built by Mehmet the Conqueror in 1472. The museum exhibits beautiful examples of the art of colored tiles. This Ottoman art reached a peak in the city of İznik, and the colored İznik tiles became world famous. These are the tiles that give the Blue Mosque its name.

The museums are open daily, 9am-5pm, closed on Mon. A ticket to all the museums costs about $1. Tickets cost about half on weekends and holidays. Due to renovations, the Üinili Kösk has been closed, and is expected to be opened to the public only once a week, on Tuesdays.

The **Church of St. Irene** (Aya Irene Kilisesi) stands on the left side of the Courtyard of the *Janissaries*. The church was built in the sixth century by Justinian and is as old as the great Ayasofia. Today the shady courtyard is used as a parking lot for tour buses. Concerts are held in the Church of St. Irene during the summer season.

Visiting the Topkapı Palace

The Gate of Salutations (Orta Kapı), built in 1524 by Sulayman the Magnificent, leads us to the second courtyard, **The Courtyard of the Divan**. Entry to this courtyard was on foot as only the Sultan had the right to enter on horseback. The *divan*, the council hall, served for assemblies of the high officials and the Great Vizier, the head of the ministers, as a place for assembling to discuss affairs of the empire. The *divan* is located on the left side of the courtyard, next to the entrance to the harem. Next to the gate is the **Executioner's Fountain** (Cellat Çesmesi). Here the executioner would wash the blood off his hands and sword after performing his job. The exe-

At the Topkapı Palace

cutioner was usually the head gardener and lived in a small building next to the Gate of Salutations.

In the palace kitchens, on the right side of the courtyard, there is an impressive display of the implements that were once used in the palace. Among them are collections of porcelain, crystal, silverware, glassware and more. On the left side of the Courtyard of the Divan, where the royal stables were located, there is a display of the Sultan's carriages. Between the royal stables and the hall of the *divan* is the entrance to the harem.

Entry to the **Harem** is allowed only with guided tours, which leave at set times between 10am-4pm. Buy a ticket in advance, due to the demand for these tours. It is advisable to visit the harem before visiting the rest of the palace. If you arrive late and there is already a large crowd waiting, buy a ticket for the time that suits you best, continue to tour the palace, and then return here for the tour.

There are many legends associated with life in the harem. Stories of the oriental pleasures of the Sultan and his thousand mistresses aroused great jealousy among men throughout the world. The truth is somewhat different: the harem was the private residential quarters of the Sultan's family, and was strictly managed by the Valide Sultan, the Sultan's mother. This influence on the life of the Sultan and his mistresses gave the Sultan's mother great power, and it was she who controlled his nocturnal pleasures.

The Moslem religion allows a man to have four legal wives and as many mistresses as he can decently support, and during certain periods, the Sultan kept over 200 mistresses. Islam forbids enslavement of monotheists, Moslems, Christians and Jews – so the mistresses were of foreign origin. These women were purchased or taken from their parents as children; at age nine they were brought to the palace, where they were taught by the other mistresses. They studied religious subjects, such as the commandments of Islam, in addition to subjects such as reading and writing, dance and embroidery. After a period in the harem, the Sultan and his mother would marry the mistress off to one of the visitors to the palace. These women were in great demand because of their education and their connection to the palace. In this manner, the Sultan's mother could easily dispose of mistresses who were too ambitious or who were no longer pleasing.

The Topkapı Palace.

At its height, more than 500 people – wives, mistresses and princes up to age 11 – lived in the harem. The residents of the harem were waited on by Black Eunuchs, who were brought from Saudi Arabia and Africa. The Chief Black Eunuch had great influence on the harem, and thus a central position in the life of the empire. There was open competition between the Sultan's wives in their ambitions to advance their sons to the Sultan's throne. The Ottoman tradition did not give preference to the oldest son of the Sultan and the way to the crown was open to any of his children, with the strongest (or the one with the most determined mother) ultimately claiming the throne

The Harem is entered via a corridor tiled in mosaics. This is known as the Golden Way, an allusion to the custom of the Sultan to give gold coins to his subjects who bowed down to him as he walked here. Past the gate to the Harem is the Hall of the Black Eunuchs, the apartment of the Chief Black Eunuch and the Princes' School. At this school the princes studied from age 5 to 11, when they were sent away from the Harem. Farther along the Golden Way the tour comes to the Courtyard of the Valide Sultan, where the Sultan's mother lived, and opposite it, the apartments of the first wives of the Sultan. The next halls are the Hall of the

The Sultan's throne in the Topkapı Palace

Emperor, the largest and most magnificent room in the palace, which served the Sultan alone, and the Salon of Murat III, in which most of the original ornate decor has been preserved. From these halls the tour continues to other rooms that served the Sultans, including the room of the crown prince. Less than 40 rooms out of 400 of the Harem are open to the public. At the end of the tour, the visitors return via the Golden Way to the Courtyard of the Divan or to the third, innermost courtyard.

The entrance to the third courtyard from the second is the **Gate of Felicity** (Babı Sade). Here the Sultans made their public appearances, in the Audience Chamber (Arz Odası). These rare appearances were the only opportunity for contact between the Sultan and his subjects. The many residential rooms in this area were used by the princes and the royal messengers. Visitors to the palace were served by the White Eunuchs, who were based in the inner courtyard. Today, these rooms house splendid displays of the Sultan's treasures, including gold, silver, precious stones and royal clothing accumulated in the Ottoman Empire. Among the many magnificent items on display in the (Imperial Treasury) you will, no doubt, be awed by the famous gold throne of Shah Ismail, captured by Sultan Selim I in a war with the Persians and the 86-carat Spoonmaker's diamond (Kaşıkçı Elması). In the **Library of Ahmet III**, there are miniature paintings, imperial seals and arms.

The fourth courtyard, with gardens, verandas and large marbled terraces, is at the back of the palace. In one of its chambers there is an exhibit of a tooth and a hair from the beard of the Prophet Muhammad. The courtyard has decorative domes, known as kiosks (*köskü*) and wishing wells. The views from all sides are breathtaking, making it an ideal spot for a rest. In the lower part, there is a restaurant which is an ideal place to stop and revive yourself if you're feeling tired.

The Old City

Ayasofia

Ayasofia stands on the ruins of a number of churches that were destroyed. The first church was built in 327 by Constantine, founder of the Empire; it burned down in 404. The second church was erected in 415 by Theodosius II. This was destroyed in the famous Nicaea revolt in January 532, when Justinian almost lost the crown. When the revolt was quelled, Justinian appointed Anthemius of Tralles, the greatest mathematician of the period, and Isidorus of Miletos, last president of the Platonic Academy of Athens, to build a church that would reflect the greatness of God and of the nation. The construction took five years, and in December 537, Justinian passed through the gates of the church and entered the hall. His first response was, "Solomon, I have surpassed thee!" The completed church, in the opinion of the Emperor, was even more beautiful than Solomon's Temple in Jerusalem.

The Ayasofia Church in İstanbul – note the four minarets in the courtyard

Open daily, 9:30am-4:30pm. Closed Mon. In July and August, open to 7pm. The galleries are open 9:30-11:30am and 1-4pm. Audio-visual programs

are presented in the gallery daily (except for Sat.) at 3pm.

As you walk into the dark church, the colored stained glass windows catch your eyes. Past the door are gold-coated mosaics depicting Biblical themes. From here you can go up to the gallery and into the inner hall, where you will find the Imperial Gate to the church. Entrance through this door was restricted to the Emperor and those accompanying him. When Mehmet conquered Constantinople in 1453, he rode his horse into the church through the Imperial Gate, and with this symbolic gesture ended the 1123-year-old Byzantine Empire.

The genius of the construction of the church is reflected in its large central dome and the surrounding half-domes. The height of the central dome is 184ft. (56m), its diameter is 101ft. (31m) and next to it are two very impressive half-domes. Four large arches support the royal dome creating a sensation of spaciousness in the rounded inner space. The dome made such a great impression on the local residents of the time, that during the first few years after it was built they were afraid to enter the church, for fear that it would collapse on their heads. The dome was originally built of hollow bricks specially prepared in Rhodes from lightweight material. Paintings and colored mosaics, depicting traditional scenes, such as the *Angel Gabriel* and the *Madonna and Child*, decorate the ceiling.

Time left its mark on the Ayasofia, and it has been renovated over the centuries. Most of the renovations were on the exterior, and the original appearance of the church has been preserved. The Ottoman Sultans added four minarets to the church courtyard.

Sultanahmet Mosque
In 1609, Ahmet I, ruler of the Ottoman Empire 1603-1617, appointed his architect, Mehmet Aga, to build a splendid mosque opposite the Ayasofia church. Construction was completed in 1616. Since then, the entire district is known by the name of the beautiful Sultanahmet Mosque.

Sultanahmet was built on Byzantine ruins, in an

attempt to complement the Byzantine achievements in building, in general, and to outdo the grandeur of the Ayasofia in particular. The mosque clearly

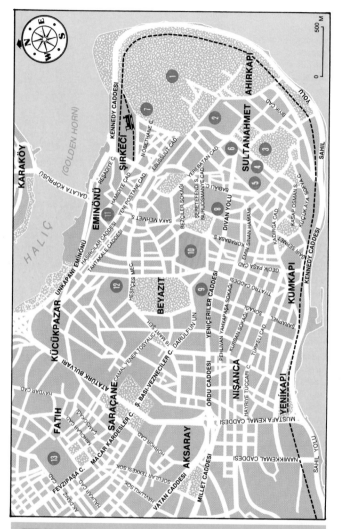

THE OLD CITY

1. Topkapı Palace
2. Ayasofia
3. Sultanahmet Mosque
4. Hippodrome
5. Museum of Islamic Art
6. Yerebetan Saray
7. Museums
8. Çemberlitas Hamami
9. The Mosque of Beyazıt II
10. Grand Bazaar
11. Egyptian Market
12. Mosque of Sulayman
13. Fatih Mosque

reflects the differences between the Byzantine and Ottoman architectural concept of space. While the emphasis in Ayasofia is on free flowing movement, the architecture of the Sultanahmet clearly favors the absence of movement and serenity. The Ottoman architect copied the dome, the arches and the pillars of the Ayasofia church, but the central dome is surrounded by half-domes on all sides. This creates a square-shaped space and closes in the Blue Mosque in comparison to the spacious airiness of the adjacent Byzantine church.

The most important part of the mosque is the **Mihrab**, a niche in the wall directing the worshippers to pray facing Mecca. To the right of the *Mihrab* is the *Mimber*, the carved pulpit of the *imam*, who preaches from it during the Friday and holiday prayer sessions. To the left of the *Mihrab* is the pulpit for reading the *Koran* to the worshippers (*Kuran kursu*). The Sultan himself used to pray at the far end of the left-hand gallery, in a place known as the "royal corner" (*Hünkàr Mahfili*). The gallery, in the inner section of the mosque, is covered with original blue and green İznik tiles. The light coming through the windows is reflected in the beautiful tiles, creating a glittering bluish mosque. This is also contrasted with the dark Ayasofia church, where the walls and the mosaics absorb the light. Because of its blue shine, the Sultanahmet mosque is best known as the "Blue Mosque".

A structure for feet-washing near the Hippodrome

The six minarets built by Ahmet I testify to the importance and centrality of the mosque in the eyes of the Moslems. This aroused bitterness throughout the Moslem world, as the only mosque at the time with six minarets was the Ka'aba Mosque in Mecca. In response to the outrage, the Sultan sent money and builders to Mecca to build a seventh minaret. In his defense, the Sultan claimed that the architect had not understood him: he had requested minarets of gold (*altin*) but the architect had understood him as saying six (*altı*) minarets... The death of the Sultan one year after completion of the Blue Mosque was attributed by the religious sages to his attempt to belittle the mosque in Mecca.

The impressive mosque built by Ahmet I, dominates the skyline of the old city of İstanbul, but despite its beauty and perfection, it seems that he did not succeed in his primary aim, to build a splendid creation that would overshadow the Emperor Justinian's Ayasofia, itself built to surpass the Temple in Jerusalem.

In the northern wing of the mosque is a small, interesting **museum**, exhibiting antique carpets woven in different periods and various regions of Turkey, and fabulous antique *kilim* – true *objets d'art*. Open Tues.-Sat. 9am-5pm. From May to October there is a marvelous audio-visual program in the Blue Mosque. Details are available at the mosque plaza and at the information offices.

The Theodosius Obelisk, brought from Egypt to İstanbul's Hippodrome in 390 AD

The **Hippodrome** adjacent to the Sultanahmet mosque was the playground of the old city during the reign of the Byzantine Empire. Chariot races and public celebrations, performances, music and circus acts, were held here. The foundations of the Hippodrome were built by Septimus Severus in the third century. After the Byzantine conquest, Constantine and his heirs enlarged the area and prepared the streets around the Hippodrome for chariot races. In between the races and circus acts, plays were presented. Audiences at the Hippodrome could also enjoy music, wine and dancing. The writers of the period testify that the Hippodrome could hold up to 100,000 people. The Byzantine Emperors tried to turn the Hippodrome into a public showcase of the empire. They brought large collections of art from throughout the kingdom to the plaza, but most of the items were destroyed and taken in invasions – some of them are displayed now in museums in London, Paris and Rome. The most prominent monuments still standing in the splendid plaza are the Theodosius Obelisk, the Serpentine Column and Constantine Porphyrogenitus' Spiral Column.

The Theodosius Obelisk was brought from Thebes in upper Egypt. The original obelisk, of which we only see the top third, was brought to the Hippodrome by Emperor Theodosius in the year 390. On the marble slabs at the base of the monument are engraved the figures of Theodosius and his family, in scenes from the life of the empire. The **Serpentine Column** is part of a monument erected at the

Temple of Apollo in Delphi in memory of the Greek victory over the Persians, in the fifth century BC. Constantine the Great, founder of the Empire, brought the monument to the Hippodrome in 330 AD. This spiral column is built of bronze, in the form of three intertwined snakes. The heads of the snakes broke and disappeared, except for one, which was found and is exhibited in the Archeological Museum. The third column is a mass of rough stone, named after the Emperor Porphyrogenitus, because it was he who gave the order to renovate it in the tenth century. According to one theory, this column was erected by Constantine the Great when the Hippodrome was built, to mark the southern end of the Hippodrome on the chariot race track. When the Sultanahmet Mosque was built, the Hippodrome was almost entirely destroyed.

On the far, western side of the Hippodrome lies the Palace of Ibrahim Pasha (Ibrahim Paşa Sarayı), the Great Vizier in the period of Sulayman the Magnificent. The palace was built in 1524, and now houses the **Museum of Islamic Art**. The museum contains a large collection of Turkish and Persian miniatures. Other interesting exhibits in the museum are verses from the *Koran* carved in wood, calligraphy and a display of antique carpets. The museum is open daily, 10am-5pm., closed Mon.

From the Hippodrome, cross the busy street, Divan Yolu. On the other side is the church **Yerebetan Saray**, Turkish for the "Sunken Palace". Entering this modest church, after descending a few steps, you will be surprised by the underground scenery that appears before you – a large hall with rows of columns sunken in water. This building is also known by its Byzantine name, the Basilica Cistern. It is a large pool built in the time of Justinian, apparently in 532 AD. The length of the hall is 460ft. (40m) and its width is 230ft. (70m). The 336 pillars are arranged in 12 rows of 28 columns each. The cistern was part of Constantinople's water system. There is no access to the cistern because of renovations, but the Turkish workers usually allow curious tourists to peek in for a few minutes.

The Cistern of a Thousand-and-One Columns (Binbirdirek Sarnıcı) is a small structure on the western side of the Hippodrome, behind the Museum of Islamic Art. It is another entrance to the underground water system of the Byzantine city. The construction of the cistern is attributed to Constantine, the founder of the empire. The hall is

A base of a column at the Cistern of a Thousand-and-One-Columns

The Cistern of a Thousand-and-One-Columns contains, in fact, only 224 beautiful columns, which are most pleasant to walk through

approximately one-third the size of the Basilica Cistern, and contains 224 columns. This cistern is completely dry, and it is pleasant to walk through it, among its lovely columns.

Along Divan Yolu

The street Divan Yolu leads us from the Sultanah-met district into the old city. This historic route crossed the old city and led to Topkapı Palace, where the *Divan*, the hall of the council, was located. Originally Byzantine, the road was used in the Ottoman period as well.

At the beginning of the street, opposite the Hippodrome, stands a lovely small mosque on the left side, **Mosque of Firuz Ağa** (Firuz Ağa Cami), built in 1491 for Firuz, the treasurer of the Emperor Beyazit the Second. Some 220 yards (200m) past the mosque we come to the grave of the Sultan Mehmet II, who died in the mid-fifteenth century. Further down the road is the **Köprülü Mosque**, built for the Köprülü family, five of whose sons attained the position of Great Vizier, the Chief Minister, in the seventeenth and eighteenth century. Opposite this mosque is a beautiful Turkish bath, the **Hamam** (Çemberlitas Hamamı), built in the late sixteenth century by the Valide Sultan Nur Banu, the mother of Murat III. Behind the *Hamam* is the **Column of Constantine**, erected in memory of the dedication of the city to the Roman Empire in the year 330 AD. The monument was subjected to storms and fires, but it still stands in its place, 1,700 years after it was built. Opposite the Column of Constantine is the **Mosque of Atik Ali Pasha**, constructed in 1496 for the Chief White Eunuch of the Sultan Beyazit II. Divan Yolu changes its name here to Janissaries Street (Yeniçeriler Caddesi).

We continue on Janissaries Cad. a few hundred meters along the road lined with mosques and other historic sites, until we come to Beyazıt Square (Beyazıt Meydanı), near the University of İstanbul. In the Byzantine period the square was called the "Forum of Theodosius," after the emperor who built it and the famous Theodosius Arch, one of the wonders of the ancient world. **The Mosque of Beyazıt II** is considered one of the first mosques to embody Ottoman architecture. This lovely mosque, built in the early sixteenth century, is certainly worth a visit.

The northeast exit from the area of the mosque leads to the **Market of the Booksellers** (Sahaflar Çarşısı). The little market was built in the eighteenth century, with ancient shops, selling paper and books here since the time of the Byzantine Constantinople. From the Market of the Booksellers we go out through the Gate of the Engravers to the large market.

The Grand Bazaar in İstanbul is the largest covered market in the world

The Grand Bazaar (Grandbazaar, Kapalı Çarşı): The markets in this guide generally appear in the chapters on shopping, but even if you don't plan to buy anything, a visit to the Grand Bazaar of İstanbul is highly recommended. This is the largest covered market in the world, it began with a small warehouse area built in the fifteenth century during the reign of Mehmet the Conqueror. In the course of time, the warehouses developed into stores. The powerful Ottoman Empire experienced economic prosperity, and the market expanded. The small stores were arranged into streets, the merchants put up a roof in order to make it possible to trade all year round, and mosques and hostels (*khans*) were built for visitors. Now, more than 500 years later, there are 4,500 stores here, on more than 60 streets, covering some 1.2 square miles (3 sq/km).

The streets of the market and the stores are arranged according to the type of merchandise they sell. The Goldsmiths' Street, with its sparkling piles of silver and gold, is located in the center of the market, as gold and silver work was one of the first trades here. Other streets display carpets, brass objects, fabric, leather products and other wares. It is very easy to lose your sense of direction here, and you will probably find yourself back on the same streets again and again.

The lively bazaar is a paradise for avid shoppers. The merchants invite visitors into their shops, and are very skilled in the art of selling. Bargaining is part of the game here, and you can get the initial price down considerably. If you get a local friend to join you and bargain in Turkish, the price may reach half or even less of the initial price. Even though the market is becoming increasingly tourist-oriented, the residents of İstanbul still come here to shop. Outside of the market are many stores that sell similar merchandise at a slightly lower price, but they don't have the special atmosphere of the market.

The Grand Bazaar is open Mon.-Sat. 9am-7pm, and is closed Sun. There are restaurants, a bank and a few mosques here. The visit may take from a few hours to half a day, and even those not intending to buy anything will probably end up with something. It is best to walk around first, and then take a rest at one of the restaurants or coffee-houses. You should always do your buying on your way out of the market – it is not worth carrying your shopping the

The Egyptian Market is considered to be the largest food market in the world

whole way, and the prices, for some reason, are lower near the exit. It seems that the merchants can sense that you are about to leave.

The northwestern exit of the Grand Bazaar leads to the **Egyptian Market** (Mısır Çarsısı), built in the seventeenth century as part of **Yeni Cami**. The rent charged from the stores was used to fund the activities of the mosque. The main

The Mosque of Sulayman, the largest mosque in İstanbul, can hold 25,000 worshippers!

entrance to the mosque is from Eminönü Square, and its doors are open Mon.-Sat. The spices in the market shops were originally brought from Egypt which is how it came by its name. It is considered to be the largest food market in the city, and you can buy vegetables, fish, meat, walnuts, pistachios and, of course, a wide variety of spices here. In the nearby mosque many Sultans and princes are buried.

Another pretty mosque in the vicinity the Egyptian Market is **Rüstem Paşa Cami**, reached from Hasircilar Cad. The mosque was built in 1561 for Rüstem Pasha, the Grand Vizier under the reign of Sulayman the Magnificent. The mosque is decorated with colored Iznik tiles. It is, undoubtedly, one of the most beautiful mosques in İstanbul.

The **Mosque of Sulayman** (Süleymaniye Cami) was built by the greatest Sultan in the history of the Ottoman Empire, Sulayman the Magnificent, on one of the hills of the old city in the Beyazıt district. It lies opposite the University of İstanbul; the best way to get here is from Beyazıt Square. This is the largest mosque in İstanbul, with a capacity to hold 25,000 worshippers. It was built by Sinan, the greatest architect of the Ottoman period. Construction took seven years, and was completed in 1557.

The large mosque encompassed many public buildings, including a hostel, a school, a kitchen, a Turkish bath and even a hospital. During the visit to the mosque you should ask the guard to let you into the burial section. Here Sulayman the Magnificent and his wife Roxelana are buried in ornate graves, among colored Iznik tiles.

Golden Horn Bay (Haliç)
On the shore of the bay dividing the old city from the new are several interesting and important sites.

The most prominent among them is the **Mosque at Eyüp** (Eyüp Sultan Cami), located on the outskirts of İstanbul at the top of the bay. Eyüp Ansaray was a close friend of the Prophet Muhammad, and was killed in the battles in which the Byzantine army broke through the Arab siege of the city in the seventh century. Legend has it that the grave of Eyüp disappeared and was found by Mehmet the Conqueror during the siege of the city in 1453. This legend aroused the fighters and motivated them in the last stages of the war. After the conquest Mehmet erected a mosque on the grave of Eyüp. After it was destroyed by an earthquake, the mosque was rebuilt by Sultan Selim III and it is this reconstructed mosque which we see today. This is one of the most sacred places for Moslems.

You can get to Eyüp by bus, *dolmuş* or taxi; however, definitely the most beautiful route is to take the Golden Horn ferry from Eminönü to the Eyüp stop. The dock signs show the way to the mosque. Another path leads up the hill to the Café of Pierre Loti.

Pierre Loti (1850-1923) was a talented writer, a French romantic who fell in love with the Golden Horn and made his home here. He fell in love not only with the bay, but also with a married Turkish woman, and the ensuing complications forced him to return to France. His romantic stories have brought the charm of the Ottoman Orient to the homes of many Europeans. A café stands on the hill to the north of the Mosque of Eyüp, at the spot where he used to sit and watch the city. The best

The Mosque at Eyüp is one of the most sacred places for Moslems

A view of the European side of İstanbul from the Bosphorus with the Galata Tower

time to visit is at sunset, a romantic hour when the last rays of the sun hide the pollution of the bay water.

Three bridges connect the old city to the new. The **Golden Horn Bridge** or **Haliç Bridge** (Haliç Köprüsü) is located at the beginning of the bay; **Atatürk Bridge** is the central bridge and **Galata Bridge** (Galata Köprüsü), which was renovated after being burnt down in 1992 – is the closest to the straits. The Galata Bridge opens every morning from 4:30-5:30am, to let ships pass.

The New City (Beyoğlu)

Settlement of the new city of İstanbul began many years ago. The city developed from a fortified settlement at the beginning of the Byzantine Empire to a center of commerce and trade during the Ottoman Empire. The name the "new city" was intended mainly to distinguish it from the "old city", and to note the merging of the city Pera and Galata and the creation of a modern European city within İstanbul. At the northern end of the Galata Bridge are the Karaköy docks, where there is a lively fish trade. The fishermen tie their boats to the dock and stand there offering their catch for sale. From the Karaköy docks, Yüksek Kaldırım boulevard leads to **Galata Tower** (Galata Kulesi), which was renovated in the fifteenth century by the ruler of Genoa. The port Galata was settled by Genoese merchants in the 11th century. The tower was originally built of wood, in the Byzantine period. It is 200ft. (61m)

Vegetables galore at the İstanbul Market

high, constructed like a thick wall. At the top of the tower is an observation point, marked with directions. An elevator goes up to the observation point, which operates from 10am-6pm. Admission is about $2. In the evening there is a restaurant here, with performances by local singers and dancers.

Further down the boulevard begins Istiklâl Cad., which continues to Taksim Square.

At 51 Istiklâl Cad., between Galata Tower and Taksim Square, is the entrance to the **Flower Sellers' Alley** (Çiçek Pasajı). This is the place to rest from touring palaces and mosques. The flower stands and the nearby fish market (Balık Pazarı) serve as the setting for cafés and small restaurants, where the local residents meet for a chat or business. In the early evening, after the stores and offices close the picturesque alley bustles; musicians walk among the cafés and play for the guests, wandering merchants offer their goods from table to table athletes and jugglers perform circus acts, and the general atmosphere is gay and friendly. Most of the waiters do not speak English, and the menus are not very clear. This is a place to use the little Turkish you know, or to let your fingers do the choosing, by pointing at what you want.

Taksim Square, the central square in the new city, inherited its name from Taksim Station, which was part of İstanbul's water system in the eighteenth century. East of the square is the **Atatürk Cultural Hall** (Atatürk Kültür Sarayı), also known as the Opera House. This is where performances of the

International İstanbul Festival are held during the summer. In the center of the square stands a memorial, the creation of an Italian sculptor to the founding of the republic. In front of the square is the prominent statue of Kemal Atatürk himself. In the square you will also find local city bus stops, where you can get a bus or *dolmuş* to any part of the city.

From Taksim Square, Cumhuriyet Caddesi, the wide, modern boulevard with dots of greenery, runs north. Along it are exclusive hotels, boutiques, travel agencies and the offices of many airlines.

The **Military Museum** (Askeri Müze) is a small and interesting museum, located near the *Hilton Hotel* and the Taksim Square. The museum houses exhibits from the numerous Ottoman battlefields. The museum is open Wed.-Sun. 9am-5pm, closed Mon. and Tues. The central attractions in the museum are without doubt the appearances of the *Mehter*, an Ottoman military band in uniform. This is the first military band in the world, and it is worth finding out its performance times from the tourist information offices.

From Taksim Square, İnönü Cad. runs to the Bosphorus Coast and to the white palace, the Dolmabahçe.

The Dolmabahçe Palace amidst luscious greenery lives up to its name – "full of gardens"

Dolmabahçe Palace

The story of the Dolmabahçe Palace (Dolmabahçe Sarayı) parallels that of the empire that lost its wealth and power, of a Sultan who lost touch with his subjects and the state of his empire. In the mid-nineteenth century, the widening gap between powerful European states and the crumbling Ottoman Empire was already clear. The Sultan Abdül Mecit sought a way to imitate the progressive Europeans and decided to build a magnificent palace in the style of Versailles. The construction began in 1843 and was completed in 1856, less than 70 years before the fall of the Sultanate. The palace was constructed from marble, at a cost which completely depleted the

Royal pink inside the Dolmabahçe Palace

country's treasury. Upon completion, the great, spacious palace became the home of the Sultans. The next Sultan, Abdül Aziz, almost never left the palace walls because his excessive bulk made it difficult for him to walk. In his room, you can still see the special bed made to bear his enormous weight.

The name Dolmabahçe means "full of gardens", and the palace gardens are indeed exquisite, and give the palace a sense of tranquillity. A white marble fence runs about a half a mile to the shores of the strait. The palace itself is magnificent and has huge rooms containing royal furnishings and enormous chandeliers. In the coronation room is the largest chandelier in the world, weighing more than four tons. You shouldn't miss this beautiful palace, typifying the decline of the Ottoman Empire.

The palace has great symbolic importance. Mehmet the Conqueror concealed his forces here before setting out for battle and to besiege Constantinople, a siege which ultimately led to the fall of the city and the Byzantine Empire, and the subsequent rise of the Ottoman Empire. Kemal Atatürk, the leader of the Turkish Republic died, in a small room in the palace, on November 10, 1938, at 9:05am. Since then, the clocks in the palace are set to the time of Atatürk's death.

At the entrance, in order to prevent any damage to the palace, visitors are divided into groups and enter the place accompanied by a guide. The tour takes about an hour and a quarter. Open daily, except for Mon. and Thurs., 9am-3pm. Admission, including the tour, is about $5. You can reach the palace by bus, *dolmuş*, taxi or by ferry to the Beşiktaş mooring.

A Trip Up the Bosphorus Strait

Sailing in the Bosphorus Strait is one of the main pleasures of visiting İstanbul. The trip is a welcome opportunity to leave the bustle of the city for a rural setting and the great outdoors. The orange and white ferry makes its way from Eminönü to the strait in a two-and-a-half hour long trip, which zig zags between the European and the Asian sides. The passengers can get off at any station and continue their trip on the next ferry. You must keep the ticket until you get back to the city.

You can take a regular ferry which sails once an hour, or a special ferry for tourists. In the summer this special, comfortable ferry leaves on weekdays and Saturdays at 10:25am and 1:35pm, leaving the last station, Anadolu Kavaği, on the way back to İstanbul at 3pm and 5:10 pm, respectively. On Sunday and holidays the schedule changes, and the ferries leave five times a day at 9:45am, 10:45am, 11:45am, 1:45pm and 4:45pm. The last ferry leaves Anadolu Kavaği for İstanbul at 7:10 pm.

The European Side

North of the Dolmabahçe Palace is the Beşiktaş mooring. The name of the suburb is Barbaros Hayrettin Paşa, named after the Admiral Barbaros, who conquered North Africa for Sulayman the Magnificent. There is a memorial for the admiral in a square in Beşiktaş. From the mooring you can get to the **Naval Museum** (Deniz Müzesi), which has an exhibit of the long narrow boats of the Sultans, which were used for efficient, quick transportation between the different palaces. Other prominent exhibits include the personal boat of Atatürk, naval cannons, and a collection of ancient naval maps.

The port of İstanbul

TURKEY

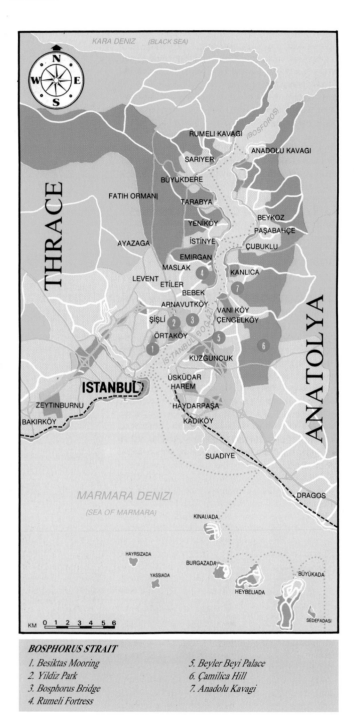

BOSPHORUS STRAIT

1. Besiktas Mooring
2. Yildiz Park
3. Bosphorus Bridge
4. Rumeli Fortress
5. Beyler Beyi Palace
6. Çamilica Hill
7. Anadolu Kavagi

The museum is open Wed.-Sun. 9am-noon and 12:30-5pm, and closed Mon. and Tues. It has two wings, and you need a separate ticket for each. Admission to each side is about 60 cents.

The Naval Museum is about a quarter of an hour's walk from Yıldız Parkı. On the way to the park you can see the ruins of the **Çıragan Palace** (Çıragan Sarayı). The palace was built for Sultan Abdül Aziz at the end of the nineteenth century, when he grew tired of the Dolmabahçe and wanted a palace of his own. Here, Murat V, the Sultan who ruled Turkey for a few months in 1876, was imprisoned after having been dethroned. The palace was burned down before World War I, evidently as a political act of arson.

Star Park (Yıldız Parkı), on a tree-covered hill overlooking the Bosphorus, is a wonderful park, cultivated for hundreds of years by the Sultans. The park boasts many varied types of trees brought from all over the world, and splendid villas were built here to serve the Sultans who loved to spend time in natural surroundings. The park was once part of a large forest that covered the European bank of the Bosphorus, and it now has gardens, a lake, fountains and expensive buildings.

Among these buildings is the palace of Sultan Abdül Hamit, who like his predecessors, hated the existing palace and built his own palace here just a few years before the fall of the empire. This Sultan designed the park in its present dimensions and form. Prominent among the magnificent villas and pavilions is the Şale Pavilion (Şale Köşkü), which was the official guest house for guests of the Republic, such as Charles de Gaulle and others. This is the place from which Mehmet V, the last Sultan, fled one morning in November 1922, when the period of the Ottoman Sultanate came to an end. The most beautiful view in the park is from the Malta Pavilion (Malta Köşkü), situated at the top of a hill, where there is also a café and a restaurant. The park is open daily from 9am-6pm. The Şale Pavilion closes about two hours before the park, and admission is about $1.5.

Bosphorus Bridge is located near Ortaköy. The bridge is named after Bogazigi Köprüsü. It is one of the five largest suspended bridges in the world – 290ft. (64m) high and more than half a mile (1km) long. The bridge spans the two continents of Europe and Asia. The newly built Fatih Sultan Mehmet

Bridge is located to the north of the Bosphorus Bridge. It is shorter – "only" 875 yards (800m).

Rumeli Fortress, situated in Bebek, built to control passage through the strait

Bebek, a picturesque coastal village, is a summer resort for wealthy Turks with a pleasant bathing beach. Near the town is the **Rumeli Fortress** (Rumeli Hisarı), built by Mehmet the Conqueror in 1452, to control passage through the strait during the siege of Constantinople. Legend has it that Mehmet the Conqueror appointed each of his viziers to be responsible for one of the fortress towers. Any vizier whose tower was not completed in time was to pay with his head. Such efficient methods worked well, and the fortress, with its 17 towers, was completed even before the planned date. The impressive fortress is open Tues.-Sun. 9:30am-5pm, and closed Mon. North of Bebek is the town **Tarabya**, famous for its luxury hotel. Further north are two more moorings: **Sarıyer**, is the town of the same name, which is famous for its baked goods, and **Rumeli Kavağı**, a small fishing village, which is the last stop on the European side before the Black Sea.

The Asian Side

Üsküdar, the Asian suburb of İstanbul, serves as a "Dormitory suburb" for the city. Tradition tells us that Kadıköy, south of Üsküdar, was the site of the first settlement in the İstanbul area, "the country of the blind" according to the oracle of the Delphi (see the section on the history of İstanbul). Near the port, south of Üsküdar, is a tiny island, and on it the **Maiden's Tower** (Kız Kulesi). The tower was used to protect the strait and legend tells of an emperor who imprisoned his daughter on the island, in order to save her from death as the oracle had prophesied. As is the way of legends, the isolation was to no avail and the girl died when bitten by a snake, which lay hidden in a basket of fruit that was served to her. Boats sail to the tower, which offers a lovely view of the bay.

Area code: 216

The route north from Üsküdar along the shore of the

strait takes us to **Beylerbeyi Palace** (Beylerbeyi Sarayı). Sultan Abdül Aziz continued in the tradition of changing palaces, and in 1865 built his palace on the forested hill, amid a fine setting. The palace was designed by the brother of the Armenian architect who built the Dolmabahçe Palace. Because of the obvious similarity between them, this palace is known as the Little Dolmabahçe. The palace is situated north of the large Bosphorus Bridge, and is easiest to reach from the European side via the bridge or by bus from Üsküdar. The palace is open daily, 9am-5pm, closed Mon. Admission fee is about $3.

Çamlıca Hill is one of the highest peaks in the İstanbul area. At the top of the hill are television aerials, and a picnic area with a café, open until midnight. On a clear day, the view from the Üamilica is fantastic. You can get here by bus, *dolmuş* or private car, over the Bosphorus Bridge. There is no ferry stop in the immediate area.

The small Anadolu Fortress (Anadolu Hisari) and other small towns are located further along the Asian bank of the strait. These villages, such as Paşabahçe and Beykoz, have preserved the splendid buildings and the beauty and glory of the gardens from the Ottoman period. The last stop on the ferry ride, **Anadolu Kavağı**, is the location of a small fishing village and the ruins of a Byzantine fortress. The last ferry leaves this mooring on weekdays at 4:45pm. Those who miss it will find it difficult to get a taxi back to İstanbul.

The Princes' Isles

The Princes' Isles (Kızıl Adalar) comprise nine islands in the Marmara Sea, near the Asian coast. The islands were once used as a place of exile for princes and courtiers who no longer pleased the Byzantine Emperor. They now serve as a summer oasis for the wealthy residents of İstanbul. Most of the houses along the coast are built in nineteenth-century style. In that century, the ethnic minorities, Greeks and Jews in particular, adopted the islands as their favorite vacation spot and built large villas there.

The Bosphorus Bridge, more than half a mile long

The largest island is **Büyükada** (large – *büyük*, island – *ada*). No private or public vehicles are allowed on the island, with the exception of emergency vehicles. The tranquillity and the old houses make a visit here very enjoyable. You can rent a carriage for a short trip (about $7) or a long one (about $9). In the center of the island is a lovely Greek monastery, St. Gregory's.

Area code: 212

At the Egyptian Market

On **Heybeli** island, you will find the Turkish Naval Academy. The small islands of Kınalı and Burgaz are the first that you see when coming from İstanbul. It is worth including more than one island in this trip, as they are quite different in character and appearance from one another. The trip to the islands is a recommended day trip for those visiting İstanbul for more than three days. The trip from İstanbul to the Princes' Isles takes about an hour, and costs about $1.5. Ferries leave dock number 5 at the Sirkeçi port from morning to the early afternoon. From the Kabataş dock there is a quick hovercraft, known in Turkish as the "sea bus." On the hovercraft, the trip takes half the time and costs about double the price. A convenient and pleasant trip begins on the morning hovercraft from Kabataş to Büyükada at 9:45am, continuing with a trip around the island, lunch and an inter-island ferry to Heybeli, finishing up with a return to Sirkeçi on the evening ferry, at 6:55pm.

General Information

Turkish Baths

Tourists favorite baths in İstanbul are the *Cağaloglu Hamamı*, in the old city between Sultanahmet Mosque and the Grand Bazaar (34 Yerebatan Cad., Tel. 522-2424) and *Tarihi Galatasaray Hamamı*, on Suterazisi Sokak, Tel. 144-1412. Both these ancient bath houses are open daily from 7am-10pm for men, and from 8am-8pm for women. The price ranges from $3 for bathing yourself to $12 for the royal treatment. It is accepted practice to leave a small tip for both the bath attendant and the masseur.

Çemberlitas Hamamı have beautiful 16th century architecture, chambers for men and women. Open daily 6am-12pm, Tel. 522-7974. Located between Vezirhan Cadessi and Diran Yolu, near the tomb of Mahmut II.

Night Life

In İstanbul today little remains of the

Sultan's many tempting pleasures. The night life in the city is really evening life – at midnight it is hard to find anything open. Details of operas, concerts and ballet performances can be obtained at the Atatürk Cultural Center, near Taksim Square. Because of the language problem, theater performances do not attract tourists. A similar problem arises in the movie theaters, which show Turkish films.

Tourists can enjoy the "Les Parisiennes" style night club. The first striptease club to open in İstanbul at 18 Harbiye Cumhuriyet. For reservations call 147-6362.

A night out is usually spent at one of the Oriental night clubs, which serve dinner accompanied by entertainment. The program includes belly dancing, magicians and local vocalists. These clubs mainly cater for visitors from the Balkan states, who are familiar with this culture, although the *Kervansaray* club near the *Hilton Hotel* tries to include performances for western tourists too. Another well-known club is located on the top floor of Galata Tower.

Other nightclubs can be found in Taksim Square and along Istiklâl

Dressed in tartan in the men's chambers at the Çemberlitas public baths

Street. After midnight a few outdated disco clubs in the Taksim District, near the large hotels, remain open.

The favorite pastime of the Turks and many tourists is a night trip on the Bosphorus to one of the fine restaurants in the distant quarters, such as the excellent *Abdullah*, at 11 Koru Cad. in the Emirgan Quarter. An evening spent in a fine Turkish restaurant overlooking the Bosphorus will leave you with a pleasant memory that will last long after your meal.

Shopping

There are three major shopping areas: The Grand Bazaar is described

At the Dolmabahçe Palace

in the section on tours in the city. A second center is located off Istiklâl street, in the Galatasaray area. The stores here sell select local products: shoes, leather coats, suits and the like. The shopping district extends from Tünel Square to Taksim Square. You must visit the confectionery store, *Hacı Bekir*, where the produce of the famous nineteenth-century factory is sold, even if only to smell the sweet *lokum* (Turkish delight).

The prestigious shopping districts are on Osmanbey and Nisantasi – where the choice is staggering: from Haute Couture to Army Surplus, from diamonds to junk jewellry. The prices are high and the stores serve the city's wealthy residents and high-class tourists. Most of the stores in the city are open from 9am -7pm. Between 1-2pm stores close for a noon break; almost all are closed on Sunday.

Postal Services and Telephones

The central post office is located off the new Post street in Eminönü (Yeni Postahane Cad., Eminönü) and this is the location of the *poste restante*.

Other post offices are located in the new city, on Cumhuriyet Cad., near Taksim Square and on Meşrutiyet Cad., near the British Consulate. The parcel post office is located in the Karaköy District. You can make international telephone calls from these offices and from the good hotels.

The major post offices are open from Mon.-Sat. 8am-12pm and Sun. 9am-7pm; Smaller branches are open 8:30-12:30pm and 1.30-5:30pm; closed Sat. and Sun.

Books, Guides and Newspapers in English

Red House Press distributes guides and dictionaries to assist the English-speaking tourist, You can find these books at *Redhouse Kitabevi* the publishers' office at Riza Paşa Yokuşu, Uzum Çarsi, in the old city, near the Grand Bazaar. Books, albums, maps and other helpful material, particularly in English and German, can be found in the store *Sander Kitabevi*, at 275 Hâlâskargazi Cad., north of Taksim Square. This store has a branch on Istiklâl Cad., near the post office. Other book and newspaper shops are located in the lobbies of the exclusive hotels.

In İstanbul you can get the daily papers that are published in Europe, such as the *London Times* and the *International Herald Tribune*. The daily Turkish paper in English, the *Turkish Daily News*, is sold at many newsstands. The paper is readable and fairly good, particularly considering the limited number of English speakers and writers in the country.

Important Addresses and Phone Numbers

Police: Tel. 055.
Ambulance (in Taksim District): Tel. 240-6886.
American Hospital: 20 Güzelbahçe Sok. Nişantaşı, Tel. 231-4050.
American Consulate: 104 Meşrutiyet Cad., Kızılay, Tel. 251-3602.
British Consulate: 34 Meşrutiyet Cad., Tepebası, Tel. 244-7540.
Tourism Police: Sultanahmet, Tel. 528-5369.

The monument at Taksim Square

THRACE (TRAKYA)

Thrace (Trakya), the European part of Turkey, represents only 3 percent of the area of the country, and is a tiny remnant of the empire which at its peak reached the gates of Vienna. Few tourists visit this region; and most of those who do so come from Europe by land – bus, train or with a private vehicle. The climate in the area is hot and dry in the summer, and more pleasant in the spring and fall.

Border Crossings

The European road E80 crosses Bulgaria and reaches the Kapıkule border just a few miles outside of Edirne. The border is open 24 hours a day, and there is a tourist information office here. From Greece, road E55 reaches Pazarkule, in the suburbs of Edirne, the second most important border crossing, after Kapıkule. Two other fairly quiet border crossings are located on the Bulgarian-Greek border. The Dereköy border crossing serves those coming from the Bulgarian cities of Burgas and Varna to the Black Sea coast. Visitors arriving from Salonika by local bus or private car will cross the border near Ipsala. There is little traffic at these passes and you should check the schedule with the Bulgarian and Greek Consular Offices. At the Ipsala border crossing, a tourist information point operates during the day.

Passengers on the train from Europe arrive at the border near Edirne. The train from Greece passes along the Meriç river in Turkish territory before reaching the border crossing, because of a peculiar section of the Lausanne treaty, according to which part of the Greek train route is in enemy Turkish

One can almost smell the familiar aroma of freshly cut grass

territory. The *Bosfor Motel* serves the border at Kapıkule; the *Ipsala Motel* is located 1 mile (2km) from the Ipsala border crossing, and there are camping sites near both.

Traditional Turkish richly colored elaborate carpets

Edirne

Edirne is the Turkish name for Adrianople, the city of the Roman Emperor Hadrian. Founded in the second century AD as a frontal defense position for the Bosphorus Strait, the city was conquered in 1363, in the struggle between the rising Ottoman forces and the crumbling Byzantine Empire. In 1365, Murat I declared the city his capital instead of Bursa, the former capital. For some 90 years Edirne was the capital of the Sultanate, until the conquest of Constantinople in 1453.

Area code: 284

Edirne continued to hold an important position even after the capital moved to İstanbul. It was the center of the *utz*, the outskirts where the wars between the heretics and the believers were centered, and it served as the bridge for conquests in the Balkans and in Europe. Following the fall of Turkey in World War I, all of Thrace, including Edirne, was awarded to the Greeks, who took over the city in 1920. Under the leadership of Kemal Atatürk, Edirne was recaptured, and the Lausanne Treaty finally set the Turkish border at Edirne. A **tourist information office** is located at Talat Paşa Asfalti, 76/1, Tel. 212-1490.

NORTH WESTERN TURKEY

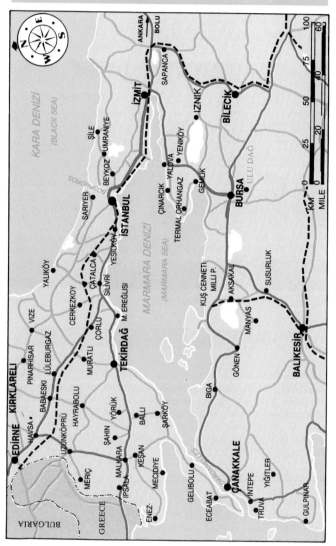

Transportation

From Europe: At the border crossings, taxis and *dolmuşes* serve tourists most hours of the day. Passengers on the train from Europe can get off at the train station in the city. Buses from Europe stop at the bus station at the outskirts of the city.

On to İstanbul

Dolmuşes pick up passengers along the route from Talat Paşa street to the central bus station Otobüs (Otobüs Garaji). The buses to İstanbul leave hourly and travel the 146 miles (234 km) in four hours. The bus travels on road E5-North, the continuation of the European road E80. The bus goes to the Topkapı station in İstanbul from the direction of the Atatürk airport. The train ride to İstanbul takes over seven hours and stops at numerous stations on the way. If possible, try to pass up on this exhausting journey, and rather take the bus. The price of the train ride from Edirne to İstanbul is slightly lower than the bus ride.

To the Dardanelles Strait and the Aegean Sea

Road E24, called road number 6 on some sections within Turkey, turns south at Havsa toward Gallipoli, Çanakkale and İzmir. There are two direct buses a day from Edirne to this area. If you miss the direct bus you can make a stop at the town of Keşan and change buses there. The distance from Edirne to İzmir is 340 miles (548km); this route is suitable for visitors who want to go straight to the western Turkish coast without passing through İstanbul.

Accommodation and Dining

The 1-star *Kervan*, Tel. 211-1382, and *Sultan*, Tel. 225-1372, hotels are located along Talat Paşa Cad., the major street. The *Onar Hotel* is located on Kaleci Maarif Cad. These three fine hotels are the best in the city. Among the inexpensive hotels, the most prominent is Rustenpasa Caravanserail, Tel. 212-0463, housed in a beautiful old building on Eski İstanbul Cad. For dining, we recommend the small, charming restaurants in the old city.

Sites to See

Few remnants of the Byzantine period remain in the city; among these are sections of the city wall. Because of the important role of the city during the Ottoman Empire, several fabulous mosques were built here.

Selimiye Mosque (Selimiye Camıı) is considered to be one of the finest examples of Ottoman mosque architecture throughout the world. The mosque is located at the top of Talat Paşa Cad. and was built, between 1569 and 1576, by the great Ottoman architect, Sinan, for Sultan Selim II. Sinan was 85 years old at the time of the completion of the mosque, which he regarded as his greatest master-piece. The structure is special because of its perfect proportions: a wide marvelous dome 148ft. (45m) high, and slender minarets, towering 262ft. (80m) high. When entering, the airiness gives one a sense of harmony. The large dome is supported by arches, pillars and buttresses. The special building technique enabled Sinan to build many windows. Sinan wanted 1,000 windows, but the Sultan suggested that he build only 999, as people would be likely to remember such a number. And he was proved to be correct.

At the bottom of Talat Paşa Cad., near the central square, is the **Old Mosque** (Eski Camii), built in

Bending under the burden

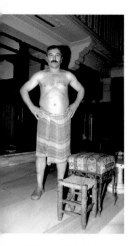

*At the Turkish Baths –
the perfect ending to a
day of sight-seeing*

1402-1413 by the three sons of the Sultan Beyazıt, who died as a prisoner of Tamerlane. Mehmet, the son who won the Sultanate, became Mehmet I and completed construction of the mosque which his brothers had begun. The mosque is built in early Ottoman style, similar to the large mosque in Bursa.

Next to the Old Mosque is the vacation home and reception hall of **Rüstem Paşa** (Rüstem Paşa Kervansarayı), built by Sinan in 1560, and today a hotel.

There are two markets in the area of the mosque: **the Covered Bazaar** (Bedesten), built by Mehmet the First, and the **Ali Paşa Bazaar**, built in 1568 by Sinan, who left the mark of his genius on the city. On the other side of Talat Paşa Street stands the **Kule Mosque** (Kule Kapışı), which is all that remains of the guard tower and large observation point built by Emperor Hadrian when he founded the city.

The **Three Veranda Mosque** (Üç Şerefeli Cami), located in the center of the city, near the central square, was built from 1437-1447. In the mosque, during the reign of Murat II, you can see the development of Turkish-Ottoman style that was beautifully expressed in the work of Sinan. Opposite the mosque is the **Turkish Bath** (Sokullu Mehmet Paşa Hamamı). The bath house was built by Sinan in 1579, here you can enjoy a bath after the long trip from Europe, in the atmosphere of Turkey 500 years ago.

A half hour walk along the Tunca river, pleasant in itself, brings you to the bridge built by Mehmet the Conqueror. After crossing the bridge you come to a winding path that leads to the **Mosque of Beyazıt II** (Beyazıt II Cami). The mosque, built by the architect Hayrettin Paşa in 1488, reflects the prosperity and success enjoyed during the reign of this Sultan.

Among the other sights of the city is the **Muradiye Mosque**, originally built as a center for the Dervish, after their leader appeared in a dream of Sultan Murat II and asked him to build the center. The mosque, located on a hill east of the city, is decorated with beautiful İznik tiles. You can get there from Mimar Sinan Cad.

The city also has a museum of antiquities and an interesting ethnographic museum. These are located near the cemetery, close to the Selimiye Mosque.

There are many other mosques in the city, and you can wander among them as an introductory course in the architecture that awaits the visitor to Turkey.

Special Events

Edirne is famous for its special fights (*Yağlı Güreslerı*), in which the contestants are rubbed with olive oil before they try to push their opponents onto the floor. The contests take place over six days at the beginning of July, on the island of Kırkpınar, which once served as a hunting reserve for the Sultans. The ruins of a fifteenth-century palace make a wonderful setting for the contests.

THE SOUTHERN SHORE OF THE MARMARA SEA

The southern shore of the Marmara Sea is known for its low green hills and its fruit and olive orchards. Despite its rural landscape, this region has known many a stormy period. In the course of history splendid cities and mighty fortresses have risen and fallen in this area. The legendary Troy served as a center of power, renowned throughout the Old World. Later the kingdom of Bithynia prospered in the area until it was assimilated into Roman culture, and it was here that the Ottoman dynasty began, with Bursa as the empire's first capital.

Yalova

Yalova is the transit point on the way from İstanbul to Bursa. You can reach Yalova by bus via İzmit, but it is better to spare yourself this trip, and sail by the fast or slow ferry from the Kabataş dock, in İstanbul. There is a regular bus service from the platform to the left of the statue of Atatürk. The price of the trip to İznik and Bursa is about $1.5. Many tourists remember Yalova as the city between the ferry and bus. There are a few simple, inexpensive hotels in the city.

Area code: 216

Termal

Approximately 7.5 miles (12km) west of Yalova is Termal, the town of the baths. Tourists with enough time can visit this town of gardens and enjoy a bath in the hot springs, whose water contains many minerals that are considered good for your health. Organized bathing began here as early as the

The lake at İznik

Roman era. You can get to Termal by *dolmuş* or by city bus number 4. The station for Termal is located next to the platform. In the town there are several pools of different standards, priced accordingly. Bathing in the "Sultan's Pool" (Sultan Banyo) costs around $4 – twice as much as in the nearby Valide Banyo.

Those interested in staying the night in Termal can find accommodation at the *Turban Hotel*, Tel. 814-4400, fax 814-4413 (not inexpensive).

İznik

The small, quiet town of İznik, home to some 20,000 inhabitants, has known many turbulent days in its rich history. Evidence found in the town indicates that it has existed since the year 1000 BC. After the death of Alexander the Great, the city prospered under the rule of Lysimachus, King of Thrace. The city was to be called Nicaea, in honor of the king's beloved wife. The prosperity continued in the days of the Bithynia Kingdom, of which Nicaea was the capital, and under the reign of the Romans, who inherited it as an independent kingdom.

An exhibit at the Municipal Museum at İznik

In 325 AD the Nicaea Ecumenical Conference was held in the city, which decried different factions in Christianity. The Seljuks conquered Nicaea in 1075 and controlled the city for 20 years. Sultan Selim the Grim brought Persian artisans as prisoners from the Tabriz region to build and decorate his palaces. These craftsmen brought with them the secret for producing tiles. The colored İznik tiles became known for their excellence and are one of the special trademarks of Ottoman architecture.

Area code: 224

A tourist information office is located at Belediye Bsaji 130-1, Tel. 757-1933.

The Church of Santa Sofia in the center of the city is nothing but a faded remnant of its glorious past. Excavations at this location indicate that the original church, built by the Emperor Justinian, was destroyed by an earthquake and the rebuilt church became a mosque under Ottoman rule. The church was renovated several times by the Sultans, and was badly damaged during the War of Independence in 1922 under Atatürk. The church has a handsome mosaic floor. Open Tues.-Sun. 9am-noon and

2-5pm, closed Mon. If the church is closed, you can get the key at the Municipal Museum.

The Green Mosque (Yeşil Cami) was built in 1378-1391 for Çandarlı Halil Paşa, the Grand Vizier of Murat I. It is built in Seljuk Style, which preceded Ottoman style. The ceramic tiles, which give the mosque its name and color, are a copy of the original turquoise tiles which have been removed over the years.

Excellent examples of İznik tiles can be seen in the **Municipal Museum**. The museum is located in the Hospice of the Lady Nilüfer Hatun, near the Green Mosque. This hospice, which fed the Dervish of the city, was built in memory of the Lady Nilüfer Hatun in 1388 by her son, Sultan Murat. The generous woman was the daughter of the Emperor John the VI, who married her to Sultan Orhan Gazi in order to make a Byzantine-Ottoman treaty. The exhibit includes remnants of the city's past, including colored tiles. The Sultan Selim I, "the Grim," wanted to establish a tile industry whose products would surpass the Persian tiles that were used in the Green Mosque. For this purpose he captured Persian artisans from the city of Trabiz, and resettled them in İznik. The special feature of the tiles is their color, prepared from various roots. Unfortunately, this secret has been lost since the eighteenth century. The museum is open daily 9am-noon and 1:30-5pm, closed Mon. Tours can be organized at

The Municipal Museum at İznik located in the Hospice of the Lady Nilüfer Hatun, which once fed the Dervish of the city

the museum for the Byzantine burial grounds (*katakom*) near the city.

Other interesting sights in İznik are the **city wall** and its gates. The most impressive of these is **Lefke Gate** (Lefke Kapişi), at the eastern end of Kil-içarslan street. You can climb the gate and get a good view of the city from above. The monumental gate was erected in honor of the visit of Emperor Hadrian. Other handsome gates are located at the two ends of Atatürk street – İstanbul Gate in the north and Yenişehir Gate in the south.

The favorite hotels in the city are those close to the lake – the *Burcum* and the *İznik* motel. In the city center you can find less expensive hotels. The best restaurants are those along the lake, and they are slightly more expensive than those within the city walls.

Buses leave for İstanbul and Bursa on a regular basis. The last bus to Bursa leaves at 6pm and the trip takes an hour and a half. The last bus to İstanbul leaves on the ferry to Yalova at 7pm.

The minaret of the Green Mosque at İznik

Bursa

The city of Bursa lies at the foot of Mount Uludağ. The mountain was formerly called the Olympus, and it is one of the mountains of the Old World that were identified as the home of the gods of Greek mythology. Bursa was named after Prusias, the king of Bithynia in the second century BC. In Ottoman history, Bursa holds the position as the first capital of the dynasty.

Today, this is the fifth largest city in the country, and its suburbs are home to some 1.2 million people. Despite its size, Bursa has managed to preserve the character of a quiet town. Its proximity to the snowy Mount Uludağ has made it the winter sports capital of the country.

History of the City

Prusias I founded the city at the beginning of the second century BC, evident-ly on the remains of an earlier settlement. In the Byzantine period, the city was called Prusa, and it became famous for its silk worm production and its hot baths. Othman, the founder of the Ottoman dynasty, surrounded the city, but he died before he managed to occupy it. In 1326 Orhan, the son of Othman, con-quered the city and made it the first capital of the rising Ottoman Sultanate.

At the end of World War I, Bursa was conquered by the Greek army and in 1922 it was recaptured by Atatürk. Today, Bursa is an important industrial center, with developed silk, textile, motor and agricultural processing industries in the city. Traditional houseware; towels, knives and other items, are also produced here.

TURKEY

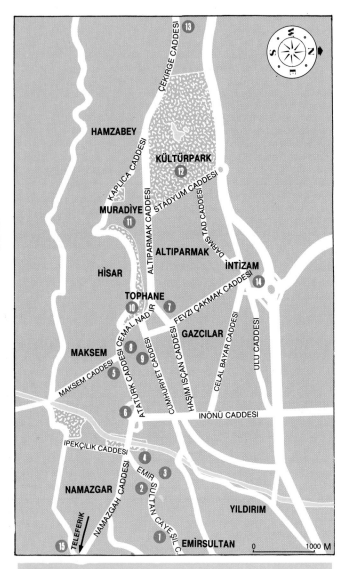

BURSA

1. Sultan Emir Mosque
2. Green Grave
3. The Green Mosque
4. The Museum of Turkish and Islamic Art
5. Post Office
6. Heykel Square
7. Tourist Information
8. Great Mosque
9. Covered Market
10. Graves of Sultans
11. Muradiye Mosque
12. Cultural Park
13. New Baths
14. Bus Terminal
15. Cable car (teleferik) to Uludağ

Tourist Services

A small information point operates during the tourist season at the Bursa bus terminal. The central information office is located at 64 Atatürk Cad., Tel. 254-2274, near the Great Mosque in the city center. There is also a **tourist information office** located at Ulucami Parkı, Atatürk Cad. 1, Tel. 220-1848. Here one can obtain much information on the area. The post office is opposite the central information office.

Area code: 224

Accommodation and Dining

The good hotels in the city are located in the Çekirge district in the western part of the city. The veteran 5-star *Çelik Palas Hotel*, 79 Çerkirge Cad., Tel. 233-3800, fax 236-1910, is considered the best in the city. The hotel was built after the First World War and was a favorite of Kemal Atatürk. It houses thermal pools of mineral spring water. The 4-star *Anatolia Hotel*, Tel. 233-9400, fax 233-9408, is also excellent, and has a good Turkish bath.

The city offers a selection of good hotels at moderately high prices. Recommended are the 4-star *Dilmen*, Hamamlar Cad., Çerkirge, Tel. 233-9500, fax 235-2568 and the 3-star *Akdoğan Hotel*, Murat Cad. 1, Tel. 233-8200, fax 236-3129, where there is a Turkish bath as well as a pool for the guests' enjoyment.

For visitors on an economy budget, we suggest that you avoid the inexpensive hotels in the area of the central bus station, because of the noise and smoke. In the city center the *Çamlibel Hotel*, 71 Inebey Cad., is recommended.

While visiting Bursa, we recommend you try the local delicacy, *Bursa kebapı;* this is lamb prepared in a special spiced tomato sauce. The local residents claim that this dish was invented at the *Kebabçı Iskenderoğlu* restaurant, located at 60 Atatürk Street. Another good inexpensive restaurant is the *Snir Lokantası*, near the *Çamlibel Hotel*. In the cultural park (*Kültür Parkı*) you will find several restaurants and a café where Turkish food is served in the pleasant atmosphere of the park.

Sites to See

The major tourist sights in Bursa are easily accessible and a convenient tour around city should begin at the major mosques in the east, continuing to the western baths via the bustling center of town and its Cultural Park.

Sultan Emir Mosque (Emir Sultan Camii) is located at the eastern border of Bursa. Buses and *dolmuşes* leave from Heykel square, the central square, and Atatürk Cad. The Sultan Emir station is the last stop on the line. The mosque is located in a forest, at a beautiful observation point. It was renovated in a fairly flamboyant style, in the early nineteenth century. From here, you can see the Yildirim Beyazıt Mosque, in the north.

The Green Mosque (Yeşil Cami), which has become a symbol of the city, is its most beautiful

Opulence inside the Green Mosque at Bursa

and prominent mosque. Built for Sultan Mehmet I in 1413-1424, it reflects the development of the Turkish Ottoman architecture, and a rejection of the Seljuk and Persian influences. In spite of its modest size, this is one of the most beautiful mosques in the country, and its colored İznik tiles are exquisite. Next to the Green Mosque, across the road, on a hill is the **Green Grave** (Yeşil Türbe). The Green Grave is actually the mausoleum of Mehmet I. Most of the tiles that gave the grave its name fell off during an earthquake in the late nineteenth century, but despite this damage, it is interesting to visit the grave of the acclaimed Sultan.

The Museum of Turkish and Islamic Art (Türk-Islam Eserleri Müzesi) is located across the road, in buildings that surrounded the Mosque of Mehmet I. The museum houses exhibits of jewellry, books and housewares from the Ottoman period, and it is open Tues.-Sun., 9am-noon and 1-5:30pm; closed Mon.

In the city center, on Atatürk Cad., is the **Great Mosque** (Ulu Camii), constructed 1396-1399 by Sultan Beyazıt I, "Thunderbolt" (Beyazıt Yildirim). The Sultan financed construction of the mosque with the spoils of his victory over the Crusaders in 1396. The architecture is influenced by Seljuk style with a central courtyard, surrounded by domes and pillars. This is the largest mosque in the city. Next to it is the **Orhan Gazi Mosque** (Orhan Gazi Camii), built in 1336 by Orhan, son of Osman, who conquered Bursa. Nearby is the **Covered Market** (see the section on shopping).

Between the city center and the western baths are

more mosques, such as the **Muradiye Mosque** and the complex of buildings around it, built by Murat II, the father of Mehmet the Conqueror. Next to the complex is a 200-year-old building that has been preserved in its entirety, with all its contents. It is worth visiting here to get an idea of daily life in eighteenth-century Bursa.

The Archeological Museum (Arkeoloji Müzesi) is located in the Cultural Park. It contains a collection of antiques reflecting the history of the city since the second century. Opposite the museum is the *Çelik Palas Hotel* and a small museum in memory of Atatürk, in a house in which he stayed on his visits to the area.

Inside the western baths (Çekirge) you will find the **Old Baths** (Eski Kaplıca), probably the oldest bath house in the world, which has been in use since the fourteenth century. The Old Baths are located at the western edge of the city. Opposite the *Çelik Palas Hotel* are the **New Baths** (Yeni Kaplıca). This elegant bath house was built in 1522 by Rüstem Paşa, the Grand

Bathing at the baths, a common pastime in Turkey

Vizier of Sulayman the Magnificent. The baths get their warm water from springs at the foot of the Uludağ. In Çekirge you can also see a number of mosques and the graves of several Sultans, including that of Murat I, situated opposite the Old Baths.

Uludağ

Mount Olympus, the Uludağ, towers to a height of 8340ft. (2,543m) over the city of Bursa. The mountain, which has been declared a national park, has a ski resort, active from December to April during the snowy season.

You can reach the top of the mountain in a *dolmuş*, which leaves the Bursa bus terminal and climbs the mountain on a charming, green winding route for 22 miles (36km), but most visitors prefer to use the cable car (*teleferik*). *Dolmuşes* and buses frequently depart for the lower cable car station from Heykel Square, west of the statue of Atatürk. The trip from the lower cable car station, to the top station, takes about half an hour and costs about $2 each way. The cable cars operate every 45 minutes, with the first car leaving at 8am. The last car descends the mountain before dusk. From the top you can get a *dolmuş* to the hotel area. On summer mornings the view from the cable car, overlooking the mountains, Bursa and the environs, is breathtaking. On top of the mountain, you can take short walking tours, go on longer hikes some taking several hours, or simply enjoy a picnic in the natural setting.

In the winter months (Dec. to April) the winter sports season is in full swing on the mountain resort (1800-1900m high), where one can find several hotels, chalets and after-ski facilities. The runs include slalom beginners' fields, free descents and a small but modern little hospital. Guides, skis, sleds and all the rest may be purchased or hired on the site. Full details are available at most travel agencies.

Area code: 224

The Bird Reserve

Near Lake Manyas (Manyas Gölü), 62 miles (100km) west of Bursa, is a bird reserve in the Kuş Cenneti national park. This is the nesting ground of water birds such as cormorants, pelicans and herons. In the reserve there are picnic areas, short hiking paths, a small museum and observation towers from which you can see some of the 200 types of birds that live here. You can get to the reserve on road 2 from Bursa west. The best seasons for a visit are March-June and Sept.-Oct.

On the way to Uludağ

Shopping

There are two interesting markets in the city. One is the **Goose Market** *(Bit Pazarı)*, located on İnönü Cad. and Cumhuriyet Cad. In this colorful and lively market you can find everything, except a goose. Even if you have no intention of buying anything in Bursa, it is worth visiting the Goose Market, and the **Covered Market** *(Bedesten)*. In order to reach the market, return to Cumhuriyet Cad., in the direction of the Great Mosque. This market was renovated after the earthquake of 1855, with the intention of preserving the original atmosphere of the late fourteenth century, when it was built by Sultan Beyazıt, the "Thunderbolt." Opposite the Great Bazaar there is a market where locally produced fruit and vegetables are sold.

Special products of the area are silk, hand-knitted socks and gloves, and *karagöz puppets*, made of dried camel skin of the kind used in the special shadow puppet theater developed in Bursa. In the markets you will find a selection of Turkish products, such as carpets and fabric,

The cable-car to the Uludağ

at prices lower than those in the İstanbul markets.

Special Events

The Bursa Folklore Festival is held in July in the Cultural Park (Kültür Park). Here the dance of swords and shields (*kılıç kalkan*) is presented. The dance is performed only by uniformed men, who create the rhythm of the dance with their steps and their weapons, without any orchestra. The dances express a feeling of power and strength, and apparently originate in the early Ottoman period.

The Dardanelles Strait

The Dardanelles Strait is located in the western Marmara Sea, connecting it to the Aegean Sea. The strait is 40 miles (65km) long and its maximum width, at Çanakkale, is only 1312 yards (1,200m).

Ever since ancient times, the strait has been a bottleneck in the sea journey from the Mediterranean to the Black Sea and by land from Europe to Asia; this has often rendered this area a bloody battle field, torn between the opposing forces of those who sought to gain control over this strategic point. There were many such attempts, resulting in huge losses and suffering, even for the victors.

According to historical evidence, the first to settle at the opening of the strait were the Trojans and the first nation who came to challenge the settlers here were the Greeks, in the twelfth century BC. Troy held out for nine years of siege until defeated by the deception of the Greeks, who succeeded in entering the city in their infamous "gift" of a wooden horse. (The story of the siege of Troy (llium) is told by Homer in *The Iliad*). However, the joy of the victors, led by Odysseus, did not last long. Many met their death in a storm

Sheep-tending

at sea on their way home to Greece (as recounted in Homer's *The Odyssey*). Thus the first attempt in history to gain control over the Dardanelles came to an end.

In World War I, some 3,000 years later, the British fought a long, harsh battle here at Gallipoli against the Turkish army, who were allied to the Germans. The British were defeated and many troops on both sides lost their lives. This has been the last attempt in history to gain control over the Dardanelles.

Between the first and the last attempt, there were many other battles here, as inscribed in the chronicles of the human race.

Today the strait is named after the city Dardanos. It was formerly called Helles Pontus (the bridge to Greece), and there was an ancient settlement here on the caravan route. The strait is the location of the Asian city of Abydos and Status, the European city. These two Greek cities became famous in the legend of Leander of Abydos and his lover, Hero of Status, priestess of Aphrodite. Abydos crossed the straits every night until he was swept away by the current and drowned. Hero, who could not stand the sorrow, drowned herself and joined her beloved for eternity.

In the area of the Dardanelles there are several interesting sights, and we set out to see them from the major city of the region, Çanakkale.

Çanakkale

The city of Çanakkale plays an important role as the central point of passage across the strait. In the First World War, the British tried to capture the strait, in order to help their ally, Russia. The Turkish army, under the command of the not so well-known lieutenant colonel, fought against the British forces, which were assisted by the armies of Australia and New Zealand. The Turks courageously and skillfully defended the strait, and the battle ended with the defeat of the British, who retreated with heavy losses in 1916, after nine months of siege. The excellent Australian film, *Gallipoli*, tells the story of the campaign. This was the only battle in the war in which Turkey was not defeated, and the name of the lieutenant colonel who earned glory and fame, Mustafa Kemal, began to echo throughout the country. This is where Mustafa Kemal, Atatürk, father of the Turks, began his career which completely altered the character of Turkey. Çanakkale is situated at the narrowest point of the strait and is an ideal base for visiting the region, especially Troy, which is situated 27km (17 miles) southwest through rolling hills.

How to Get There

A bus arrives in Çanakkale once an hour throughout the day from Bursa. The trip from Bursa takes about six hours and costs approximately $4. A bus to İzmir leaves frequently, passing through Ayvalık and Bergama. Direct buses connect Çanakkale with Keşan and Edirne in Thrace. You can also get to Thrace by the ferry, which leaves hourly from the Çanakkale dock to Eceabat, on the European side of the strait. Another ferry, further north, operates between Lâpeski and Gallipoli (Gelibolu). The ferries take both passengers and cars, and the price for crossing the strait is about 15 cents per person.

Area code: 286

Tourist Services

There is a **tourist information office** in the central square (Tel. 217-5012), and next to it is a ferry ticket office (Iskele Meydanı). The police and post office are about half-way between the bus station and the ferry dock.

Accommodation and Dining

The 3-star *Anafartalar Hotel* at Iskele Meydani, Tel. 217-4454, fax 217-4457, north of the ferry dock, is well-established and recommended. On the roof of the hotel is a fine restaurant. Inexpensive hotels can be found in the area of the clock tower; among them are the *Kervansaray Hotel*, which has a lovely garden and old-fashioned rooms. On the road to Troy there are several motels, such as *Tusan Truva*, Tel. 217-4987, located approximately 9 miles (15km) south of Çanakkale. In the area of the clock tower is the usual selection of small, inexpensive restaurants. To the left of the ferry dock, along the water, there are some good, reasonably-priced restaurants.

Sites to See

The principal sight here is the fortress built by Mehmet II the Conqueror, in the fifteenth century, in an attempt to control the strait. The fortress was reinforced in the 17th century, and another fortress was built on the European coast opposite Çanakkale. The fortress, which is still used for defense of the strait, is situated in a military zone, as part of the Military Naval Museum. You can visit the fortress and see the forti-

Turkish folk dancing

fications, cannons, and rotating exhibits in the gallery. The museum is open Tues., Wed. and Sun., 9am-noon and 1:30-5pm. Another museum is the new Archeological Museum, located at the exit from the city, facing Troy. The museum contains exhibits of the city's past and the remains of nearby Troy. Open daily 10am-noon and 1:00-5pm. closed Mon.

Special Events
The Troy Festival is held in Çanakkale in mid-August. The festival includes Turkish folk dancing and the ceremonial selection of Helen of Troy. There are many nice beaches, with adjacent camping sites and motels, in the area. The beaches are quiet, as most tourists prefer to take their vacations in the sun further south.

Troy
"Ilium was to the Old World what Jerusalem is to the Christians," wrote McLaren, the first scholar to discover the lost Troy. Troy was the center of power and wealth, well-known throughout history until this day: Troy, the heroic city immortalized in the *Iliad*, which endured years of wars and was defeated only by a shrewd trick.

In 1822, Charles McLaren published a study in which he identified the legendary Troy as the Turkish mound, Hisarlik. Heinrich Schliemann, a German merchant and amateur archeologist, who made his fortune in the California gold rush, obtained permission to excavate the mound, at his own expense.

For 20 years, from 1871 to 1890, Schliemann excavated the site, uncovering seven layers; he identified Troy in the second. Later excavations revealed additional layers, and many cities. Today it is widely accepted that there were 47 different cities on the spot, built one on the other in nine principal layers, and most experts identify Troy at the seventh layer, Troy VIIA.

The Legend
The story begins with a golden apple, which an unkind goddess declared as intended for the "fairest of all." Many goddesses, entered into contests to win the golden apple, until only three remained: Hera, wife of Zeus, Athena, the goddess of war, and the delicate Aphrodite. The natural choice of the judge of the contest, Zeus, head of the gods, wisely refused the task and elected Paris, a young shepherd, to serve as judge.

Now Paris was not a simple shepherd, but rather Prince of Troy, son of King Priam and Queen Hecuba. Paris had been sent away from Troy because Priam was warned that this son would bring a curse on his homeland. The goddesses tried to influence the young shepherd: Hera promised him control over Asia and Europe, Athena promised him military victories and the destruction of Greece, and Aphrodite promised him the most beautiful of all women. The romantic Paris, chose Aphrodite as the beauty queen in the heavenly contest.

However, as fate would have it, the most beautiful woman, in the world, Helen, was married. The exquisite Helen was the wife of Menelaus, King of Sparta. Aphrodite, the Goddess of love and beauty, directed Paris to Sparta, where Menelaus welcomed his guest and then left to attend to matters in Crete. Paris and Aphrodite succeeded in confusing Helen, and convinced her to flee with Paris to Troy. The angry and betrayed Menelaus called his brother Agamemnon and the other princes of Greece to join forces and return his beautiful wife. The Greek rulers were pleased to enter into an alliance that would destroy the power of Troy. The forces recruited the cunning Odysseus and Achilles the hero, who tried to avoid going to war by disguising himself as a woman.

A thousand ships set sail for Troy. The campaign continued for nine years and the losses were great. While the earthly war was being fought, a heavenly battle was being waged – between Aphrodite and Apollo, who favored Troy, and Hera and Athena, who had been insulted by Paris's choice, sided with the Greeks. Zeus remained balanced, favoring different sides at different times. Hector, the Trojan hero and brother to Paris, slew Patroclus, Achilles's close friend, in battle. This angered Achilles who enlisted the aid of the Goddess Athena and a heavy weapon to kill Hector. Achilles, whose strength came from the waters of the legendary Styx river, had one vulnerable spot, on his heel, where his mother had held him when she immersed him in the Styx. When Achilles led the Greeks to battle, Apollo aimed an arrow from Paris's bow at Achilles's heel, where it mortally wounded the hero.

When all the attempts of the Greeks failed, Odysseus, King of Ithaca, suggested a ploy. The amazed Trojans saw their Greek enemies abandoning their camp and returning to their ships, leaving behind a huge wooden horse. The joyous

The ferry from İstanbul to Yalova

Trojans brought the horse into the city walls, and began a joyful celebration with wine. In the early hours of the morning, the Greek soldiers hidden within the horse jumped out and opened the gates of the city to the Greek army, which had secretly returned. The desperate battles in the streets were to no avail. The great Troy fell.

Most of this story has come to us through Homer, the blind Greek poet who chronicled the war. There have been many debates about Homer and his works, *The Iliad* and *The Odyssey*: Scholars pondered whether it was a true story, or a great epic masterpiece, written by different authors. The discovery of lost Troy was a significant finding, as it was the first time that it was possible to examine the story of *The Iliad* in a scientific and archeologically sound manner.

The Site

Many tourists are disappointed with what they find at Troy. The greatness of the past is not reflected in the ruins that we see today. It seems that were it not for the legacy left to us by Homer these remnants would have been long forgotten. Nevertheless, it is worth visiting the site, and wandering among the ruins, thinking about the great war and the words of Euripides, who asked, "what were the consequences of this war, which was glorified throughout the world? Piles of ruins, a dead baby and a few miserable women who remained alive."

Dolmuşes travel the 17 miles (27km) from Çanakkale to Troy once an hour. The entrance to the site is from the parking lot, where a huge wooden horse stands. At the entrance there is a small museum.

The city is divided into nine major layers:

Layer I 3200–2800 BC
Layer II 2800–2200 BC
Layer III–V 2200–1800 BC
Layer VI 1800–1275 BC
Layer VII 1275–1100 BC, the city of Homer
Layer VIII 700–600 BC
Layer IX 350 BC – 400 AD, the Hellenistic-Roman Period

A path leads from the museum at the entrance, to the excavation site, where you can see the different layers. Walk around and try to imagine the glory of the past, think how Hector "walked on and into Priam's palace, fair and still, made of ashlar, with bright colonnades. Inside there were fifty rooms of polished stone, where the sons of Priam slept beside their wives; Across an inner court were twelve other rooms of polished stone all in one line, where slept the sons-in-law of Priam and their wives" (*The Iliad*, Book 6, "Interludes in Field and City").

Another interesting tale is the story of the jewellry that Schliemann found and identified as the "jewels of Helen of Troy." Schliemann claimed that he found the jewels in Troy and that he gave them to his wife, who kept them for many years, much to the disapproval of others. The scientists claimed that Schliemann did not find the jewellry in Troy, while the Turkish authorities, on the other hand, were most angry that the jewels had been smuggled out of the country. In the end, Schliemann gave the treasure to the Berlin Museum and during the Russian occupation in 1945 it was taken to Moscow. Today, it is believed that the jewels were found in the mound, although it is impossible to know whether Helen ever wore them. Scientists are still angry with Schliemann, who in his amateur excavations damaged several important layers.

The Uludağ Mountain

FROM İSTANBUL TO ANKARA

The distance between İstanbul and Ankara is 284 miles (458 km) and a comfortable toll-road connects these two major cities. Parts of the road pass through settled areas, which are not especially interesting (particularly those closer to İstanbul), but other sections pass through rolling green hills.

The settlements along the highway are relatively modernized, but short deviations from it, on secondary roads, take you to an entirely different world – small, poor villages, without electricity or running water, with mules their sole means of transportation and the locals garbed in traditional clothing.

İzmit (Kocaeli)

Road E5 connects İstanbul with İzmit. Today this city is a crowded industrial center, with a serious air pollution problem. The present İzmit is situated on the ruins of Nicodemia, the city of Nicomedes I, who made it the capital of ancient Bithynia instead of İznik. The city was destroyed and rebuilt a number of times. It was here that the Roman Emperor Hadrian lived. The Ottomans conquered it in the fourteenth century and changed its name to İzmit.

The only ancient remains are the acropolis in the eastern part of the city and the Roman aqueduct. Lake Sapanca (Sapanca Gölü), 9 miles (11km) north of the city, is a popular vacation spot, with bathing and fishing. Near the lake there is an impressive bridge dating to the time of Justinian.

Area code: 262

Lake Abant

The **tourist information office** in İzmit is located on Ankara road (Ankara Asfalti), Tel. 321-5663.

Bolu

Approximately 75 miles (120km) past İzmit, road E5 brings you to the village of Bolu. The last 18 miles (30km) of the ride are noteworthy, as the road is very lovely here, climbing through a natural forest to a height of 3,280ft. (1000m), to the Bolu Pass. Our interest in the village, apart from its several attractions, lies in its being a point of access to two pleasant and lovely natural sights – Lake Abant and Seven Lakes Park (Yedi Göller).

Since its establishment under the rule of the Hittite kingdom, Bolu was an important stop on the ancient caravan route from Europe to Asia. After the death of Alexander the Great, Bolu became an important Bithynian city, and even served as its capital for a short period. During this period Bolu was called Claudiopolis; the name Bolu is a distortion of the Greek word *polis*. In Bolu there is an ancient mosque and a Turkish bath that were built in the late fourteenth century, during the period of Beyazıt I. There is also a museum, with an exhibition on the history of the city since the seventh century BC, and a tourist information office, Tel. 215-5479.

The *Köroğlu Hotel*, Tel. 212-5346, fax 212-5345, in the village is a comfortable, moderately-priced place to stay.

Four km south of Bolu, on the Ankara-Istanbul highway, there is a cluster of thermal sources (44°C) rich in mineral salts, used in the therapy of a wide range of ailments.

Area code: 374

Lake Abant (Abant Gölü)

Seven miles (12km) before Bolu a narrow path winds from the main road to the right, through green hills. About 12 miles (20km) along, the road reaches Lake Abant, a blue lake surrounded by high hills covered with huge pine trees. The lake is situated 4,920ft. (1,500m) above sea level.

This is a wonderful tranquil spot, and the road around the lake leads to camping sites and a few hotels. The road climbing from the southwest to the lake and up to the towering hills leads to some exceptional observation points.

Yedi Göller Parkı

The Seven Lakes Park, Yedi Göller in Turkish, lies some 18 miles (30km) north of Bolu, between the town and the Black Sea beaches. This is a mountainous park, with forests of fir, pine and styrax, and seven beautiful lakes hiding among the trees. It is particularly beautiful here in the autumn, when the leaves give the entire area a reddish hue.

The road to Yedi Göller Parkı turns off road E5 exactly opposite the town of Bolu (the turn is sign-posted). This is a difficult road to drive on, and much of it is unpaved. On dry days you can travel on the road in any vehicle, but on rainy days and for a short while afterwards, the dirt path is muddy, and only a jeep can get through.

Off the road connecting İstanbul and Ankara there are many traditional small villages, where technology has still not arrived

The beginning of the road is paved, and it passes through small pastoral villages, where time seems to stand still. There is no electricity here, and water is fetched from the river. A few miles on, the road becomes a difficult but charming dirt path, climbing into the green mountains. A few miles up, at 4,920ft. (1,500m) above sea level, the road begins to descend, to the fabulous park.

ANKARA

Ankara has been the capital of the Turkish Republic since it was founded by Kemal Atatürk, in 1923. He moved the capital from its historic location in İstanbul to the open plains of Ana-

tolia. Ankara is a symbol of Atatürk's desire to depart from the magnificent Oriental past, and to establish a future-oriented society – a modern, industrialized, liberal society, belonging to the entire Turkish people rather than to a privileged minority. The location of Ankara in the center of the country affords it greater protection; the city is not exposed to attack from the sea, as is İstanbul.

Today, Ankara is a modern Turkish city, with a population of some 3.7 million. In spite of the international influence of business people, foreign embassies and diplomats who visit the city, Ankara lacks the luster of İstanbul, whose thousands of years of history make the modern city's 70 years seem meager. It is nevertheless worth visiting Ankara, with its wide boulevards and museums, and to see Atatürk's dream come true.

History of the City

From 28,000 in 1923, the city's population has grown to 3.7 million residents in less than 70 years. Until the twentieth century, Ankara was a remote little town in Anatolia. Evidence shows that this location was first settled during the Hittite period. Midas, King of Phrygia, ruled the city after the Hittites and called it Angoro, ("anchor"), because according to legend, It was here that Midas found the ancient anchor of Noah's Ark, which landed in Ararat. The Greek name is still preserved in the name of the high-quality wool produced from the angora sheep that are common to the region. The city became famous in 1402, when a great battle was held nearby. The rising Ottoman forces under the command of Sultan Beyazıt, "Thunderbolt," was preparing to defeat the Byzantine Empire and conquer Constantinople when the Mongols appeared under the command of Tamerlane, the heir of Genghis Khan, bringing blood and fire to Asia in their wake. The battle between the two imperial rulers ended with Tamerlane's victory. Beyazıt was taken prisoner to the court of Tamerlane. In 1405 Beyazıt died in captivity, most probably by suicide. Tamerlane died in the same year, and his death made the recovery of the Ottoman dynasty possible. Ankara regained its obscurity for 500 years, until Atatürk convened the National Assembly here in April 1920, after the parliament in İstanbul was dissolved by the occupational forces in the First World War. In October 1923, Atatürk declared the establishment of the republic, with Ankara as its capital and himself as its president. Since then, the city has developed rapidly, with the assistance of European architects and city planners.

The Layout of the City

The old city is called Ulus. This is all that existed of Ankara from the Roman period until the end of the War of Independence in 1923. The new city is located south of Ulus. The main artery, Atatürk Boulevard (Atatürk Bulvarı) begins at Ulus Square and cuts across the new city, leading from Ulus to the hotel area (Kızılay, Bakanlıklar). It runs to the prestigious Çankaya district, where the foreign embassies are located.

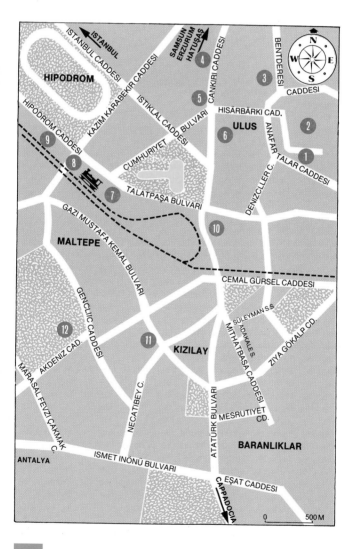

Atatürk's Mausoleum

Climate

It is most pleasant to visit Ankara in the spring (May-June) and fall (mid-Sept.-Oct.). In the summer the weather is dry and hot, with temperatures reaching 40°C. Like the rest of Anatolia, located 2,720ft. (850m) above sea level, the temperatures drop in the evening, even in the burning hot summer. The winter is cold and snowy: in January, the coldest month, it sometimes reaches 20°C.

How to Get There

Ankara is a major junction point serving all parts of the country. Visitors can include Ankara as a stop on their way to another destination, as many plane, bus and train routes stop there before continuing on to their final destination

By air: The Esenboğa Airport is about 18 miles (30km) from the city center. International flights from Europe and 13 other locations in Turkey, such as Van in the east, Trabzon on the Black Sea, İzmir in the west and, İstanbul land here. The air connection to İstanbul is particularly good. There are many daily flights between the two cities; the trip takes 70 minutes. Ankara's centrality is reflected in the flight prices: approximately $50 to any destination in Turkey.

The *Turkish Airlines (THY)* terminal on Talat Paşa near the train station serves as the stop for buses to and from the airport. The city terminal operates 7am-8pm, and the bus timetable coordinates with the flight schedules. Details are available from Tel. 311-8841. Reservations for flights can be made in travel agencies and at the terminal booths.

ANKARA

1. The Museum of Anatolian Cultures
2. Ankara Citadel
3. Temple of Augustus and Rome
4. Roman Baths
5. Museum of War
6. Central Post Office
7. Railway Station
8. Turkish Airlines Terminal
9. Bus Station
10. Ethnological Museum
11. Turkish Tourism Office
12. Atatürk Mausoleum

By bus: The main bus station (*otogar*) in Ankara is an interesting sight in itself. The station is located on Hippodrome Cad., west of the city terminal. It is worth taking a moment to look around at the dozens of platforms and rows of ticket stands, with thousands of people passing through at all hours of the day. At the station one can see the enormous variety of people who populate Turkey – country folk who have came to sell their products in the city, Kurdish farmers, city high-school students on vacation and young European tourists wearing traditional baggy Turkish pants and braids.

Direct buses leave for the different Turkish cities, large and small. Buses to İstanbul leave every 15 minutes; The ticket costs about $5. International buses leave for the east to the neighboring Moslem countries. Tourists with a visa to Iran can get to Teheran for less that $25 on their way to India. Many travel agencies have opened offices in the center of Ankara; you can buy your tickets there and guarantee a place on the bus before you get to the station.

By train: The train service to Ankara is fast and efficient. The trip on an express train from İstanbul takes about 8 hours. There are comfortable night trains between Istanbul and Ankara, with sleeping cars and a restaurant. The basic price for the journey is similar to that on the bus.

The train ride to İzmir is also recommended (the trip takes about 14 hours) and has a special dining car, where dinner and breakfast are served. The slow trains are liable to take days to reach their destination, and only devoted train lovers with plenty of time on their hands will take anything other than the express line (*Ekspres*). The eastbound train goes to Adana and Gaziantep and to Van.

By car: Road E5, which in most parts is a good highway, connects İstanbul to Ankara (284 miles 458km). The drive takes around 4 hours. The road then continues to Adana (300 miles 486km). The E23 connects Ankara to İzmir (360 miles 583km).

Area code: 312

Tourist Services

The central tourist information center is located at the **Turkish tourism office** at 33 Gazi Mustafa Kemal, west of Kizilay, Tel. 488-7007. Another office is located at the Esenboğa Airport (Esenboğa Havaalanı).

International telephone calls can be made from the fine hotels and from the central post office on Atatürk boulevard, near Ulus Square. There is also a post office in Kızılay, for the convenience of tourists in the hotel area.

There are many banks in the new city. A currency exchange is situated in the Turkish Airlines city terminal, near the train and bus station.

Cars can be rented at *Hertz*, 1 Kızılırmak Cad., Tel. 118-4440 and *Avis*, 68/2 Tunus Cad., Bakanlıklar, Tel. 467-2314. These agencies also have offices at the city airport.

Getting Around

Taxis: There are many taxis in Ankara. The traffic flows properly on the wide streets, unlike the narrow streets of İstanbul.

Buses: An efficient bus system covers the city. Journeys throughout the city are very low priced, tickets must be purchased in the booths near the bus stops before boarding the bus. Important lines for the tourist are line 8, running along Atatürk Boulevard, line 59 from the bus and train station to Ulus and line 63 from Ulus to Atatürk's Mausoleum. Detailed maps of the bus lines in the city can be obtained at the tourist information offices.

Accommodation and Dining

In Ankara there are many hotels, as one would expect from the capital of Turkey. The good hotels are located along Atatürk Boulevard, midway between the old city and the prestigious area of the foreign embassies. Most of the hotels are modern, but they lack the old Ottoman charm. They were built in a grey, functional design.

Merit, and Tandoğan Meydan, Tel. 231-7760 is a deluxe hotel.

Expensive hotels

Büyük Sürmeli: 183 Atatürk Bul., Tel. 231-7660, fax 229-5176. This excellent hotel has a casino, which tourists who are not guests at the hotel may also enter.

The Vakif Suluhan Çarşişi Mosque at Ankara

Ankara Hilton: 12 Tahran Cad. Kavaklıdere, Tel. 468-2888, fax 468-0909. 670 beds in 327 rooms.

Dedeman: on Büklüm Sok., Tel. 417-6200, fax 417-6214. 4 stars.

Kent: 4 Mithatpaşa Cad., Tel 435-5050. Also an *Etap* hotel, it has an excellent restaurant.

Recommended among the more **moderately priced hotels** are:

Bulvar Palas: 142 Atatürk Bul., Tel. 417-5020, an excellent and established hotel, centrally located.

Erşan: 13 Meşrutiyet Cad., Tel. 418-9875.

Inexpensive hotels – Simple hotels and pensions can be found in the Ulus quarter and in the area of the central post office. On Posta Cad., near the PTT, are the *Zümrüt Palas* at No. 16 and the *Oba* at No. 9. There are more hotels on the adjacent streets.

There is a **camping site**, *Kervansaray Susuzköy Mokamp* – approximately 12 miles (20km) outside of Ankara, along Road E23 – westward.

Expensive **restaurants** can be found in the fine hotels and in the prestigious Çanakaya district. Among the restaurants in Çanakaya, *R.V.*, 12 Tahran Cad., Tel. 427-4344, is particularly well-known. Less exclusive and much less expensive restaurants, include *Beyaz Saray* near Sihhiye Square (Sihhiye Meydanı); *Liman*, at 11 İzmir Cad. and the *Körfez* restaurant, 24 Bayındır Sok., in the Kızılay district.

In the Ulus district in the old city, there is the usual selection of small, inexpensive grill houses and self-service restaurants. It is worth trying the *Yavuz*, 13 Konya Sokak, near the Museum of Anatolian Cultures.

Sites to See

Unlike other large cities in Turkey, Ankara does not offer the visitor many palaces and mosques. Here the tourist will find several museums, the most special of which is the Museum of Anatolian Cultures, known also as the Hittite Museum. This museum has one of the richest exhibits of ancient cultures in the world. In addition to this museum, the tour to Ankara also includes the mausoleum of Atatürk.

On a hill near the prominent museum stands the **Ankara Citadel** (Hisar). A visit to this sight should be made before entering the Museum of Anatolian Cultures. The fortress was built on the fortifications of the acropolis from the Hellenistic period. The inner fortifications were apparently erected after the Byzantine conquest of the city in 630 AD, under the Byzantine Emperor, Heraclius; the outer walls were reinforced and renovated by Emperor Michael III in 859, as the inscriptions on the wall indicate.

An exhibit at the Museum of Anatolian Cultures

Entering the Ankara Citadel, one can sense for a moment the Ankara of the Ottoman Empire. Inside the citadel is a small Ottoman quarter, with narrow alleyways, old houses and mosques. There is a lovely view of the capital from the eastern tower (Şark Kulesi). Ankara Citadel is located at the end of Hisar Parkı street, east of Ulus.

The **Museum of Anatolian Cultures** (Anadolu Medeniyetleri Müzesi) provides a fascinating display of the glory of Turkey: It presents the visitor with the country's ancient history beginning with the bronze age, continuing with the Roman Province in Asia,

the Hittite, Assyriano and Helenistic eras and much more. Among other things, the museum exhibits the beautiful frescoes found in Çatal Hoyük, the first city in the world. The exhibits are arranged chronologically, and visitors to the museum can follow the development of human cultures through the different displays. The impressive Hittite exhibit is the museum's best, with statues of lions and the Sphinx that guarded the gates of the Hittite cities. Another notable exhibit deals with the Uraritan kingdom that was located in the eastern part of the country. The last exhibit is from the Greek and Roman period, some 7000 years after the period of the first exhibit.

Inside the Museum of Anatolian Cultures at Ankara

The museum is open daily 8:30am-12:30pm, closed Mon. The museum is located next to the citadel, east of Anafartalar Cad. You can get there on foot or by taxi from Ulus. It is located in a covered market (Bedesten) which was built in 1464-1471 by Mehmet Paşa, the Grand Vizier of Mehmet the Conqueror. If your feel tired, you can take a rest from the treasures of the Anatolian past in the special cocktail bar at the end of the eastern hall. It is a good idea to tour the museum with a Turkish guide, but ask him only to answer your questions, otherwise, you will be overwhelmed with dates, names and periods.

The Atatürk Mausoleum (Anıt Kabir)

When Atatürk died in 1938, his body was taken to Ankara, and buried in the Ethnological Museum. At the end of the Second World War construction began on a monumental mausoleum in honor of the beloved leader of the republic. Statues of lions line the boulevard leading to an awesome plaza inscribed with the words "Beyond all doubt, government belongs to the people." The entrance to the grave is through huge bronze doors. Inside, a sacred atmosphere prevails, and it is obligatory to remove your hat. The reverence and honor that the Turkish people hold for their leader to this day is evident on the faces of the visitors to the mausoleum.

You can get to Atatürk's Mausoleum by taxi or by bus. The young and the hearty can walk from the train and bus station. In the tourist season an interesting audio-visual show is presented.

Roman Ankara

A tour of the northern part of the city, in the Ulus quarter, takes us to the **Temple of Augustus and Rome**. On the walls of this temple, Emperor Augustus engraved the summary of his political and cultural activity. The temple became a Christian church under Byzantine rule, and in 1427, the Mosque of the Holy Hacı Bayram (Hacı Bayram Camıı) was built next to it. In the quarter you will also find the **Roman Baths** (Roma Hamamları) from the third century AD and the **Column of Julian** (Belkis Minaresi), erected in honor of the visit of the Byzantine Emperor Julian to the city in 362 AD.

The Atatürk Mausoleum, the burial place of Turkey's beloved leader

Other Museums

The **Ethnological Museum** (Etnografya Müzesi),

at the corner of Atatürk boulevard and Talat Paşa, covers the Seljuk and Ottoman periods with collections of jewellry, weapons, art work and housewares. Next to this museum is the Museum of Art (Resim Ve Heykel Müzesi), which contains paintings and sculpture by Turkish artists from the fifteenth century to the present day. The **Museum of the Republic** (Cumhuriyet Müzesi), located on Cumhuriyet boulevard, near Ulus Square, documents the establishment of the republic, in photographs and documents. The adjacent **Museum of War** (Kurtuluş Savaşı Müzesi) is devoted to the War of Independence. This was the site of the first Great National Assembly, which convened after dispersion of the parliament by the occupying forces in the First World War. The museums are open daily 8:30am-12:30pm and 1:30-5:30pm, closed Mon.

Atatürk's automobile at the Atatürk Mausoleum

Shopping

Shopping In Ankara is generally done in the city shopping centers, and not in the open and covered market places common to other cities in Turkey. There are large shopping centers on Atatürk boulevard in the hotel district in Kızılay. In Ulus there is a produce market (*Yeni Haller*) and behind it is a tastefully renovated rest house (*Vakîâ Suluhan Çarşısı*), where clothing and accessory stores have opened. Turkish handicrafts such as *kilim*, carpets, jewellry and embroidery can be purchased at the Association of Turkish Crafts on Selanik Cad.

Night Life

In addition to the casino in the *Büyük Ankara Hotel*, the exclusive hotels in Ankara offer performances of folklore and belly dancing to tourists and residents. Another popular form of entertainment is dinner with a Turkish entertainment program. The *Gar Gazinosu Club*, in the Central Station square (Istasyon Meydanı), presents such programs

At the *Set Club* in Kızılay you can dance until the wee hours. There are also theater performances (only in Turkish) and opera in Ankara (details are available at the tourist information offices).

The Land of the Hittites

The Hittite tribes came to Anatolia at the beginning of the second millennium BC, and conquered the land from the Hattian rulers. At its height, the Hittite realm was one of the greatest powers in the Old World, and included not only Asia Minor but also the kingdom of Aleppo and Babylonia. The development of the Hittite culture led to the construction of large fortified cities, with open temples and enormous palaces.

Hattuşaş

The Hittite capital was built on the foundation of the Hattian capital in the seventeenth century BC. The location was evidently chosen because it offered control over the surrounding plains. In Hattuşaş it is possible to discern a lower city, an upper city, the northern citadel and the large citadel. In the lower city there is a temple of the god of the storm, and above it the large citadel where the royal palace was housed. Measuring 443ft. by 525ft. (135m x 160m), this is the largest of all Hittite structures. Hittite cities were typically enormous; this site is about one mile long and over half a mile wide, and the ancient city wall is almost four miles long. It is best for the visitor to decide which part of the city to tour because a visit to the entire city can be absolutely exhausting.

A sight worth seeing is the **Temple of the Rock** (Yazılıkaya). The Hittite religion recognized 1,000 gods, some borrowed from Babylonian mythology. Some 100 of them are engraved on the exposed rock and the temple next to it, approximately one mile northeast of Hattuşaş. An ancient road connected the northern gate of the lower city with the Temple of the Rock, and was evidently used for religious parades of agricultural rituals.

Another Hittite site near Hattuşaş is the city of **Alaca Höyük**, one of the largest Hittite cities, located approximately 18 miles (30km) north of Hattuşaş. The most interesting objects have been taken from here to the Museum of Anatolian Cultures. At the site you can see the ruins of the fortified city, including time-worn Sphinxes.

An exhibit set on red at the Museum of Anatolian Cultures

Boğazkale

The town of Boğazkale, near Hattuşaş, is the central base for visits to Hittite sites. The village is located 130 miles (210km) east of Ankara and about 2 miles (3km) from Hattuşaş. You can arrange a guided bus tour to the land of the Hittites through agencies and at the exclusive hotels in Ankara. The tour takes a full day, and costs about $35, including lunch. Those traveling by public transportation should take the bus from the Ankara bus station to Sungurlu, 110 miles (175km) from the capital. At Sungurlu you can rent a taxi for a tour of Hattuşaş for about $20, or continue to Boğazkale by *dolmuş*. A tour of the sites by taxi from Boğazkale costs about $8. The trip takes about 4 hours and is not easy.

To get to Nevşehir in the Cappadocia region, take the bus to Yozgat, from there take a *dolmuş* for a tour of Hattuşaş and back to Yozgat, to the bus station. From here there is a direct bus to the Cappadocia region.

Those interested in staying in the area can find inexpensive accommodation in Boğazkale, at the *Aşikoğlu Turistik Moteli*, where there is also a restaurant. There are also inexpensive hotels in Sungurlu (the *Hattuşaş Hotel* and the *Hitit Hotel*) and the *Yılmaz* in Yozgat.

Ankara Citadel near the Museum of Anatolian Cultures

CAPPADOCIA

A trip to the area of Cappadocia is one of the high points of a visit to Turkey. Nature's workshop has created a particularly spectacular sight here; and the beauty of this area will remain with you for many years after your visit to Turkey. The ancient inhabitants of the region conformed to their natural surroundings and built their churches, homes and underground cities into the soft rock in marvelous harmony with the moon-like landscape. This is nature at its best!

The Cappadocia triangle is bounded by **Kayseri** in the east, **Aksaray** in the west and **Niğde** in the south. The secret of Cappadocia's appeal lies in the layer of tuff covering the area. The volcanic mountains, Erciyas, near Kayseri (*Erciyas Daği*) and Hasan (*Hasan Daği*) covered Cappadocia in a thick layer of volcanic dust. The dust, earth and water, together with the sun, formed this layer of soft tuff, and the rivers, streams and winds sculpted the famous moon-like Cappadocian landscape in the soft rock.

Hard rocks that got caught in the tuff protected the soft layers under them, creating the erect cones, crowned with rock hats. A landscape of fantasy fortresses, or magic chimneys, known as "fairy chimneys" (*Peri Bacaları*) was formed. The layer of tuff enriched the soil and agriculture in the region prospers.

The Layout of the Region

Three centers attract the interest of visitors: the **Göreme Valley** and the rock churches in the small Cappadocian Ürgüp-Avanos-Nevşehir triangle are the major sight. The **underground cities** of Derinkuyu and Kaymaklı near Nevşehir, and the **Ihalar Canyon**, near Aksaray, are the two other spots of interest for tourists in the area.

Quaint Göreme Village in Cappadocia

Visitors to the region may choose their base in one of Cappadocia's cities or villages. Most stay in Ürgüp, Nevşehir or Avanos and set out from there on day trips to the local sights. Aksaray serves as a convenient base for visiting Ihalar Canyon. Kayseri, the large city of the eastern part of the region, offers tourist attractions in addition to being a base, although a bit far away, for touring Cappadocia.

Climate
The spring and fall are the most comfortable seasons to visit. The Cappadocian heights are located 3,780ft. (1,000m) or more above sea level, and the weather is dry and clear in the summer, while in the winter it snows. Göreme Valley is most beautiful when covered with a light blanket of snow, between December and February.

How to Get There
By air: There are flights from İstanbul and Ankara to the Erkilet Airport near Kayseri. From the airport you can take a bus to the city center.

By train: The train from Ankara to Adana stops at Kayseri and Niğde. Due to the length of the train journey and the inconvenient schedule, the bus is generally preferable.

By bus: A good, efficient bus service links the various cities of Cappadocia with the rest of the country. The connections to Ankara and to Konya and Adana, both near the Mediterranean shore, are particularly good.

By car: Road E5 from Ankara to Aksaray (142 miles, 230km) is the best road leading in to the region. On this route you can enjoy the seemingly endless plains of the Anatolian plateau. The road runs along the bank of the large salt-water lake, Tuz Gölü. In Aksaray, turn east to Nevşehir and Ürgüp onto highway 73. You can also take highway 60, which branches off road E5 at Çakal, 18 miles (30km) outside of Ankara, and reaches Kayseri which is 176 miles (284km) away.

Getting Around
The best means of transportation here is the *dolmuş*; the minibuses provide efficient service throughout the region. There is also a good inter-city bus service, but the *dolmuşes* are preferable and faster – the trip from Nevşehir to Kayseri by bus takes an hour longer than by *dolmuş*. but, the *dolmuş* costs less. Tourists who have more time than money can reach all destinations in the area by hitching rides with the friendly Turkish drivers, most of whom speak no English, or with European drivers, who come here en masse by car.

Kayseri

At the foot of the inactive volcano Erciyas, which towers 12,850ft. (3,918m) high, lies Kayseri the largest city in the area. The city has served as the capital of Cappadocia for many years, and has some half a million residents. It has managed to preserve

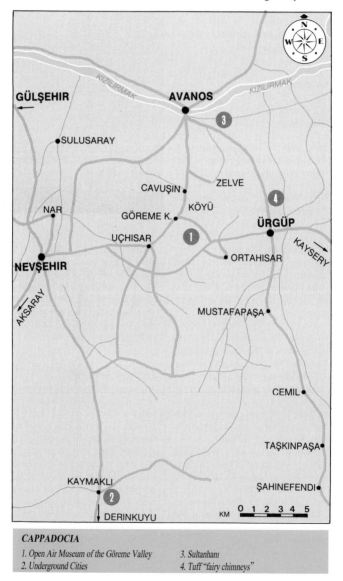

CAPPADOCIA

1. Open Air Museum of the Göreme Valley
2. Underground Cities
3. Sultanhanı
4. Tuff "fairy chimneys"

its traditional character and is an excellent base for touring the Cappadocia region.

The importance of Kayseri lies in its position at an important crossroads. Here the ancient trade route from Europe to Asia met with the route from the Black Sea to the Mediterranean. When the Cappadocian realm was established, after the death of Alexander the Great, the city (then called Mazarca) was made capital of Cappadocia. The last king of Cappadocia, Archelaus, who ruled under the auspices of the Romans, changed the name at the beginning of the Christian era of the city to Ceasaria, in honor of his patron, Augustus Caesar.

The village of Uçhisar

Ceasaria was later declared the capital of the Roman province of Cappadocia, and it became an important bishopric during the Byzantine period. From the eleventh century on, the city changed hands among the Turkish tribes, Mongols, Mamelukes and Seljuks. The Seljuk period was particularly prosperous, and the city has many magnificent mosques and public buildings which date back to that time.

Most of the mosques and other sights are located in the old city near **Cumhuriyet Square** (Cumhuriyet Meydanı) in the center of the city. The **Citadel** (Hisar), built partially from black basalt stones, is an excellent example of the Seljuk military architecture. In the thirteenth century, the Seljuk Sultan Keykâvus I constructed an impressive fortress on the foundation of a Byzantine fortress which had been built by Justinian in the sixth century.

The fortress is opposite the post office (PTT), just a short walk from Cumhuriyet Square. On the other side of the square is **Sahibiye Medresesi**, a characteristic Seljuk religious center, built in 1268, containing a religious studies center, a mausoleum and a Turkish bath.

Tourist Services

The tourist information center is located opposite the citadel, near 61 Huand Medresesi, Tel. 231-9295. The post office is located between the tourist information office and the central square, Cumhuriyet. The Erkilet Airport is north of the city, and buses and taxis run between the airport and the city in coordination with the flight schedules. There are many buses and *dolmuşes* to the city center from the *otogar*, the bus station west of the city.

A cave cut into the stone, which served as a residence in Zelve

Area code: 352

Accommodation and Dining

In Kayseri there are several good, moderately priced hotels; the *Hatat*, 1 Istanbul Cad., Tel. 231-9331 is modern and comfortable; the *Turan*, 8 Turan Cad., Tel. 231-8214, is older and more traditional. These hotels also house the most expensive restaurants in the city.

Among the inexpensive hotels, we highly recommend the *Sur* near the Citadel, 12 Talas Cad., Tel. 231-9545. You can find good restaurants, in addition to those in the hotels, along May 27 street (27 Mayis Cad.), near the Citadel. In the gastronomic realm, Kayseri is famous for its spicy salamis, among them *sucuk* and *pastirma*, which are just right for a picnic in the Göreme Valley. Another special delicacy is *güveç* – which consists of slices of mutton cooked with tomatoes, eggplant and pepper in a clay pot.

Shopping

Kayseri is a paradise for carpet and *kilim* lovers. The alert merchants will try to sweep you off the street into their stores. Next to the Citadel is a lovely bazaar, which is a must on any visit to the city. The carpet merchants are located in closed courtyards, creating for their merchandise a flattering background that they will probably not have in your home.

Because the number of tourists is small, the merchants are happy to invite potential buyers to a cup of tea and a short discussion on current affairs. Many of these merchants have branches in other European countries. The carpets in Kayseri are much less expensive than in İstanbul.

Ürgüp

The town of Ürgüp is located in the heart of Cappadocia, and it is a favorite base for many visitors to the area. Many buses and *dolmuşes* link Ürgüp with Kayseri (50 miles, 80km) and Nevşehir (14 miles, 22km), from the early morning until night. Many of the houses in the city are built of soft limestone, reminiscent of ancient caves. The town's economy based on agriculture and tourism. Although small (8,000 residents), the town has a decidedly international flavor, due to the many tourists who stay here. The **tourist information office** is located close to the center of town, at 37 Kayseri Cad., Tel. 341-1059.

Area code: 384

In Ürgüp there are several hotels at moderate and low prices. The **Büyük**, Tel. 341-8990, in the town center is friendly and reasonable. In order to find a room in one of the inexpensive pensions, walk east from the bus station on Dumlupınar Sok. Along this street you will find well-established hotels, and next to them inexpensive pensions, such as the *Kale* at No. 26. If you do not find what you want on this street, continue on to the next one, Elgin. Camping is permitted next to the inexpensive hotels and in camping sites along the road from Ürgüp to Nevşehir.

Göreme Valley

Göreme Valley is the most well-known area of Cappadocia, it is also its geographical centre and therefore the best place to stay. Travel agencies in Urgüp offer a guided tour but you can also organize a group yourself and rent a taxi or minibus to Göreme Valley, the caves at Zelve and the village of Avanos. For hikers, we recommend taking the

The Open Air Museum in the Göreme Valley

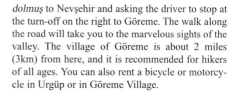

dolmuş to Nevşehir and asking the driver to stop at the turn-off on the right to Göreme. The walk along the road will take you to the marvelous sights of the valley. The village of Göreme is about 2 miles (3km) from here, and it is recommended for hikers of all ages. You can also rent a bicycle or motorcycle in Ürgüp or in Göreme Village.

Another short walk takes you to the mouth of this special valley. On the left of the road is the **Open Air Museum** (Açik Hava Müzesi), where some of the most beautiful churches built into the rock are located.

The soft tuff has attracted settlers since ancient times. Settlement of the Göreme Valley developed with the introduction of Christianity in the area, in the fourth and fifth centuries. It was during this period that the first churches were built in the valley. Christian settlement here reached its peak in the seventh century, after the Moslem conquest, when many monks and large groups of Christians fled here from Egypt and Palestine. The oppressed Christians found refuge in Cappadocia, and particularly in the Göreme Valley, which in Turkish means "I hope you can't see." The beautiful churches in the Göreme Valley were carved into the stone, and were in use until the Mongolian conquest of the area in the thirteenth century.

The Church of John the Baptist, carved out of a large rock

The **Church of St. Barbara** (Barbara Kilisesi) is one of the oldest churches in the valley. In the **Church of the Apple** (Elmali Kilise) you can view beautiful paintings which depict scenes from the life of Jesus. **Tokali Church** (Tokali Kilise) is the largest in the valley and the **Dark Church** (Karanlik Kilise) is the most impressive, because of the superb state of preservation of the fresco in the dark hall. These churches, and others, have been declared a national museum. You can visit the churches daily, 8:30am-5:30pm.

At the entrance to the Göreme Valley is the *Paris Motel* and *camping site*. The hotel has a swimming pool and restaurant. Between the Open Museum and Göreme Village is the modern *Kaya Hotel*, designed to blend in with the valley landscape. This is the best hotel in the region, and it is particularly suitable for those planning to stay just one night.

Göreme Village

In the village of Göreme the roads forks – north to

Remains of living-quarters hewn out of stone at Zelve

Avanos and southwest to Nevşehir. The village is a good spot for a rest in a café or restaurant after touring the valley. The village is well-known by its former name, Avcılar. You should stroll through the alleyways of the village and look at houses that were built out of stone, and which still serve local residents as warehouses and workshops.

Area code: 381

From Göreme Village to Avanos

The road to Avanos from Göreme Village runs some 7.5 miles (12km), and along it are two more tourist sights. **Çavuşin** is situated about 3 miles (5km) from Göreme; the primary sight of interest in this quiet village is the **Church of John the Baptist**, carved out of a large rock above it.

About 2 miles (3km) further on the road, a turn to the right leads to **Zelve**, another place where caves were cut into the stone along a narrow canyon, to serve as homes for the locals. Zelve was inhabited until modern times, but then the residents were forced to leave their homes carved into the rock for fear of their collapse and flooding. Extensive reconstruction is currently underway here. The sight is very impressive, including numerous churches and the only remaining Moslem mosque of this type.

There is no regular transportation between Göreme Village and Avanos. You must wait for an available *dolmuş*, or hitch a ride for the short trip. The local

Potters busy at work in the village of Avanos

drivers are friendly, and they are usually pleased to have a chance to host a tourist in their car.

Avanos

The village of Avanos is situated on the bank of the Kızılırmak river, approximately 7 miles (12km) from the village of Göreme. The town is a center for alabaster production, and the shop owners here will be happy to show you the production process and typical ornaments. The little town has 10,000 inhabitants, most of whom make a living from tourism or agriculture.

Area code: 384

Avanos has a **tourist information office**, Tel. 511-1360, next to the *Hotel Venessa,* Tel. 511-1201. There is also a bank and several hotels in town, among the least expensive in the area. After Ürgüp, Avanos is the region's most important center of tourism. From here, you can get buses and *dolmuşes* to Kayseri and other cities.

There are a few touring routes between Avanos and Ürgüp. On the easternmost road, you will find the Sarı Han, "The Yellow Khan," 3 miles (5km) outside of Avanos.

This ancient inn is a lovely example of Seljuk architecture. Past the khan, the road to Ürgüp continues through a charming area of tuff "fairy chimneys" (*Peribacaları Vadisi*).

A large underground city has recently been opened to the public at Ozkonak, approximately 12 miles (20km) from Avanos on the northern road to Kayseri. There is no regular transportation to the underground city, so you should hire a taxi in Avanos for this tour.

From Ürgüp to Nevşehir

On the 14 mile (22km) route between Urgüp and Nevşehir, there are two interesting sights. Four miles (6km) from Ürgüp lies the "Middle Citadel" (*Orta Hisar*). The inhabitants of this area farmed here for many generations, as indicated by the lemon storehouses and the agricultural scenes depicted in frescoes in the **Church of the Grapes** (*Uzun Kilise*) and the other churches in the area. The town of **Uçhisar**, whose name means "the three citadels," is built around a huge rock. Climb to the top for a spectacular view of the Göreme Valley. Don't miss it! The houses of the town are built around the natural citadel, blending in with the special landscape. The town is located at a crossroads, and can also easily be reached from Göreme Village, less than two miles (3km) away.

Nevşehir

Many tourists choose Nevşehir as their base for touring the region, as it offers good transportation to both Ankara and Konya, as well as proximity to the Göreme Valley and the underground cities of Derinkuyu and Kaymaklı.

Time has taken its toll on the beauty and special character of the ancient city of Nevşehir. In the central square is a statue of Damat Ibrahim Pasha, the most famous native of Nevşehir. Born here in 1670, Ibrahim Pasha served as the Grand Vizier to Sultan Ahmet III. There is an acropolis and a Seljuk fortress in the city, but these are not particularly interesting.

Area code: 384

A **tourist information office** is located at 22 Lale Cad., Tel. 212-3659, and another at the bus station in the northern part of the city. The post office is located on Atatürk Street, next to the *Göreme Hotel* in the city center. At the

central bus station you will find buses to Ankara, Konya and Antalya (11 hours). Three small *dolmuş* stations serve those traveling within Cappadocia.

The *dolmuş* service to the underground cities leaves from opposite the city museum. It also leaves from a point east of the museum, along Gazhane Sok. bound for Uçhisar, Göreme Village and Avanos, and slightly to the east you can find the *dolmuşes* traveling to Ürgüp and the Göreme Valley.

A moderately priced but very good hotel is the Orsan Kapadokya, Kayseri Cad., Tel. 213-2115. Another fine establishment is the centrally located Epok Hotel, 39 Hükümet Cad., Tel. 213-1487, which is closed for the winter from Nov.-March. One of the less expensive hotels, the Viva, Tel. 213-1326, is located next to the Orsan on Kayseri Cad. Several inexpensive hotels are located near the central bus station. The best of these is the Uçhisar Hotel, Tel. 213-5672. The central Lale Hotel, Tel. 213-1797, offers adjacent bathrooms and an elevator. On the main street, Atatürk, you will find the Kermer, an especially friendly and inexpensive pension.

Special Events
The Nevşehir tourist festival, with Turkish folklore and folk dance performances, is held in late June. The Wine Festival is held in Cappadocia in mid-September; the festivities include the harvest celebration, wine-tasting, folk dancing and exhibits of traditional crafts in the towns and villages.

The Underground Cities
South of Nevşehir, along the road to Niğde, some amazing and unusual settlements await the visitor: these are underground cities, cut into the soft tuff. Stairs lead you from the small, very regular town into rooms and passages in the belly of the earth. In some areas in these cities as many as 10 stories were dug, one on top of the other. The upper floors were used for residences, the lower ones for storage and hiding.

It is not certain who created these cities, which include small squares and chapels. A Greek historian mentions them as early as the fifth century BC.

The use of these caves apparently intensified between the seventh and tenth centuries, during the Arab invasion of the area, when local Christians hid in them. During that period, regular city life carried on here beneath the ground. The structures included places of residence, trade and religion, and special quarters were used for burial. The last time these underground cities were used was in 1839, when the local residents hid from Ibrahim Pasha and the Egyptian army.

Of the numerous underground cities in the area, two are open to the public: **Kaymaklı**, 12 miles (19km) from Nevşehir, and **Derinkuyu**, 6 miles (10km) further south. The underground cities are open to visitors daily from 9am-noon and 1:30-6:30pm. The two cities are fairly similar; if you want to visit just one, choose Derinkuyu, as it is slightly further away and somewhat less crowded with tourists.

Aksaray

Aksaray is a good place to stay when touring the Ihlara Canyon, and it is an important crossroads. You can get to the city by a direct bus from Ankara, Nevşehir or Konya. There is a tourist information office on Bankalar Cad., Belediye Işhani, Tel. 213-2474.

Area code: 382

Among the moderately priced hotels is the *Ihlara*, Eski Sanayi Cad., Tel. 213-1482, and the centrally located, recommended *Vadi Hotel*, Tel. 213-4326. There are also simple hotels in the center of the city. On the outskirts of town you will find some good motels and roadside hotels, for organized groups and tourists traveling by car.

Ihlara Canyon

Ihlara Canyon was cut into the tuff of Peristerma Valley by the Melendiz river (Melendiz Suyu). A tour through the narrow channel, between the steep walls of the canyon, leads you to churches, small groves and ancient graves. The canyon extends from the village of Ihlara (Ihalar Köyü) to Selim's grave (Selimiye Türbesi), a distance of some 7 miles (12km). Most of the beautiful churches are located upstream, between Ihlara and Belisirma.

Sultanhanı, the Khan of the Sultan – a Seljuk construction

The easiest point to enter the canyon is from the restaurant on its southern bank, one mile from the village of Ihalar. Buy a ticket to the site at the restaurant, and from there walk down the steep steps to the bottom of the canyon. The walk along the canyon takes about half a day, and you should bring food for the way. Open to visitors daily, 8:30am-5:30pm. It is prohibited to sleep and cook here.

The road leading to the start the walk passes through Ihalar village. The turn to the south is located a few miles before Aksaray (for those coming from Nevşehir). It is 18 miles (30km) long and goes through the picturesque villages of Selime and Yaprakhisar.

South of Aksaray is a mountaineers' attraction, the Hasandagi Mountain (3250m). It is a surprisingly unsophisticated climb, particularly enjoyable from its Taspinar approach. Maps and lists of local guides are available at the Aksaray tourist information office.

From Cappadocia to Konya

From the crossroads at Aksaray, the tourist can get to the Mediterranean coast by a number of roads. One turns southeast, toward Adana, but the most interesting route is by road 73 from Aksaray to Konya, an ancient city and important religious center.

Sultanhanı

Some 25 miles (40km) from Aksaray along the road to Konya is the Khan of the Sultan (Sultanhanı). The Seljuk Sultan Keykûbad I built the magnificent khan here between 1232-1236. The khan was designed as a resting place and safeguard for the merchants on the ancient trade routes, and the caravan staff stayed here without charge. The khan included bedrooms, bathrooms, a kitchen, a café, a mosque and workshops for repairing the wagons and equipment that were damaged along the way. Stables and troughs were set up for the horses and animals. The Sultanhanı is the largest of its type in the country and a prime example of Seljuk construction.

Konya

Konya, 62 miles (110km) from the Sultan's Khan, was a truly splendid city in the mid-thirteenth century. At the southwestern edge of the Anatolian plateau, 163 miles 263km) south of Ankara, 87 miles (140km) southwest of Aksaray, it is one of the oldest cities in the world. The city serves as a religious center, and numbers over half a million inhabitants, who make their living in trade and agriculture.

History of the City

Some 30 miles (50km) from Konya is **Çatal Höyük**, the oldest city in the world. There was an urban settlement in Çatal Höyük as early as the Neolithic

Pastoral scenery on the way to Konya

period, in the seventh millennium BC. Some five thousand years later, in the second millennium BC, the Hattians settled in Konya, and in the first millennium BC, the city was conquered by the Phrygians. According to Phrygian tradition Konya was the first place to be revealed to man after the flood. For centuries Konya changed hands, being controlled by the Persians, the Seleucids and the Romans, and its name was changed with each conquest: Koana in the Hattian period, Koanya under the Phrygians and Iconium during the Roman period. The Roman Iconium was the capital of the Karamania region, and an important crossroads of trade routes. Paul the Apostle visited the city in the year 47 AD, and Konya became one of the first centers of Christianity in Anatolia. The Romans lost control of Konya to the Byzantine Empire, and during this period the city suffered terribly from frequent Arab invasions. Konya's golden era began in the twelfth century, when the city was made the capital of the Seljuk Sultanate of Rum.

The Seljuks were originally part of the Turkish tribes who came from the Asian plains. They converted to Islam in the tenth century and split from the other tribes, who remained pagans. Under the leadership of Seljuk, the founder of the dynasty, they began their conquests and established themselves in the area of Bukhara and Caspian Sea, today in Uzbekistan. In the eleventh century, the Seljuks reached the peak of their power, under the rule of Alp Arslan and Malakhshah, and the boundaries of their kingdom extended to Samarkand, China, Yemen and Jerusalem.

In 1071, the Seljuk victory over the Byzantines, in the battle of Manzikert, opened the gates of Anatolia to the Moslem fighters, and with the subsequent disintegration of the great Byzantine Empire in the twelfth century, the Seljuks continued to rule Anatolia as an independent dynasty, leaving only Constantinople and its environs under the Byzantine Empire. This conquest is what led to the transformation of Turkey into a Moslem country, and opened the way for the Turkish-Ottoman tribes.

Konya was the capital of the Seljuk Empire until it fell to the Mongols in the fourteenth century. During the Seljuk rule, Konya gained status as an important religious and cultural center, and the Seljuks saw themselves as the protectors of orthodox Suni Islam, and built numerous mosques and public institutions in the city.

In the thirteenth century, the religious poet and philosopher, Celaledoin Rumi, who developed a system of religious Moslem mysticism, and founded the order of Dervishes, lived in Konya. The members of the Dervish order called their leader *Mevlâna*, meaning "our guide." Their worship ceremony (*sema*) symbolizes their rebirth in a mystical union with God. This ceremony consists of a ritual dance, in which the worshippers reach an ecstatic state by whirling round and round on a revolving stage. Their ritual costumes compliment the content of the ceremony; red conical hats and long white robes represent their tomb-stones and shrouds as they relinquish earthly life and are reborn in union with God. Mevlâna's grave is a central tourist attraction in the city. Konya was ruled by the Ottomans, from the mid-fifteenth century.

The Layout of the City

Most of the tourist sights in Konya are concentrated in a single square kilometer in the center of the city. From the central hill, Alaeddin Parkı, Alaeddin Cad. runs east, and continues as Mevlâna Cad. Most of the important sights of the Seljuk capital are located in the vicinity of these streets.

How to Get There

By bus: The bus station is about half a mile from the city center. You can get there by bus from Ankara, Nevşehir, Aksaray, Isparta and the other cities of Cappadocia. There are good bus links with Adana, Alanya and Antalya, on the Mediterranean coast.

By train: The Meram Express (*Mera Ekspresi*) connects Konya with Istanbul. The train travels the 435 miles (700km) dividing the two cities in 13 hours, and it has a dining car. The train leaves Konya in the morning and reaches İstanbul at night, and vice versa.

By car: Road 73 from Nevşehir to Aksaray leads to Konya via Sultan-hanı. From Ankara, take road E5 and then road 35 until the entrance to Konya. Road 35 continues from Konya to Silifke, on the Mediterranean coast, where it meets coastal road 24, leading to Mersin and Adana. Road 31 leads to Antalya and Alanya. Road 80 goes from Konya to Afyon, and from there to İzmir or Bursa.

It is interesting to note that the network of modern roads to and from Konya in many places follow the Roman roads, which themselves followed the most ancient caravan routes.

Tourist Services

The **tourist information office** is located opposite the Mevlâna Museum, at 21 Mevlâna Cad., Tel. 235-1074. The post office is situated next to Hükümet Square (Hükümet Meydanı), between Alaeaddin Cad. and İstanbul Cad. The police station is opposite the Selimiye Mosque, next to the Mevlâna Museum.

Area code: 332

An Important Note

Konya is an important religious center for orthodox Moslems, and the level of religious sensitivity here is higher than just about anywhere in the country. Be sure to dress modestly when visiting the mosques and sacred graves. During the month of Ramadan most of the restaurants and cafés in the city are closed during the day, and you should eat in the hotel restaurant, not outside, until nightfall. On Mondays all the main museums are closed, so this is not a good day to visit Konya.

Transportation

Because of the concentration of the city's sights in a small area, the tourist does not usually need the transportation services within the city. Between the bus station and the city center there are many buses and dolmuşes, which you can find outside the station, next to the *Park Hotel*. Buses frequently leave the train station for the center of the city.

Accommodation and Dining

The *Özkaymak Park*, Otogar Cad., Tel. 233-3770, near the bus station, is considered the best hotel in town, but the centrally located *Başak Hotel*, 3 Hükümet Meydanı, Tel. 351-1338 and the adjacent *Şahin* Tel. 351-3350 are built in a more old-fashioned style, more in the spirit of the city, and their prices are much lower.

Many Turks make pilgrimages to Konya from throughout the country. This has led to the development of inexpensive tourist services. There are numerous simple, inexpensive hotels which can be found along Alaeddin and Mevlâna streets, particularly in the area of the central Hükümet square. Examples are the *Şeref Palas Oteli*, next to the *Başak*, and the *Saray Oteli* at 15 Mevlâna Cad.

A good restaurant in central Konya is *Köşem*, 26 Aleatin Cad. next to the *Başak Hotel*. Many of the restaurants in the city serve local delicacies, including baked mutton (*Fırın Kebap*) and a bread-and-cheese pastry (*Peynirli Pide*).

The beautiful turquoise cap at the Mevlâna Museum

Sites to See

The **Mevlâna Museum** (Mevlâna Müzesi) is the main attraction in Konya. The Dervishes of Mevlâna lived in Tekke, a sort of dervish monastery. The Tekke of the Whirling Dervishes became a museum in 1927, by order of Atatürk. The tomb dates back to the Seljuk period, and the other parts of the hall were added during the Ottoman era, by the Sultans and grand viziers. The silver doors of the Tekke, for instance, were a gift from Hassan Pasha presented in 1599.

The life of the Whirling Dervishes is depicted at the Mevlâna Museum

Inside the museum is an exhibit depicting the life of the Dervishes, their costumes, their books, as well as fabulous glass *objets d'art* and displays of sacred objects. This is also the eternal resting place of some of the Dervish saints, including Celaleddin-i Rumi, or Mevlâna, who died in 1273. Take note of the colorful and interesting visitors to the museum, which is also a sacred Moslem site.

The museum is open daily 9am-noon, and 1:30-5:30pm, closed on Mon. **Note: Modest dress required**.

Alaeddin Mosque (Alaeddin Cami) is centrally located on Alaeddin hill. The construction of the mosque, which is the largest Seljuk mosque in the city, took 70 years to complete. Completed in 1221, the mosque was built during the reign of Sultan Alaeddin Keykûbad I, one of the greatest Seljuk Sultans to rule Anatolia. Note the architectural differences between this ancient Seljuk mosque, influenced by the Arab-Oriental style, and the magnificent Ottoman mosques in İstanbul and Edirne. Alaeddin Mosque has been renovated several times, and a number of Seljuk Sultans are buried here. This central hill was the location of the acropolis during the Roman period, when the city was called Iconium, and many columns dating from that era are still found on the hill.

The **Karatay Museum** (Karatay Müzesi), located opposite Alaeddin Mosque and the ruins of the Seljuk palace, is the large Karay theological college (Büyük Karatay Medresesi). This college served as a theological study center and was built by the Emir Karatay in 1251. The exterior of the impressive building is a good example of the Seljuk craft of stone engraving. The central room in the seminary is particularly striking, with a dome 40ft. (12m) in diameter looming over a pool of water. The room is decorated with extraordinary turquoise and blue tiles, with gold decorations symbolizing the sun and the stars. The museum also houses an exhibit of lovely colored tiles. One of the rooms contains the tomb of Seljuk Karatay. The museum is open daily 8:30am-noon and 1:30-5:30pm, closed Mon.

On the western side of Alaeddin hill is **Ince Minare Museum,** a special museum, which was also erected in 1258 as a theological college. The museum has a high, slender minaret, from which name, Ince Minare, "the slender minaret" is derived. The minaret, by the way, was hit by lightning at the beginning of the century so only half of it remains. The carved entrance is one of the most exquisite found in a Seljuk construction in the entire country. In the center of the college is an interesting exhibit of stone and wood carvings, from the Seljuk period. The museum is open during the same hours as the Karatay Museum.

In Konya there are other museums, such as the archeological and ethnographic museums and the Museum of Culture, devoted to the memory of Atatürk, as well as a number of Seljuk and Ottoman mosques. The city of Konya, located on the tourist route between the marvelous Cappadocia and the resort beaches of the Mediterranean, is a suitable place to stop before visiting the religious sights.

Shopping

There is a large market in Konya, behind the central post office (PTT). In the market and elsewhere in the city there are many shops selling carpets at low prices. The market has many stores selling shoes and clothing. A few stores sell colored hand-woven straw mats typical of the Konya region.

Special Events

The annual Rose Festival is held in Konya in early June. The central event of the festival is a competition among rose growers. The end of October brings with it a week of poetry competitions for Turkish

At the Mevlâna Festival in traditional clothing

poets, following an old tradition similar to that of the troubadours in Europe. In addition to poetry there are competitions in less lyric realms, such as horse racing.

The largest event in the city and indeed in this area of the country is the Mevlâna Festival. This festival is held in mid-December, and revolves around the celebrations of the Whirling Dervishes. These dances abound in mystical symbols, and are performed in traditional clothing, including wide white capes and long red turbans. During the festival it is very hard to find accommodation in the city, so you should reserve a hotel room and tickets for the festival well in advance.

On to the Mediterranean Coast

There are two alternative routes from Konya to the Mediterranean Sea. The one way is to turn south toward Silifke (on the main coastal road), passing through Karaman and Mut. The other is to turn west from Konya toward Beyşehir, a picturesque town on the lake of the same name. The road continues along the lake, to its southern shore, and turns south toward the Taurus mountains. From here the beautiful road narrows and becomes difficult, to pass as it winds around the mountains and pine forests. Drive slowly and with great caution here. About 120 miles (190km) further along the road joins up with the main coastal road, where you must turn right to reach Antalya and left in the direction of Alanya.

Another possibility is to turn from Beyşehir west, and to go around the lake from the north, toward the city of **Isparta**. This road goes along the shore of the Eğridir Lake, the fourth largest lake in Turkey, known for its blue waters and the towering mountains which surround it. The city of **Eğridir**, situated on a peninsula, offers a charming vacation and recreation spot.

Continuing to Antalya, the road turns south from Eğridir, and crosses the Taurus mountain range. Those who want to skip the Mediterranean coastal area should turn west from Eğridir to Pamukkale and Kuşadası (see "The Aegean Sea").

A fountain at Konya

THE MEDITERRANEAN COAST

The shores of the Mediterranean Sea stretch from Antakya, in southeastern Turkey, to Marmaris, in the southwest, and can be reached from anywhere in Turkey by bus, by train to Adana and by air to Antalya, Adana, and Dalaman, near Marmaris. Transportation within the area along the coast consists of buses and *dolmuşes*.

The enchanting seaside village of Kaş – one of many along the Mediterranean coast

The climate along the coast is, as might be expected, decidedly Mediterranean. Temperatures reach 40°C in the hot summer months, and drop to 10-12°C in the rainy wintertime. The tourist season along the shores is from March to November. Considerable portions of the shore are not suitable for bathing because the pebbly beaches make it hard to enter the water. Small sandy beaches can be found in the little bays between Alanya and Marmaris.

The Mediterranean seashore prospered during the first century BC. After the Trojan War, in the eleventh and twelfth centuries BC, the coastal area was conquered by Ionian and Aeolian immigrants, who came from southern Greece. The new cities that they founded were united in an alliance, similar to the confederation of the Lycian cities. The coastal area was known to the Greeks by the name Pamphylia, "the land of the tribes." After the fall of Alexander the Macedonian, and the division of his territory, the powerful Seleucid Empire was established here, with Antioch, today Antakya, as its capital. With the Roman conquest and the birth of the Byzantine Empire, the golden age of the Mediterranean shores ended, and the center of affairs moved to Constantinople and the shores of the Marmara Sea.

Since the 1970s there has been a tremendous flood of sunshine tourism in the area. Many European vacations take advantage of the climate and the beaches for sunbathing and vacationing. This has affected the lifestyle and the customs of the local inhabitants. The Turks try to preserve their religious ways and their

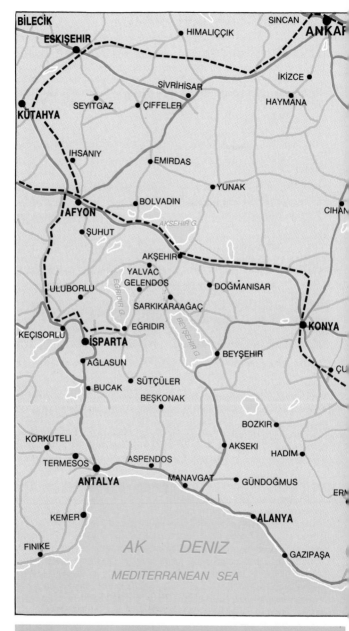

CENTRAL ANATOLIA AND THE MEDITERRANEAN COAST

unique culture. For instance, bathing in the nude, partial or full, is forbidden on the beaches of Turkey and is allowed only in the large resort villages. Because of the many tourists, some of the coastal cities have lost their special charm, and, unfortunately, a lot of the youth try to imitate the behavior and norms of the tourists.

In the resort villages along the coast the prevailing atmosphere is cosmopolitan, and the accommodation like similar places throughout the world. These resorts offer swimming pools, restaurants and discotheques. The hotel accommodation in the cities and towns is part of the experience: some are housed in historic buildings that have been carefully renovated, while in small villages there are hotels that still have no running water. It may be worthwhile traveling some distance from the international resort centers, in favor of an unmediated encounter with the Turkish experience.

In this chapter we shall travel along the Mediterranean seaside resorts, from Adana westward to Marmaris. The regions east of Adana, as well as the Antakia District, will be covered in a later chapter (see Index).

The Ancient Delta

The Seyhan and Ceyhan rivers run down from the Taurus mountains, creating the Kilika plain, which is, for the most part, a delta formed from the silt of these rivers. A group of British archeologists identified 150 ancient settlements in the fertile delta, some from as long ago as the Neolithic period. Arab geographers called rivers the "rivers of Paradise." Today nothing remains of these cities but a heap of ruins, and the major segment of the population of the Kilika plain is found in the large city of Adana.

Adana

Adana is the fourth largest city in Turkey, with a population of some 1 million. The Seyhan river passes through the eastern part of the city, and most of the city lies west of the river. Adana was founded in the early part of the first millennium BC, but only a few ruins remain from its glorious past. Today Adana is a bustling, industrial city, and is no frequented much by tourists.

Area code: 322

A **tourist information office** is located at 13 Atatürk Cad., Tel. 431-1323, next near the city center. The post office (PTT) is located next to the clock tower on Gürsel Cad.

How to Get There

By air: Adana's airport is situated west of the city, on road E5. Buses link it with the city. Daily flights arrive here from İstanbul (about $80) and Ankara (about $60). There are direct flights between Adana and Lefkosia, which is the Turkish side of Nicosia, Cyprus.

By bus: From the Adana bus station, there is particularly good service to the city of Antalya, a trip of approximately 8 hours. Another direct bus goes to Antakya and Haleb in Syria. For those traveling to the western Nemrut mountain, there are two buses a day to Kâhta; the ride takes seven hours. The *otogar*, the bus station, is located about a 15-minute walk from the center of the city, on the northern side of road E5.

By train: Visitors to the area can use the train service to nearby Tarsus and Mersin. The trip to farther destinations, such as Ankara, Kayseri and Istanbul, is much longer than the same trip by bus. The train station is located at the northern end of Ziya Paşa bul, where you can take a *dolmuş* or taxi to the city center.

By car: Road E5 cuts across Adana from east to west. Adana is situated some 305 miles (490km) from Ankara, 345 miles (556km) from Anatolia and only 176 miles (284km) from Nevşehir in Cappadocia.

Accommodation and Dining

As befitting a large commercial city, Adana has a number of exclusive hotels. The finest is the central *Adana Sürmeli*, 151 İnönü Cad., Tel. 351-7321. The nearby *Büyük Sürmeli*, Özler Cad., Tel. 352-3600 is older, and its prices are slightly lower.

Among the well-established hotels, the most prominent is the *Zaimoğlu*, Tel. 351-3401, located between the two hotels mentioned above. The *Ipek Palas Hotel*, Tel. 351-8741, is at 103 İnönü, next to the *Divan*. All the hotels

mentioned are air-conditioned, which is a necessity during the hot summers.

Around the bus station you will find a number of simple hotels, which are fairly noisy. Another area where there are several inexpensive hotels is on the centrally located Inönü Cad.

Try the *Mehtap Hotel*, opposite the *Divan*.

Excellent meals are served in the good hotels. The local speciality, spicy Adana kebab, can be found in the restaurants along Atatürk Cad., in the vicinity of the tourist information office.

Sites to See

Adana was founded in the first millennium BC. There are a few remains of its former glory, among them a long stone bridge (Taş Köprü), built by the Emperor Hadrian. The bridge crosses the Seyhan river, close to the Great Mosque (Ulu Cami). This mosque was built in 1507 by the Emir Halil Bey, the ruler of the area preceding the Ottoman conquest. The mosque houses the grave of the Emir and has some very lovely tiles.

In Adana there are three museums. The **Ethnographic Museum**, located to the left of the *Divan Hotel*, houses some historic artifacts and lovely handicrafts, such as antique carpets and *kilim*. This is the most interesting museum in the city; the **Archeological Museum** and the **Atatürk Museum** are less interesting. It is also worth visiting the **covered market**, to see the colorful crowds.

Tarsus

Twenty four miles (38km) west of Adana, the coastal road E24 between Adana and Antalya meets road E5 from Aksaray and Kayseri in Cappadocia. Near this intersection is **Tarsus**. Formerly an important city, it was here that Mark Anthony and Cleopatra met to discuss important matters. This meeting sparked the imagination of Plutarch, Shakespeare and thousands of viewers throughout the world, who were intrigued by Elizabeth Taylor taking the role of the Egyptian queen. Today, you can see one Roman gate in the center of the city, which is of course, named, Cleopatra Gate.

Mersin

Mersin, called Içel in Turkish, is a large city with the largest port on Turkey's southern shore. Ancient Mersin was located a few miles north of the new city and has continuously been settled since the Neolithic period. Almost nothing is left of the old settlement, and the new Mersin is a modern city of apartment houses, with 320,000 residents.

You can get to Mersin from the Mediterranean coastal cities by bus. Other buses reach the city from Konya and Cappadocia, and the bus and train service between Mersin and Adana is excellent.

Mersin tries to attract some of the "sunshine tourism" which is drawn to the Mediterranean coast. The city is adorned with green gardens and boulevards of palm trees. The *Mersin Hotel*, 10 Cami Şerif Mah, Tel. 232-1640 is the city's finest hotel, except perhaps for the new *Mersin Hilton*, 5 star, Menderes Blvd., Tel. 326-5000. The Mersin is located on the sea shore, overlooking the harbor. Among the recommended well-established hotels are the *Toros*, Tel. 231-2201 on Atatürk Cad., and the central and modern *Ege*, Tel. 332-1419 on Istiklâl Cad. Inexpensive hotels can be found near the bus station. The low-priced *Nobel Hotel* is located at 101 Istiklâl Cad., Tel. 237-2210. The *Kent Hotel* is at number 51 on the same street.

Area code: 324

The **tourist information office** in Mersin is located near the port, on Inönü boulevard. The post office (PTT) is next to the Mersin hotel.

Ferries sail from the port in Mersin to Famagusta in Cyprus. The ferry to Famagusta (or its Greek name Magosa), leaves at 10pm from Mersin on Monday, Wednesday and Friday nights, arriving at 8:30am the next morning. The Friday ferry continues to Latakia in Syria. The ferry takes both passengers and cars, and costs from about $30 for a lounge chair on the deck to $60 per person in the best cabin. It costs about $25 to transport a car on the ferry. It is currently possible to continue from Turkish Cyprus to the Greek part of the island.

From Mersin to Silifke

The coastal road from Mersin to Alanya passes several sandy bathing beaches. Just over 6 miles (10 km) west of Mersin is the ancient Roman city that was known as Soli, and is today called **Viranşehir.** There is an impressive street of columns here leading to a pleasant, sandy beach. Of the 200 original Corinthian columns only 20 remain, but it is still a lovely sight.

Further along the road to Alanya is the famous **Maiden's Castle** (*Kız Kalesi*), a fortress standing in the sea; the remains of another fortress stand on the shore. A common wall once connected the two fortresses, which were built in the twelfth century by the Armenians who established an independent kingdom in the region. The place derives its name from the ancient legend of a king who wanted to protect his daughter, after it was prophesied that she would die from a snake bite, by isolating her on an island; the princess nevertheless died when bitten by a snake which was hidden in a basket of fruit that was sent to her. The moral is that it is impossible to flee your fate.

A number of small islands in Turkey are named after this story. The local inhabitants do not like to visit the fortress, for fear of the snake, for according to the legend, it still lives there. There is an excellent beach for bathing here, a few restaurants, a camping site and a few inexpensive pensions.

From Narlıkuyu, near the Maiden's Castle, a narrow road leads north. This road continues about one mile to **"Heaven and Hell"** (*Cennet Ve Cehennem*), two large caves. Heaven is a huge cave adorned with a Byzantine entrance, and inside there are stalactites and stalagmites and an underground river. The local inhabitants make pilgrimages here, to request remedies and forgiveness. Hell is a dark, dangerous chasm, which you should not enter without a guide. You can eat lunch at one of the fish restaurants in Narlıkuyu. In the village there is a small museum, preserving a beautiful mosaic floor, found among the ruins of Roman baths, dating back the third century AD. Silifke lies about 13 miles (20 km) west of here.

Silifke

Silifke is the site of ancient Seleucia. Founded by Seleucus Nicator in the third century BC, it was situated on an ancient crossroads, which linked the coastal road with the Taurus road to the Anatolian plateau. In the center of the city runs the Göksu River, in which Emperor Frederick Barbarossa drowned in 1190, during the Third Crusade. Today some 40,000 people live in the city, mainly subsisting of agriculture.

Area code: 324

The **tourist information office** is located at 2 Atatürk Cad., Tel. 712-1151, on the northern bank of the river. The post office, police station, bus station and most of the hotels are located on the southern bank. In the city there are only simple hotels. You can find motels and hotels of a higher standard along the road between Silifke and the nearby harbor village of Taşucu; try the *Lades Motel* on the sea shore, five miles (8km) west of Silifke. You can get a dolmuş to Taşucu at the Silifke central bus station.

Boats set out from the Taşucu dock for Kyrenia in Turkish Cyprus. The ferry ride takes five hours, and costs about $30, while the trip by hovercraft takes about two hours, and costs about $35. The boats leave daily, except for Friday, at 10am (Monday, Wednesday and Friday on hovercraft; Tuesday, Thursday and Saturday by ferry). Further details are available at the tourist information office.

The most prominent attraction in Silifke is the fortress towering over the city. It was built in the seventh century by the Byzantines and renovated by the Crusader knights of Rhodes.

In the city you can see remnants from the Roman era such as a stone bridge spanning the river and the ruins of a temple dedicated to Jupiter. The city also has a rather unexceptional archeology museum.

You can take an interesting day trip from Silifke to Uzuncaburç. The dolmuşes leave Silifke from the northern side of the river, near the tourist information office. The lovely trip along the winding road is about 25 miles (40km), reaching the ancient Diocaeşarea. This old city was built by the Seleucids in the third century BC; and it attained the height of its prosperity during the first century AD, under the rule of the Roman Emperor Vespasian, father of Titus. The most outstanding sight in the city is the temple of Zeus Olbius, apparently built by Seleucus Nicator. Other interesting sights are the amphitheater, the Corinthian columns and an ancient tower 154ft. (22m) high, for which the village is named (*Uzuncaburç* means "the high tower").

A quaint restaurant on the shores of Alanya

From Silifke to Alanya

The road from Silifke to Alanya winds through the Taurus Mountains, which in this area almost reach the water line. The road is a difficult one and you must be extra careful in the dangerous sections. Along the way, there are splendid views of the small sandy bays at the mouths of the rivers that flow across the Taurus range.

The **Anamur Fortress**, 85 miles (138km) west of Silifke, is the largest and best-preserved fortress along the southern coast of Turkey. It was built in the twelfth century by the Armenians and renovated in 1840 by the Ottomans, who used it until World War I. Another Armenian fortress is located 7.5 miles (12km) east of Anamur Fortress. The Softa Fortress, dates back to the same period, but is less impressive. On a clear day you can see the coast of Cyprus from this area.

At the southernmost point in Asia Minor, almost four miles (6km) west of Anamur, are the ruins of the ancient city of Anemurium, founded by the Phoenicians. Many buildings in this "ghost town" have remained in good condition, as though the ancient inhabitants only left for a short time and will return at any minute.

From Anemurium the road continues winding for another 81 miles (130km) to Alanya.

Alanya

The city of Alanya, lies at the foot of a rocky peninsula that juts out into the sea, with a tremendous fortress on top. Settlement here began as a fortification for pirates, in the second century BC, who made their living by robbing the ships that sailed the Mediterranean between ancient ports. The city's golden era was between the years 1220-1304, when the Seljuk Sultan Alaeddin Key kûbad built the city as a central fortified port, to serve the capital, Konya. Alaeddin named the city after himself, Alaiyya, and Atatürk changed the name to Alanya in 1923. Today, the population of the city numbers some 40,000, who derive their living from agriculture, fishing and tourism.

The **tourist information center** is located on Iskele Cad., Tel. 512-1240, opposite the city museum. To the east, along Atatürk street, is the post office. In the center of the city you will find a dolmuş stop, where you can get a ride to the bus station (*otogar*) some three kilometers from the city center in the direction of Antalya. You can buy tickets for the bus near the dolmuş station. Buses up to the fortress leave during the day from the tourist information center.

Area code: 242

Accommodation and Dining

Many hotels have been built in Alanya in the last few years, some in the city and most of them along the beaches. The best hotel in the area is *Club Alantur*, Tel. 518-1740, 3 miles (5km) east of Alanya on the coastal road. Less expensive hotels on the eastern coast include *Merhaba*, Tel. 513-1251 and *Banana*, Tel. 513-4394. These hotels have private beaches and swimming pools. On the western shore are the moderate-standard *Turtas* hotel, and mediocre hotels such as *Mini*. Every year several new hotels open in this area, and you should check with the tourist information office for an updated list.

The *Kaptan Hotel*, at 62 Iskele Cad., Tel. 513-4900, is high-priced, but definitely the best hotel in the city. The more modest *Alanya Büyük Hotel* is a good choice, Tel. 513-1138. The *Kent Hotel* at number 12 on Iskele St. charges about $12 for a double room with adjacent bathroom.

Sites to See

The **fortress** (*kale*) that towers over the city and the coast is undoubtedly the central tourist attraction in this area. The fortress is situated almost 2 miles (3 km) from the city, and you can get there by bus from the tourist information office, by taxi, in a private car or by foot, although the walk is fairly exhausting on a hot summer's day.

The fortress at Alanya built in Seljuk style by Abu Ali

Construction of the fortress began in 1225, four years after the Seljuk conquest. It was built on top of Crusader foundations in Seljuk style by Abu Ali from the city of Aleppo. Four and a half miles (7 km) of fortified walls were built around the old city and the fortress itself. Today only the walls remain, but the view from above is extraordinary.

The **Red Tower** (*Kırmızı Kule*) was among the first fortifications built to defend the port. To this day the impressive tower is a tourist attraction and a symbol of the city. It contains a museum that displays weapons and objects from the region, and you can climb to the top of the observation tower. Along the walls there are 145 other towers, intended for full protection of the fortified city.

At the other end of the peninsula is the **City Museum**, containing a collection of ancient artifacts and a beautiful display of household objects and traditional carpets. The museum closes for an afternoon break, from noon-1:30pm. Next to the museum is the **Damlataş Stalactite Cave**, which was discovered by chance, by a local laborer in 1948. The cave maintains a constant temperature of 23°C and the humidity is high. The local residents believe that the climate of the cave is an effective remedy for respiratory diseases, such as asthma and bronchitis. During a visit to the cave you will see many who have come for the cure, breathing in the air, three hours a day for three weeks running. Despite its stalactites, the cave is small and disappointing; it is located at the eastern end of a sandy bathing beach which is pleasant for bathing.

The Red Tower with an observation point at the top

A delightful boat trip around the Alanya Peninsula – a glance into the Pirate's Cave

From the lovely fishermen's harbor, you can take a delightful boat trip around the peninsula. This is a marvelous angle from which to see the rocks of the fortress, and you can also see the grottoes at the foot of the rock, where the blue sea water takes on another dimension. The names of the caves here are inspiring (such as the Pirate's Cave and Cleopatra's Cave).

From Alanya to Antalya

The road from Alanya continues west along the coast toward Antalya. Approximately an hour out of Alanya you come to the **Manavgat Waterfalls** almost two miles (3km) inland from the city Manavgat. These waterfalls have been violated by the tasteless construction of a restaurant almost atop the falls themselves (not to mention the souvenir shop). Yet, their beauty is retained and a visit here is recommended. A short trip from the waterfalls brings us to Side.

Side

The little resort town of Side has become a busy tourist center. Thanks to its antiquities and beaches, Side developed from a small tranquil fishing village into a town and it is now the destination of many a tourist in search of sunshine. Many tourists come back here year after year for the sun and fun.

Despite the many tourists, Side has managed to preserve a Turkish atmosphere, perhaps due to the integration of the ancient ruins with the homes of today's town.

Archeologists from the University of İstanbul excavated Side for twenty years. This is the only site on the Mediterranean shores that has been systematically excavated, and the results are striking. In the ancient past the people of Side cooperated with pirates, who were known for their cruelty, and the small port was used for slave trade. Under Roman rule the town flourished and the ancient amphitheater, which was built at that time, is the largest of its type in Anatolia, giving us some indication of the importance of the city. Most of the ancient artifacts that were found in the city are from the Roman period.

The **tourist information office** in Side is located less than a mile outside the village walls, in Side Yolu Üzeri. Passengers traveling from Antalya and Alanya alight from the bus at Manavgat, and use the regular *dolmuş* service from there to Side. From the bus station outside the village there are direct buses to Ankara and İstanbul. Those arriving in private cars are not allowed to enter the bustling village in their vehicles during the peak tourist season, and must leave them in the parking lot at the bus station.

If you plan to visit Side during the tourist season it is essential to make reservations in advance, as the number of hotels in the area do not always meet the burgeoning demand. The exclusive *Asteria Hotel*,

The Manavgat Waterfalls

Tel. 753-1830 was recently opened; the *Defne*, Tel. 753-1905, and the *Turtel*, Tel. 746-2226 are less expensive, but also fairly high-priced. All these hotels are located on the western coast, which almost constitutes a city in itself with restaurants, stores, swimming pools and the like. The prevailing language here is German, and many of the prices are noted in German marks.

Inside the village is the *Köseoğlu Hotel*, which offers modern rooms at a reasonable price. The *Hermes* and *Çiğdem* hotels are less expensive. The local residents know all the hotels, and they will be happy to guide you in your search for a vacant room.

Sites to See

In Side the past mingles with the present, and all the sights in the village are within a short walk from the center. The **Street of Columns** leads from the gate of the old city to the central square, (*agora*) where you can see the ancient city hall, dating back to the second century BC. Next to the agora is a large Roman **amphitheater**, built in the second century AD, and containing 60 rows of seats. This amphitheater can hold between 15 and 20 thousand people, and is considered one of the largest of its type in Anatolia. From here one can get a fantastic view of the old city.

Opposite the *agora* is a Roman bath, which today houses a **museum**. The museum contains many

Archeological remains at the beach-resort of Side

sculptures that were discovered while excavating the area, and it is open 9am–noon, and 1:30-3:00pm. You should visit the museum after your tour of the city, where there are also ruins of ancient sanctuaries, Byzantine churches, a small port and other Roman baths.

Beşkonak

Approximately six miles (10km) past Side, along the coastal road, is a turn-off to the village of Beşkonak. The paved road to the remote villages, situated between forested hills, runs 23 miles (27 km), along the Köprü river. From here the road, which leads to the heart of the Taurus mountains and to many beautiful spots, is not paved. This area is the Köprülü National Park, and we continue along the road for about 4 miles (6km) until the point where it crosses the Köprülü canyon, on a Roman bridge. Near the bridge there is a restaurant, where one can arrange a trip on rafts for small or large groups. Upriver is a deep, narrow canyon, where water rushes,

Köprülü Canyon, situated in the Köprülü National Park – a great place for canoeing

mixing with that of the many wells, which gush from under almost every rock. It is worth devoting a few hours to a pleasant walk amid these unspoilt natural surroundings.

Aspendos

Some 17 miles (28km) west of Side is Aspendos, also known as Belkis, the site of the ruins of a Roman city and a famous amphitheater. Aspendos was founded after the Trojan War, at the beginning of the first millennium BC. The Roman amphitheater was built here, apparently by Marcus Aurelius, in the second century AD. An ancient legend tells us about King Aspendos who promised the hand of his beautiful daughter to the man who could beautify the appearance of the city. And thus, his daughter's beauty led to the construction of many beautiful buildings. In the end, only two men remained in the contest: the builder of the aqueduct and the builder of the amphitheater. The king could not decide which of the two to choose as the winner, and so he decided to split the prize in two and give half of the princess to each competitor. The builder of the amphitheater, who feared for his beloved, conceded his half to his opponent. The king then declared him the winner, of course, and married him to the lovely princess. It seems that King Aspendos was a graduate of King Solomon's school of law.

A modern king arriving in the area today would undoubtedly award his daughter's hand to the builder of the amphitheater. This is considered to be the most beautiful Roman amphitheater in the world. Here too, as in Side, 20,000 spectators can be seated. It is the best preserved amphitheater in Turkey, and was renovated under order of Kemal Atatürk. The amphitheater is open to visitors daily from 8am-7pm. Performances are held here in August during the tourist season, as part of the Anatolia Festival.

Visitors to Aspendos tend to take a look at the amphitheater and then leave, but it is worth devoting some time to the old city, especially the acropolis above the theater. The difficult climb up the hill of the acropolis brings you to the gates of the city, where there are some interesting remains of the past. An easier way to get up the hill is on the path north of the amphitheater. From the hill you can see the ancient stadium to the east and the aqueduct to the north.

Perge

Perge, like other cities in the area, was founded by the Greeks who came upon the area after the fall of Troy. The city, and the entire region, prospered during the Greco-Roman period, and declined from the Byzantine period on. During the Seleucid rule of the city, the mathematician Apollonius, known for his study of the behavior of the ellipse, lived in Perge.

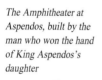

The Amphitheater at Aspendos, built by the man who won the hand of King Aspendos's daughter

Perge is located about one mile north of the main road, 11 miles (18km) before Antalya. A *dolmuş* from Antalya will take you to the town of Aksu, a mile from Perge. Outside its walls are the amphitheater and the stadium, the latter; has been well preserved, and is one of the most prominent ruins here. You enter Perge through gates that were cut out of the wall in a later period. The gates of the Hellenistic city are located inside the walls, at the beginning of an ancient, impressive street, between the central plaza (*agora*) and the Roman baths.

Paul the Apostle, who came from Cyprus, held the first religious Christian ceremony in Perge's basilica, marking the beginning of Christianity. To the left of the basilica are more baths and a street of ancient graves.

Antalya

Today, Antalya is the central tourist city of the Mediterranean region, known as the "Turkish Riviera." The founder of the city, King Attalus II of Pergamon, named it after himself, in the second century BC. Antalya did not play any special role in Turkish history, and its only importance lay in the local harbor, where the Crusaders began their journey to the Holy Land. Today, the city has some 400,000 inhabitants, who make their living from agriculture, industry and tourism. Thousands of vacationers come here on charter flights from Europe to spend a sunny vacation on the city's wonderful beach.

The Layout of the City

The old city, Kaleiçi, is built on the slope of an impressive rock, surrounding the ancient harbor The new city developed northwest of the old city; its main streets are Anafartalar Şarampol and Akdeniz Boulevard, which continues west along the coast.

The bathing beaches and resort hotels are located along Lara Beach, east of the old city. Approximately one mile west of the city, opposite the sea shore and the new port, is another, less expensive hotel area.

How to Get There

By air: International flights arrive in Antalya from Europe and the Near East. Some of these are direct, and others go through İstanbul and Ankara. The domestic flights to Ankara and İstanbul leave daily, and take about one hour. The airport is approximately ten minutes east of the city. Taxi and *dolmuş* service link the airport to the city.

By sea: The boat that sails from İstanbul to Alanya also anchors in Antalya.

TURKEY

By car: The coastal road E24 connects Antalya to Mersin in the east, and to Pamukkale, Kuşadası and İzmir in the west via the inland. Road 30 continues north along the Mediterranean coast to Marmaris.

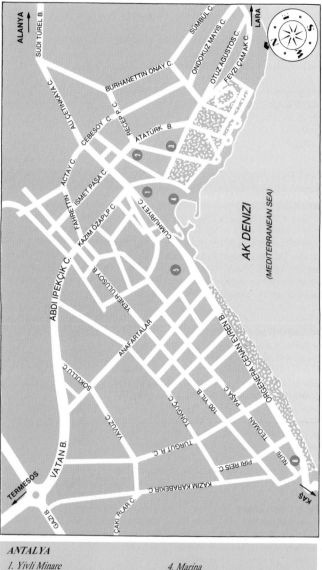

ANTALYA

1. *Yivli Minare*
2. *Hadrian's Gate*
3. *Broken Minaret (Kesik Minare)*
4. *Marina*
5. *Tourist Information Office*
6. *City Museum*

Antalya is 345 miles (556km) away from Adana, 338 miles (545km) from Ankara and 293 miles (472km) from İzmir. There is an excellent bus service between Antalya and the other cities and sights in western Turkey. Buses come to the Oto Garaji, on Şarampol Cad., opposite the Murat Pasha Mosque. The *dolmuşes* to the coastal cities and the archeological sites between Antalya and Side leave the new station (*Doğu Garaji*), at the eastern end of Ali Çetinkaya Cad. A recommended car rental service is *URENT*, Tel. 241-9683, fax 248-7184.

Area code: 242

Tourist Services

The **tourist information office** is on Selcuk Mah., Mermerli Sok, Tel. 247-0541, by the corner of Anfartalar Cad. and the post office. Nearby is a statue of Atatürk, and opposite it a bank that is open for foreign currency exchange until evening.

In recent years, Antalya has grown into a major tourist resort with many new hotels. For updated information, enquire at the address above.

Accommodation and Dining

Tourists coming to Antalya may choose to sleep in the city, or west of it, opposite the port, or in one of the resort hotels on **Lara Beach**, 7 miles (11km) east of the city center. The best hotel in the city is the *Talya*, Fevzi Cakmak Cad., Tel. 248-6800, fax 241-5400, east of the old city on the beach in the direction of Lara. It is considered to be one of the finest hotels in the country. Other hotels, such as the *Bilgehan*, 194 Şarampol Cad., situated near the bus station, Tel. 248-7950, and the centrally located *Büyük*, 57 Cumhuriyet Cad. near the statue of

Atatürk, Tel. 241-1499, are not very expensive and offer reasonable service.

A visit to the *Turban Adalya Hotel*, Tel. 241-8066 in the old city is a special experience, but it is not inexpensive. The hotel is housed in a carefully renovated building dating back to 1869.

A busy electricity post in Antalya

Of the expensive hotels on Lara Beach, we should mention the *Club Hotel*, Tel. 323-1170, which offers a cosmopolitan atmosphere and a disco club. More modest hotels are the *Lara*, Tel. 323-1460, which has a private beach, and the *Antalya Prince*, Tel. 323-3070, mid-way between Lara and the city.

You will find simple and pleasant hotels in the old city. Of these we recommend the *Tunay Pension*, Tel. 242-4677. Most of the rooms in the simple hotels in the old city do not have adjacent bathrooms. In the new city there are a number of inexpensive hotels south of the bus station, including the *Tatoğlu*, 91 Şarampol Cad. The *Turban Kızıltepe* camping grounds are located 23 miles (37km) southwest of the city.

A number of excellent restaurants, with ambience and fairly high prices are located in the old harbor. Of these we recommend the *Yat*, Tel. 242-4855 and the *Kral Sofrası*. The *Hisar*, Tel. 241-2198, is more expensive than the harbor restaurants, but it offers diners the experience of a meal in an ancient citadel which has been converted into a modern restaurant.

Everyone, especially those on a tight budget, should not miss the picturesque lane, Eski Sezer İçi Sok.

This lane, located parallel to Atatürk street, consists entirely of little restaurants and kebab stands, one next to the other, creating an abundance of color and aromas.

Sites to See

In the center of the old city stands a handsome minaret, constructed of pink stone and designed as a group of pipes. This is Yivli Minare, the "fluted minaret," built in 1219 by the Seljuk Sultan, Alâeddin Key-kûbad. The minaret has, over the years become the symbol of the city. The Sultan built the minaret next to a Byzantine church which was converted into a mosque after the Seljuk conquest in 1207. In the upper courtyard of the mosque there is an eighteenth-century Dervish monastery or Tekke.

Hadrian's Gate built in 130 AD in honor of the Emperor's visit

Another Seljuk minaret erected next to the converted mosque, is **Kesik Minare**, located alongside the public park, east of the harbor. You can easily identify this minaret by its missing upper part. From the two Seljuk minarets you can continue on a tour of the romantic marina and the nearby restaurants.

In the eastern part of the old city, on Atatürk Cad., is a prominent ruin from the Roman era, **Hadrian's Gate**, built in honor of the Emperor's visit to the city in the year 130 AD. At the gate you can see remnants of the marvelous towers and Corinthian columns.

The City Museum is one of the most outstanding museums in the country. Arranged chronologically, it contains exhibits covering the whole of southern Turkey, including costumes, weapons, musical instruments, ancient carpets and statues from the Stone and Bronze Ages to the Greco-Roman era and the magnificent Ottoman period. Don't miss it. Open daily 8am-noon and 1:30-5pm, closed Mon. The museum is located on Akdeniz Boulevard, in the western part of the city. It is a 15-minute walk from the tourist information office or a short bus ride along the boulevard.

You can spend many hours on a pleasant walk through the old city, along the old harbor and through the winding alleyways and beautiful ancient Ottoman houses, which impart the special charm of the city. In many of the alleyways there are handicraft stores.

Shopping
In the old city of Antalya there are several stores that sell carpets and other handicrafts to tourists, but they are quite pricey. The market, located opposite the clock tower, has many stores which close in the early afternoon during the hot summer.

Special Events
The Antalya Arts Festival is held every October. The central event of the festival is a contest for the best Turkish film of the year, but it also includes theater performances, some of which are held in the marvelous amphitheater of Aspendos.

Around Antalya

Eight and a half miles (14km) north of the city are the upper **Duden Waterfalls**. (Open 8:30am-5:30pm). You can reach the falls by *dolmuş* from the city. The falls are lovely, but the public park built around them detracts from the pleasure. The lower Duden Waterfalls are located west of the city, near Lara Beach. The gush of water falling straight into the sea creates a rare, breathtaking sight.

Karain Cave, with Turkey's oldest rock paintings dating back to the Paleolithic period, is situated 17 miles (27km) northwest of Antalya. Only tourists who are very interested in prehistoric archeology will find this interesting. Next to the cave is a small museum that reconstructs the life-style of this pre-historic period.

The **Saklilkent** winter sports resort is situated on the slopes of the Bakirh Daği (on the Beydağ chain). In March and April the morning's ski descent might be concluded with a swim at one of Antalya's beaches.

Termessos

A visit to Termessos is one of the high points of a trip to the Mediterranean coast of Turkey. Termessos, also known as "the Eagles' Nest," was the city of courageous fighters, who preferred to go to battle rather than surrender to forces greatly superior to them. The residents of Termessos called themselves "Solymans," after the mountain Solymos, at the foot of which their town lies.

Termessos was never excavated systematically, and the site is covered with dense Mediterranean forest, hiding many of the ruins. It is not known when the city was founded or by whom, and the first reference is from the year 333 BC. In his campaign to conquer the entire area, Alexander the Great came here as well, but the inhabitants of Termessos did not surrender, and Alexander's attempt ended unsuccessfully. After stopping for a short while, Alexander decided to move on. A visit to the area makes it clear why Alexander did not insist on conquering the fortified "Eagles' Nest," and how it succeeded in maintaining its independence for centuries to come.

Burial caves at Termessos

How to Get There

Termessos is located 21 miles (34km) northwest of Antalya, at an altitude of 4,920ft. (1,500m) above sea level. From Antalya there is a good road leading north towards Burder and Denizli. After driving about 7.5 miles (12km), turn west on road 8 toward Korkuteli. From this road, just a few miles on, you'll find a direct road that runs about 5 miles (9km) to Termessos. If travelling with public transportation, take the bus or *dolmuş* to Korkuteli, get off at the turn to Termessos and wait for a ride. You can also get a taxi from Antalya. After paying the admission fee to the site, continue up the steep road.

The Site

Even Before reaching Termessos itself, you arrive at the ruins of the **city walls** and gate. According to one legend, these walls were built by the residents of the Pamphylian plain, in recognition of the independence of the residents of Termessos. The road ends at a parking lot, from which you must walk. Opposite are the ruins of the **Temple of Hadrian**, a pile of stones on which the ornate gate stands. King Cad., the main street of the city, begins here and climbs up to an ancient **gymnasium** and a well-preserved **amphitheater**, notable for its unusually beautiful location. After catching your breath, you have a choice of direction in which to continue: right to the ornamented burial caves, or further up the mountain, to additional temples, including a Corinthian one.

If you still have the energy, continue up to the **necropolis** (the city of the dead). The slope is covered with dozens of large sarcophagi, decorated with the symbols of the Sulaymans. And if you've come this far – continue to the top of the mountain, to the forest ranger's cabin. This is a fabulous observation point, fully justifying the name "the Eagles' Nest." The forest ranger, who guards against fires, will welcome you in true Turkish tradition, with hospitality and a cup of *çay* (tea).

From Antalya to Kaş

The road continues from Antalya west, to Kaş, mainly along the coast, and it is one of the loveliest coastal roads in Turkey: green mountains and cliffs leading steeply to the blue sea. Marvelous sandy bays, suitable for swimming or for a short rest, hide between the mountains.

The **Kemer** resort site is located approximately 25 miles (40km) southwest of Antalya. The location is suitable for a vacation and sunbathing in an international atmosphere. There is no hint or memento here of the Turkish past and culture, and it lacks anything to distinguish it from numerous similar places around the world. The hotels in Kemer were mainly built by German investors and they do not really blend with the beach landscape.

Among the resort villages in the region are Palmiye, Milta, Robinson, as well as the Club Méditerranée. The price for a vacation package, which generally includes a round trip air fare from Europe to Antalya, transportation to Kemer and a week in a luxury hotel, is about $1,000, and you can stay longer for a small addition. The resort villages are self-sufficient units, complete with swimming pool, a private beach, a discotheque and other facilities. In Kemer there are also several less expensive beach hotels, such as the *Olimpos Princess Hotel*, 33 Deniz Cad., Tel. 814-1280, fax 814-2290. The **tourist information office** in Kemer is located on Belediye Binasi, Tel. 814-1495.

The Chimaera – flames from natural gas escaping from deep in the earth

West of Kemer is the Lycian city of **Olympos**. The city was named after the adjacent mountain, one of

the twenty mountains in Greece and Turkey that bear this name. In the ancient city there are not many remains, and a visit here focuses on the strange natural wonder known as *Chimaera* in Greek and *Yanar* in Turkish. This is a natural flame, coming out of a hole in a rock a yard in diameter. The flame is from natural gas escaping from deep in the earth.

Archeological relics at the city of Olympos

When extinguished with water or dirt, it flares up again after about ten minutes. This phenomenon made a big impression on Homer, and in *The Iliad* he claimed that this was the breath of an underground monster. The *Chimaera* is located in the Temple of Hephaistos, about a half-hour walk from Olympos. The effort involved in the walk deters many visitors, and justifiably – the sight is something of a disappointment.

Next to the city of Olympos is another Lycian city, **Phaselis**, founded by Dorian of Rhodes in the seventh century BC. The city benefited from its natural harbor, and Alexander the Great stopped in the city in the winter of 333 BC, during his campaign against the stubborn city of Termessos. The inhabitants of the Lycian city were arch enemies of the people of Termessos and fought against them for many years. The ruins of a temple, a theater and an aqueduct can be seen at the site. There are also several small restaurants here, which serve *phaselia*, a green pea dish named for the city.

Finike

The little town of Finike was evidently founded by Phoenician seamen in the first millennium BC. In the town you will find several simple pensions and friendly restaurants, such as the *Deniz* restaurant, next to the *Sedir* Hotel. You can make a short trip from Finike to **Limyra**, a Lycian city situated some 6 miles (10km) north. An amphitheater and a large necropolis (one of the largest in the region), which probably contains the grave of Pericles, are all that remain of the ancient city. You can visit the city of Arycanda, founded by the Persians in the fifth century BC, and which was an important member of the Lycian alliance. The city is located 21 miles (35 km) north of Finike, on the road to Elmalı. Visitors

Beautifully decorated remains from the amphitheater at Myra

here can enjoy the ancient city located off the regular tourist tracks, where they will find temples, a large Roman bath and a well-preserved Greek-style amphitheater.

Demre

Demre lies between Finike and Kaş, next to the ancient city of **Myra**. The ancient city is best known as the home of Saint Nicholas, better known as Santa Claus, who in the fourth century distributed gifts to the children of the city, thereby beginning the Christmas tradition as we know it today. A church named after him was built here in the fifth century AD, and has been renovated several times since. Nicholas, who was the bishop of Myra, was buried here, but his bones were stolen in the eleventh century by merchants from Bari, Italy. The bones that were left were taken to the museum in Antalya. Nicholas festivals are held in the city in December, before Christmas.

Other sights in old Myra are the Roman amphitheater and some impressive rock tombs, carved with images depicting burial and death rituals. The quiet town of Demre lies across the valley. There are a number of simple, inexpensive hotels here, including the *Kıyak*. There are camping grounds west of Demre, on the Çayağzi Beach.

The buses from Antalya to Kaş stop at the bus station in the center of town, which is full of pubs and has a great night life.

Kaş

The last section of the road to Kaş turns and climbs up the mountains. The sea disappears from sight, but is suddenly revealed in its full glory as you ascend the mountains above the enchanting village of Kaş. The road winds down to the small, pleasant village, which has recently prospered from the growth in tourism. In the 1970's Kaş was no more than a little fishing village, with only a single hotel. In recent years it has developed into a lively tourist center, full of pubs and with a great night life. Despite its many tourists, Kaş still preserves a quiet, rural atmosphere, in contrast to Kemer and Antalya, which have become cosmopolitan tourist centers.

Area code: 242

Just pull up a chair and order – the inviting cafés of Kaş

The bus stop is located at the entrance to the village. Buses arrive here from the other coastal cities, such as Marmaris and Antalya. The **tourist information office** is located in the central square, Tel. 836-1238, and nearby you will also find a post office and a bank for exchanging currency. There are modest and comfortable hotels in the village, such as the 4-star *Aqua-Park Hotel*, Tel. 836-1901 (slightly expensive), and the more modest *Medusa Hotel*, Tel. 836-1440. Many hotels have opened near the bus station and on the eastern side of the village, on the hillside. There is a camping ground at the end of Hastane Street, past the old theater, a 10-minute walk from the village center.

Lycian ruins partly covered by the sea at Kekova

Until the beginning of the century, Kaş was called Andifli, a distortion of the name of the Lycian city, Antiphellus, which was established in the fourth century BC. Among those sights that have survived the ravages of time are the amphitheater west of the village and a Doric grave cut into the rock on the hill beyond the amphitheater stand out.

The pebbly village beaches are not suitable for swimming. A highly recommended activity is to take a boat ride to the beaches and sights around Kaş, including **Kekova** and **Üçağız**. In the course of the journey you discover Lycian ruins covered by water, which create the impression of cities sunken into the sea.

Another wonderful boat trip is to the Greek island **Kastellorizo**. The island, located opposite Kaş, boasts an ancient church and beautiful scenery. It is forbidden to continue from this island to Greece or the Greek islands, and passengers must return to Kaş before evening. The trip west reaches the Patara and Kalkan beaches, and the Blue Cave (*Mavi Mağara*). The price is from about $6 per person in one of the groups that form at the port and about $100 for renting a boat for the entire day. Remember to equip yourself with food for the way, as well as plenty of water and a hat in hot weather.

From Kaş to Marmaris

The road from Kaş to Marmaris passes through ancient cities and some of the most beautiful beaches in Turkey. This area was controlled by the Lycian confederation, and many cities were established here. The wave of tourism to the golden shores in the area has given a boost to the development of tourist services in the villages and towns, which had been sleepy little settlements for hundreds of years.

Kalkan, about half an hour's ride west of Kaş, is a

small village built on the slopes of a hill leading down to a picturesque bay. You can get here by the coastal road or by boat from Kaş. The village has a number of hotels, the best of which are the *Kalkan Han*, Tel. 844-3151, located in a lovely old building (fairly expensive) and the pleasant *Paşa Inn* pension, Tel. 844-3077.

Patara, 7.5 miles (12km) from Kalkan, is an ancient port with a marvelous beach that stretches for many miles. Patara served as the largest port in the ancient Lycian kingdom. The ruins of Patara include a royal stone arch and Lycian tombs. It is located at the mouth of a river, and silt has covered half of the amphitheater and entirely buried the old port. The *Beyhan Patara Hotel*, Tel. 843-5096, is somewhat expensive, but it is clean and modern, and makes an effort to appeal to the sun and sea seekers.

Some 6 miles (10km) west of Patara, we come to two ancient cities. **Letoon** is located on the sea shore next to the village Kumluova, and has many temples, evidence that it was once a large religious center. The city was named after the Goddess Leto, and Ovid writes that on her way to Olympos to bring the infants Apollo and Artemis to the Goddess Hera, Leto became tired and came here to rest. The farmers tried to chase her away by yelling, and as punishment Leto transformed them into frogs. In Letoon are the ruins of a large temple dedicated to Leto.

Northwest of Letoon, next to the mountains is

The quaint village of Kalkan

Xanthus, one of the capitals of ancient Lycia. According to Homer, this was the oldest of the cities of Lycia. The city went through many wars, and one of them, against Harpagus, the commander of the army of Cyrus, is recorded by the Greek historian Herodotus: after their defeat, the Xanthians assembled in their city, gathered all the women, children, slaves and valuable objects in the city citadel, and burned them so that they would not fall into the hands of the enemy. Afterwards they set out on their final battle and were killed.

The people of Xanthus were famous for their love of freedom and objection to foreign domination. In the year 42 BC, when Brutus was about to conquer the city after a fierce war, the townspeople burned their families and killed themselves in front of Brutus, who, according to the Roman historian Plutarch, broke down crying.

The remains of Xanthus are located near the village Kınık, along the Koca river. The ruins of the city include very impressive Lycian pillar-tombs, an amphitheater, palaces and temples, some of them almost totally destroyed. The ruins are spread over a fairly large area, and you should devote a few hours to touring this site.

Another Lycian city, **Pınara**, is located 21 miles (35 km) west of Xanthus. Pınara offers the visitor lovely rural landscape and many tombs, among

Remains at Xanthus

them the "royal tomb." There is no public transportation to this spot.

Fethiye

Fethiye is a quiet seaside town, with a pleasant bay, a boardwalk, public gardens and facilities for the many tourists who come here all seasons of the year. Near the town are the ruins of Telmessos, an ancient Lycian city that was almost completely destroyed. Fethiye suffered serious damage in the earthquake that shook Marmaris in 1958, and most of the buildings here were built after that.

Fethiye

The bus station in Fethiye, about a fifteen-minute walk from the town center, operates a bus service between the town and Antalya and Marmaris. Other buses leave directly for İzmir, Ankara and İstanbul. The dolmuş to nearby Ölüdeniz leaves from opposite the post office on Atatürk Cad. The **tourist information office** is located at the end of Atatürk Cad., in Iskele square, Tel. 613-1527, near the port and the Dedeoğlu.

Area code: 252

In this town there are over a hundred hotels and pensions. The *Likya*, Tel. 616-6010, is located next to the yacht mooring. It is highly recommended, but quite expensive. The *Dedeoğlu*, Tel. 614-4010, next to the tourist information office, offers comfortable rooms at a lower price. *Kaya*, next to the *dolmuş* station, is a simple, inexpensive and clean hotel. There are good restaurants along the beach, near the statue of Atatürk.

A walk thorough the streets of the town reveals several ruins of the Lycian city, such as a sarcophagus next to the post office. A group of graves cut into stone, among them the splendid tomb of a nobleman named Amyntas, are located south of the city. On a hill above the town are the ruins of a Crusader fortress, which was used by the knights of the Order of St. John. The fortress was built on the ruins of the Lycian acropolis from the fourth century BC.

Ölüdeniz

This small village, situated between an inviting lagoon and luxuriant pine groves, is an excellent base from which to enjoy the beaches and ancient cities in the area. The village lies between a fabulous lagoon and pine forests. Ölüdeniz get is name from the tranquil water of the lagoon – it means "the lake of the dead." The nearby seashore is better for swimming than the shallow, crowded lagoon. The seaside beaches in the area are long, and even at the peak of the tourists season the visitor can find a quiet spot on the beach with some privacy.

The exclusive hotel here is *Meri*, Tel. 616-6060, next to the lagoon; it is highly-priced. The meals in the hotel are closer to international standards than to the Turkish cuisine. Less expensive accommodation can be found in bungalows in the many camping grounds along the shore, at the entrance to the village on the east. There are also simple, inexpensive hotels in Fethiye, the adjacent coastal village.

You can continue by car east from Ölüdeniz on a difficult, dangerous dirt road that climbs along the shore up the steep mountains. After a few miles the road reaches a beautiful bay which cuts into the enormous rocks. On the road, above the bay, is a remote, primitive village; it is fascinating to see how its residents live.

THE AEGEAN COAST

The Aegean coast between Marmaris and the Edremit bay was the cradle of modern Western civilization. Greek immigrants fleeing invasions by various tribes and the difficult economic situation in their country, settled on the Aegean coast. The Aeolians were the first to arrive in the area, followed by the Ionians, who set up the Ionian confederation of cities along the shore, with Miletus as their center.

The Greeks, who landed on these narrow shores were forced to show spiritual flexibility and adaptability in order to survive, and they had a great influence on the local residents who experienced incredible progress and new directions of thought. Telos of Miletus developed the study of the heavens and the sea, and this is also where the first silver and gold was minted for use in trade. The Aegean coast was covered with strong Ionian settlements, which became wealthy as a result of trade on the beaches, and the development of the roads to the east and to inner Anatolia.

The Aegean coast offers visitors an abundance of ancient cities and archeological ruins. Efes, the main site along the shoreline, gives you an amazing sense of ancient times. Just as the Mediterranean coast is the ideal place for recreation, natural scenery and ruins, the Aegean coast, and its capital İzmir, is a wonderful area for relaxing amid the landscape of the past.

The climate in the coastal region is temperate Mediterranean, and the temperatures are slightly lower than those on the Mediterranean coast. The most comfortable months for a visit here are May to September. Transportation in the area is excellent, and the roads are wide and make for easy driving. There is regular air service to the international airport in İzmir. Many boats link the Turkish coast with the different Greek islands.

Marmaris

The sight welcoming those arriving in Marmaris by ferry from Rhodes is superb; the boat, which just a moment ago was rocking in the currents of the Aegean Sea, enters a still, fjord-like bay, with steep, forested rock walls. The natural beauty of the spot, situated between the sea and the mountains, the convenient yacht mooring and the climate of Marmaris, have all made this a fashionable tourist and vacation center for Turkey's elite.

Strolling along the harbor at Marmaris

WESTERN TURKEY

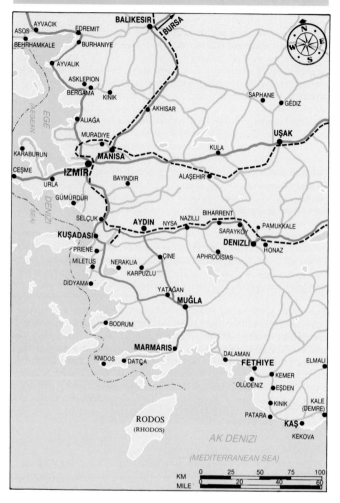

Historically, two primary factors contributed to the historic development of the city: the convenient mooring and its proximity to Rhodes. The Dorians of Rhodes conquered the region and set up a Hellenistic stronghold here. As early as the fourth millennium BC, Marmaris served as a port of the Carian kingdom, and was known as Physkos. Alexander the Great attacked the city in 334 BC, and the residents, preferring to die rather than surrender, razed the city themselves. Sulayman the Magnificent invaded Rhodes from this port in 1522 and Admiral Nelson anchored in the bay with all his ships in 1798, before sailing to Egypt to defeat the French army in the battle over the Nile. In 1958, the area was severely damaged in an earthquake, and many of its buildings collapsed and were rebuilt during the 1960's.

The town of Marmaris, with a population of 11,000, centers around the harbor. The main street along the sea is Atatürk Cad. and between Iskele Square and the statue of Atatürk is a strip of tourist and recreation services that developed along the shore.

How to Get There

By air: Dalaman airport is 62 miles (100km) east of the city. The airport serves charter flights from Europe and daily flights from İstanbul. From the airport you can get to Marmaris by taxi (about $35) or by a city bus (about $1.50). The direct buses between Marmaris and the airport stop for passengers along the way.

By sea: In summer a boat sails daily from Rhodes in the afternoon, reaching Marmaris by dark. The boat trip in the opposite direction leaves in the morning. Out of season and on Sundays, the boat sails on request only. The trip takes three and a half hours, and costs about $20 one-way.

You can also reach Marmaris by a boat that sails from İstanbul to Alanya, departing from İstanbul on Wednesdays during the summer.

A regular boat line links the city with the coastal city Bodrum.

By bus: As befitting a tourist center, there are numerous buses that connect Marmaris with the other Turkish cities, with many direct lines from İstanbul, Ankara, İzmir, Bodrum and Denizli, near Pamukkale. If you want to tour around the nearby coastal cities, you can get to Fethiye by a bus which departs every 20 minutes. A bus leaves once an hour for Datça. Marmaris has no central

The town of Marmaris

Fishing boats at the marina in Marmaris

bus station, and the bus companies have ticket offices near the statue of Atatürk, from where they take you to the bus waiting outside of town.

By car: Road 6 goes to distant İzmir, 6 hours northwest of Marmaris. This road continues east along the coast to Antalya. Road 23 takes you to Pamukkale, 143 miles (230km) northeast of the coast.

Area code: 252

Tourist Services
The **tourist information office** is located at 39 Iskele square, near the gates to the port, Tel. (252)412-1035. The bank and post office are located close by, along Atatürk Cad. and the lanes leading from it. Here you will also find some car rental agencies.

Accommodation and Dining
There are several 5 star hotels, among them the *Aqua Hotel* (Tel. 455-3633) and the *Marmaris Altinyunus* (Tel. 455-2200). There are other good hotels outside of town, along the coast, such as the *Lidya Hotel*, Tel. 412-2940.

There are less expensive hotels near the tourist information office. At the *Kalyon Hotel*, there is a friendly staff that tries to be helpful to tourists. Less expensive accommodation can be found in private homes, where rooms are rented to tourists. Further details are available at the local information office. Near the *Lidya Hotel* there is a comfortable camping site.

There are good restaurants along the dock. The yachting tourists here have brought the prices of these restaurants up to a level unusual in Turkey. The *Birtat* and *Liman*, along the coast, are good, expensive restaurants. There are many less expensive restaurants in the market area, which serve pizza, lamb on the spit and other Turkish dishes.

Sites to See
Few historic sites have survived the ravages of time and the earthquakes that have hit the area. The main attraction here is yacht sailing; one can rent a yacht, with or without a crew, and take a sailing trip for a day or more. The prices begin at $400 per day for a boat which can take 7 to 10 passengers. In May and October the prices are usually lower than in midsummer. The leading yacht company is *Yeşil Marmaris*, Tel.412-2290 in Marmaris and Tel. (212)528-5510 in İstanbul. The agency rents yachts, crews and other equipment, and its staff will also help you choose a route, give out maps and advice. There is a shuttle-ferry that operates daily at 9am and 4pm. A three-hour cruise is equivalent to a 230km journey by car.

Datça

The resort town of Datça lies at the tip of the peninsula that juts out from Marmaris. This is an excellent spot for those who want a break from the masses of tourists along the Mediterranean coast, and especially in Marmaris. The road to Datça passes through 46.5 miles (75km) of mountains and streams flowing down to the sea, but you can also reach the town by yacht on a day trip from Marmaris. You can wander through the little town on foot, enjoy the scenery and bathe at the local beach. There is hotel accommodation of every standard here.

Twenty two miles (35km) west of Datça, at the end of the peninsula, is the ancient city of **Knidos**. The ancient city was established by the Dorians in the fourth century BC, and is known for the statue of Aphrodite that stood in the temple of Aphrodite. It was created by the great Greek sculptor, Praxiteles, and at the time represented the symbol of the beauty of women. The statue, which attracted tourists from throughout the ancient world, disappeared in the course of time. The city was also the birthplace of one of Plato's students, Eudoxus of Knidos, who was one of the developers of Greek geometry and a pioneer astronomer. The observatory that he built here was the first in the Greek world. Today, the city offers interesting artifacts to visitors. Popular transportation from Datça to Knidos is a boat that leaves in the morning and returns in the afternoon. There is also a bus and motor-cycles are available for rent. The road between the sites however is unpaved and difficult although not impossible to use. Taxis charge about $25 for a half-day tour of the site.

An archeological artifact at Knidos

Shopping

Marmaris has a colorful market and many stores that sell carpets, leather coats and other Turkish products. The quality of the products is high, as are the prices, because these stores serve the yacht owners who come ashore.

From Marmaris to Bodrum

The road from Marmaris to Bodrum climbs up to **Muğla**, the district capital famous for its honey. The city has an ancient Ottoman quarter and a colorful market. The information office is located on

Belediye Atapark Sitesi, Tel. 214-3127, near the square in the city center. Few tourists stop here, the atmosphere is somewhat different from that of classical ruins and touristy vacation beaches.

From Muğla, road 30 turns west to Bodrum. If you have some time, you can continue on road 6 to **Çine** before turning to Bodrum. Near Çine are the ancient cities of **Alinda** and **Alabanda**, the capitals of the Carian kingdom, which flourished in the mid-fourth century BC, under the rule of the Queen Ada, the friend of Alexander the Great. The most outstanding ruin here is the market building in Alinda. This is an interesting stop for those traveling directly from Marmaris to Pamukkale.

The road from Muğla to Bodrum turns west near Yatağan. Next to the village are the ruins of Startoniceia, a Hellenistic city from the third century BC. The city, which was a prosperous commercial center, was completely destroyed in an earthquake and today only visitors with a deep interest in archeology visit the site.

Milas is the last stop, 43 miles (70 km) before Bodrum. Once called Mylasa, this city was one of the capitals of the Carian kingdom, during the fourth century BC, under the rule of the Persian Mausolus. In the fourteenth century, the city served as the center of the Turkish Menteşe tribe, one of the nomadic tribes that came from central Asia and settled in this region. The Menteşe tribe controlled the area and built the Peçin fortress here, which is spectacular even today. The fortress housed the rulers of the city for a long time after the Menteşe tribe surrendered in 1391 to another Turkish tribe, the Ottomans. You can visit the fortress and the ruins of the ancient city on your way to Bodrum or on your way to Kuşadası.

Bodrum

Bodrum is the tourism capital of the Aegean coast. From a population of 15,000 local residents in the winter, the city grows to some 100,000 people at the height of the tourist season. The atmosphere of the city is open and liberal, in spirit with the tourists, and you can find fast food stands and disco clubs, operated by local entrepreneurs throughout the city. The city and its environs are the bridgehead to the nearby Greek islands, and a convenient point of departure for tours on land and sea.

The narrow peninsula on which the Bodrum fortress is built divides the sea line into two bays. Bodrum developed around the natural mooring in the western bay. Neyzen Tevfik Cad. leads from the bus station to the yacht harbor along the western seashore, while Cumhuriyet Cad. continues along the eastern bathing beach to the entrance of the fortress.

Bodrum lies on the ruins of the ancient city of Halicarnassus, founded in the fifth century BC as one of the first Greek colonies in Asia. In 485 BC, the father of historians, Herodotus of Halicarnassus, was born here. The most glorious period of the city was during the mid-fourth century BC, when its ruler, the Persian governor Mausolus, declared Halicarnassus the capital of his kingdom, Caria. After his death, his wife Artemisia, who was also his oldest sister, built a grand tomb for her husband, which was the largest and most splendid of Greek tombs. The mausoleum was considered one of the wonders of the ancient world, the word *mausoleum* is derived from the name of this Persian

Bodrum as seen from atop the walls of the fortress

ruler. When the knights of the Order of Saint John of Rhodes captured the area in 1415, the mausoleum had already been destroyed; its stones were taken to build the fortress that stands on its mound to this day. In 1522, approximately a year after the conquest of Rhodes by Sulayman the Magnificent, the knights vacated the fortress and sailed to Malta.

How to Get There

By bus: There is a regular service connecting Bodrum and the Aegean coastal cities with Ankara and İstanbul. The bus station is located in the center of the city, next to the Adliye mosque and the local market.

By car: From Bodrum there is a very comfortable road to Kuşadası, 93 miles (150km) away.

By sea: The ferries to the Greek island of Cos leave daily, except for Sunday. The trip takes only an hour and 40 minutes. Travel agencies in the city offer tickets for the trip – look for the signs in their windows.

Area code: 252

Tourist Services

The **tourist information office** is located at 12 Eylül square, Tel. 316-1091. The square is situated between the fortress and the harbor, and there is also a police station next to it. The local post office is located near the bus station, along Cevat Şakir Cad.

Accommodation and Dining

On the eastern shore, there are several good hotels: *Cesars Hotel*, 5 star, Tel. 316-6434. *Club Hotel*, 5 star, Tel. 316-6100. and *Club Marveude*, 4 star, Tel. 374-5400.

More inexpensive hotels can also be found in the neighborhood: *Martı* at number 84 and *Merlan* at number 88, which only charge about $12 a night. Other hotels of this level can be found on the inner streets that run to Cumhuriyet Cad. **Note**: It is difficult to find a room in Bodrum in the peak season during July and August, and we strongly recommend that you reserve your accommodation in advance, or ensure that you arrive in the morning and can start looking right away. The *Ayaz* camping ground is located on the beach between Bodrum and Gümbet.

There are some fine restaurants in the center of the city along the shore overlooking the castle, which when lit up makes an enchanting background to a waterside dinner. The *Körfez* Restaurant on Neyzen Tevfik Cad., specializing in fish and seafood, is very good but expensive.

A mosaic floor inside the fortress at Bodrum

Sites to See

The castle is the most impressive sight in the city. It was built by several orders of Crusaders, with each group building its own section. The French tower is

the highest, and commands a beautiful view of the bay. Other towers are those of the English, German and Italian orders. The fortress houses an interesting museum, with exhibits that try to give you a sense of the daily life of the ancient world, such as the annual wages of a worker in various periods. Another exhibit shows artifacts uncovered in underwater archeological excavations along the coast. The museum is open daily, 8:30am-noon and 3-7pm in season. Off-season the museum is open in the morning and in the afternoon from 1:30-5pm.

The Bodrum crafts festival is held in the first week of September. It includes concerts and various crafts exhibitions in the castle.

The good bathing beaches here are located outside of Bodrum. **Gümbet Beach**, equipped with tourists facilities, hotels and restaurants, is situated some two miles (3km) from the center of town, and **Turgut Reis** beach is about 12.5 miles (20km) from the city, and can be reached by a short *dolmuş* ride.

From Bodrum to Kuşadası

From Bodrum, the road goes back to Milas and from there turns north. Nine miles (15km) past Milas the road passes by the ruins of the city **Euromos** of Caria. In an olive tree grove on the roadside is a **Temple of Zeus** from the second century AD, the only ruin of interest remaining from the city.

Some twelve miles (20km) further down the road to Kuşadası is **Bafa Lake**, with small restaurants along its shores that specialize in fresh fish from the lake. Mount Latmos towers 4,920ft. (1,500m) above the lake, and opposite it, on the other side of the lake, is the city **Herakleia**. This city was founded on the northern boundary of the kingdom of Caria. During that period there was no lake, but a natural bay of the Aegean; over the years the bay has been closed by silt brought by the large Meander river, and today the lake which was created serves tourists as a pleasant stop for eating and bathing. From the point where the road meets the Meander river, the road turns west to Priene, Miletus and Didim.

Didim

The Temple of Apollo in Didim was a highly important religious center. It was the largest Greek temple in Anatolia, and the seat of the oracle, who for a long time was regarded equal in status to the oracle

at Delphi. The importance of Didim was more religious than civic. According to early evidence, the Temple of Apollo stood on the ruins of another temple, and it houses a sacred spring from the period prior to the Ionian conquest in the tenth century BC. In the sixth century BC, a Didimian ritual was held in the temple which became known throughout the ancient world. After the unsuccessful rebellion of the Ionian cities against the Persian regime in 494 BC, the temple was destroyed and the bronze statue of Apollo was taken by the Persian conquerors.

Area code: 256

Legend tells us that for two hundred years following the destruction of the Temple of Apollo, the sacred spring, whose waters gave inspiration to the oracle, ceased flowing. On Alexander the Great's birthday, the spring began flowing again, and a divine voice told Alexander that he was the son of

The Temple at Didim, whose construction took over 500 years and was never completed

Zeus and that he would overcome the Persians. And indeed, after the prophesy was realized, Alexander reinstated the ritual, taking revenge on the descendants of the priests, who surrendered to the Persians, and began to rebuild the temple.

Construction of the temple continued for over 500 years, and in fact was never completed. Most of the temple we see was built in the late third century AD by Seleucus, who also returned the bronze statue to the temple. Construction was continued by the Emperors Tiberius and Caligula. The Byzantine Emperor Justinian fortified the temple and made it into a refuge. The temple was damaged badly in a number of earthquakes, especially that of 1436.

The impressive structure was surrounded by 120 columns, and its exterior walls were over 82ft. (25m) high. At the site you can see a statue of the mythological Medusa and visit the small museum, which houses statues that were found during the excavations. The most important statues were taken to the British Museum in 1858. The temple is beautifully lit at night, a sight that shouldn't be missed. A night spent on the actual site is a good idea. Next to the temple is the Medusa House Pension. A 300 year-old building with a warm and pleasant atmosphere and most recommended.

Two and a half miles (4km) south of Didim is the **Altınkum beach**. A tourist center has been developing on this beach in the last few years, and includes hotels, restaurants and a bathing beach. Transportation in the area is by *dolmuş*, which go from Altinkum to Söke.

Miletus

Almost nine miles (14km) north of Didim lies Miletus, which was the largest Ionian city. Settlement here evidently began in the thirteenth century BC, with settlers who arrived from Crete. The Ionian invaders arrived here in the tenth century BC, and according to Herodotus, they consisted only of males, who subsequently murdered the men and wed their wives, as was the custom of those times.

In the seventh and eighth centuries BC, Miletus was one of the central cities of the Hellenistic world. The city set up almost 100 colonies along the Mediterranean, the Aegean and the Black Sea coasts, thereby disseminating Greek culture to Asia Minor. Miletus served as a cultural and art center, and singing and drama contests were held in the large theater here. The famous philosopher Thales, who began to develop and teach the philosophy of nature and the order of the universe, lived here.

Miletus was spared during the Persian conquest in 546 BC, because of an earlier agreement with the conquerors. The city came under Persian rule, but freedom of ritual was allowed. In the rebellion of the Greek cities against the Persian rule, Miletus joined the rebels, and when the rebellion failed in 494 BC, Darius ordered the destruction of the city.

A column of the Temple at Didim

After the overthrow of the Persians, some twenty years later, the Greeks began rebuilding Miletus. The city once again prospered, but not for long: Alexander the Great conquered the city and it was again destroyed in 334 BC. After the death of Alexander the city came under various rulers in the area, until it again flourished during the Roman period. The Roman emperors, especially Hadrian and Augustus, glorified the city and most of the remnants we see today date from their empires.

The most prominent sight in Miletus is the large amphitheater which held as many as 15,000 spectators. There is also a race track here, two main squares, the northern *agora* and the southern *agora*, and Roman baths. Among these is the bath house of Faustine, established by the wife of the Emperor Marcus Aurelius. In addition to the Roman ruins, there is also a Byzantine fortress on the hill of the theater, the Ilyas Bey Mosque, built in 1404 by the Turkish Menteşe tribe, and a museum of the antiquities of the city. The site is open daily 9am-6pm.

Remains of the amphitheater at Priene

Priene

Here we find the ruins of an ancient Greek port, situated some 15.5 miles (25km) north of Miletus. Priene was set up on the ancient coast, and was a member of the confederation of Ionian cities, maintaining excellent neigborly relations with Miletus. Due to the accumulation of silt at the mouth of the Meander river and the movement of the coast west, the residents of the city moved their homes to the present spot in the fourth century BC.

The city is located 492ft. (150m) above the Meander valley. Its strategic location and the Temple of Athena have made Priene an important center. The city was built with a grid of parallel and perpendicular streets, with the heart of the city, the *agora*, in the center. Most of the remains of the city are Greek, unlike the Roman remains of Efes and Miletus. The site is open daily 9am-6pm.

Söke

The road from Priene to Kuşadasi goes through Söke, some 10.5 miles (17 km) north of Priene. The *dolmuşes* from Didim, Miletus, Milas and Priene reach the central bus station in the city. From the station you can go by bus to Kuşadası, İzmir, Bodrum, Marmaris and Pamukkale. Passengers to Aphrodisias and Pamukkale will find travel by *dolmuş* preferable because it is faster than the bus.

The Temple of Athena at Priene

Those interested in archeology and ancient cities can visit nearby **Magnesia**, on the banks of the Meander river. The city was established by the Greek tribes, and it protected the road from Efes into Anatolia in the Meander valley. Legends portray that the city was founded by Amazons, women warriors, under the patronage of the Goddess Artemis. The city was ruled by the Lycian and Persian kingdoms, and was declared a free city in the Roman province of Asia Minor, in return for its aid in the campaign against Mithradates, King of Pontus. Today, you can see a large agora, a temple of Athena and the remains of streets.

Kuşadası

Kuşadası, just 55 miles (90km) south of İzmir, is an international resort, the largest of its type along the Aegean coast. The city's name, which means the "island of the birds," is derived from the nearby island now connected to the land. Boat passengers headed for the beach get off at the island mooring. The Italian fortress built by Genoan merchants in the fifteenth century protected the entrance to the mooring. This is the only historic sight in the city.

Ferries sail from Kuşadası to the Greek island Samus, a two-hour ride. In the tourist seasons there are two ferries a day – one in the morning and one in the afternoon. Off-season there is only one ferry a day, and in the winter it stops completely. The price of the trip is about $35 one-way, and $40 round trip on the same day. You can buy tickets from travel agents in the city, who will also handle the arrangements for your exit from Turkey. In any case, you must leave your passport at the port office one day before the trip. *Dolmuşes* to the Kadınlar Beach, south of the city, leave from Barbaros Hayrettin Cad., next to the town hall.

Atatürk Boulevard along the coast connects the northern beach with the center of the city. The **tourist information office** is located along the boulevard, at Iskele Square, Tel. 614-1103, opposite the docks and passport control. The post office is located on Barbaros Hayrettin Cad., in the center of the city. You can change money at the Tütün Bank, at 20 Barbaros Cad. Buses and *dolmuşes* to Seljuk, Efes and İzmir leave frequently from the bus station in the eastern part of the city near the market. This is the station where the *dolmuşes* from Söke arrive, bringing passengers from Priene, Miletus and Didim.

Area code: 256

Accommodation and Dining

Almost all the hotels in Kuşadası, regardless of standard, are modern, built in the 1970's and 1980's, and are 25% less expensive off-season. In contrast to Bodrum, it is not difficult to find a vacant room here. The most impressive hotel in the city is *Club Caravaserai*, Tel. 614-4115, located in the city center, in an old khan (inn) built in 1618. The khan constitutes a tourist attraction in its own right, as it is a marvelous example of Ottoman architecture. The rooms have been carefully renovated, and the *kilim* reinforce the Ottoman feeling. The hotel houses an excellent restaurant, which is highly recommended. Another expensive fine restaurant is *Tusan*, Tel. 614-8073, which has a private beach outside of the city, on the road to the village of Seljuk.

The *Efe Hotel*, Tel. 614-3660, offers a lovely view from its veranda. The *Akman* Hotel, 13 Istiklâl Cad., Tel. 614-1501, about half a mile from the city center, both are highly recommended.

A quieter atmosphere and less expensive accommodation can be found at the *Kuşadası*, at the end of Barbaros Cad. next to the *Akdeniz Hotel*. Nearby there are several other inexpensive hotels. Camping grounds can be found along the northern coast, opposite the yacht mooring. Picturesque fish restaurants are located next to the fishermen's wharf. The *Diba* restaurant is one of the most highly recommended. Less expensive restaurants can be found in the market area, north of Kahramanlar Cad.

The fortress at Kuşadası

Efes

The visitor to Turkey who plans to visit at least one historic site in the country should go to the ancient city of Ephesus, known today as Efes. Throughout Turkey there are better preserved theaters and larger temples, but here, in Efes, a large and important city has been preserved, and with a little imagination and some explanation, you can get a sense of the life of the residents of the beautiful city. The best hours to visit here are during the morning or the late afternoon, until sunset. At noon the heat and the many visitors make it difficult to tour Efes.

How to Get There

Efes is located 13.5 miles (22km) north of Kuşadası, very close to the town of Selçuk, and 48 miles (78km) south of İzmir. You can reach the site by bus or *dolmuş*, which leave every half hour from Kuşadası and İzmir.

The History of Efes

The history of Efes begins in the mid-second millennium BC, when it was settled as part of the Carian kingdom, and in the early first millennium BC, the Ionians, led by Androculus, ruled the city. During the great wars between Greece and Persia, Ephesus maintained good ties with both sides. After the death of Alexander the Great, in the fourth century BC, the area became the territory of Lysimachus. From that time on, through the Roman era and until the mid-third century AD, the city prospered, at its peak numbering 300,000 residents, and it became the most important port on the Mediterranean sea. The city served as the capital of the government of the Roman province of Asia, and there was an important Christian center here. The apostle Paul lived in the city for over thirty years and here wrote his famous sermons which he delivered to the people of the city. When the Goths invaded, in 263AD, the city begin to decline, and in the Byzantine era it was completely abandoned, and the area became a marsh.

Excavations of the city were begun in 1863 by the English engineer J.T. Wood. Wood dreamed of discovering the Temple of Artemis, one of the Seven Wonders of the Ancient World. During the excavations, he found an engraving in the amphitheater that described ritual parades along the Sacred Way, from the amphitheater to that temple. According to the clues found in the ancient engraving, Wood continued to search, and in 1869, after many years of

A statue in the façade of the Celsus Library

excavating, his dream came true and he found the ruins of the temple. He devoted the next five years to uncovering the site. The archeologist David Hogarth continued excavation of the temple and the city in the early twentieth century, and smuggled his findings to the British Museum.

Selçuk

You can start your tour in the town of Selçuk, 3 miles (5km) east of Efes. The town was built on the ancient location of Ephesus, and you can see some important remnants of the city's past here. The town now serves as a tourist center, with hotels and restaurants. The **tourist information office** is located in the center of the town, Tel. 892-6945.

Area code: 232

The visit here focuses on Ayasoluk and the Ephesus Museum. According to tradition, John the Apostle lived on this hill in the second half of the first century AD. The Emperor Justinian built a church here in the sixth century AD, known as St. John's Basilica. A church of great importance to the Crusaders, it was completely destroyed in an earthquake and had to be reconstructed by archeologists. Above the church a Byzantine citadel was built. This was renovated by the Seljuks, who acquired the area in 1304, and used it as their principal stronghold. From the citadel you can see the Isabey mosque with its double dome, which was built in 1375 by the Turkish prince who ruled the area

The ornate façade of the Celsus Library – Ephesus

between the Seljuk and Ottoman periods. Next to the hill a single marble column marks the place of the famous Temple of Artemis.

The **Archeological Museum of Ephesus** is located in the center of Selçuk. It contains some very inter-

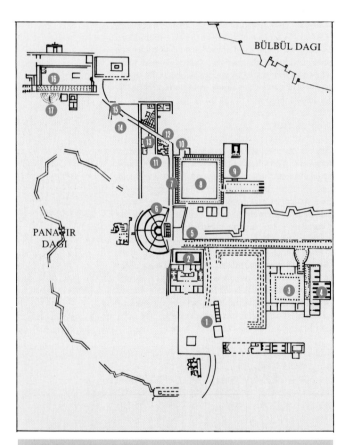

EFES (EPHESUS)

1. Entrance
2. Gymnasium and theater
3. Harbor gymnasium
4. Harbor baths
5. Arcadian way
6. Amphitheater
7. Sacred Way
8. Lower agora
9. Temple of Serapis
10. Celsus Library
11. Brothel
12. Baths of Scholastika
13. Temple of Hadrian
14. Fountain of Trajan
15. Street of Curetes
16. Upper Agora
17. Odeum

esting objects that were found at the site, such as marble statues of the goddess Artemis. The museum is open daily from 9:30am-6:30pm.

From Selçuk you can get to Efes by *dolmuş*, which leaves from the bus station. Another interesting possibility, particularly suitable for hikers, is to walk there, along the ancient **Sacred Way**, which was used for ritual parades. Start at the Temple of Artemis and walk about a hour toward the ancient city.

The Temple of Artemis, which is considered one of the Seven Wonders of the World, stands outside the walls of the Hellenistic city. The temple is the oldest site in the city, and was apparently erected in the eighth century BC. The structure was destroyed and its reconstruction, completely out of marble, was completed in 550 BC. According to evidence, this temple was the largest and most impressive in the Greek world. In 356 BC, the temple was burned by Herostratus, who sought a way into the pages of history, and in fact succeeded in his strange desire.

Remains of the Temple of Hadrian

After the fire, the work was renewed, and a new and more splendid temple was built on the ruins of its predecessor. Its size was 180ft. x 377ft. (55m x 115m), and it had 127 columns, 66ft. (20m) high. Artemis, in honor of whom the temple was built, was the goddess of nature and hunting, the twin sister of Apollo and the daughter of Zeus. In Ephesus, responsibility for fertility and youth were also ascribed to Artemis. Only one column remains at the site of the temple under the citadel, and it is surrounded by green pastures and fragments of columns.

The Site

Some twelve miles (20 km) from Kuşadası, the road turns right. For those who come by public transportation, this is the place to get off and continue on foot a short way to the parking lot, where those coming by car must park.

From the entrance to the site (there is a fee), a short path leads to the Arcadian Way – a wide, marbled path, which leads to the Magnesia Gate, at the far end of the city. This path was the main street of the city, and it led to the harbor and the amphitheater. Here the sea, like at the other locations along the Aegean coast, has drawn back over the years because of erosion, so you shouldn't expect to be able to reach either the sea or the harbor ruins. There is not much to see at the western ruins; the marble floor was laid in 550 AD, and on either side of the main street, public halls and baths and a gymnasium for the use of the city's residents were found. Today, decorated columns and statues line the way.

The **amphitheater**, the largest of its type in Asia Minor, was designed to hold 25,000 spectators. It was built in the third century BC, and was renovated and expanded in the Roman era. It is worth climbing to the top for a view of the city. From the amphitheater the marble **Sacred Way** leads to the upper *agora*, passing by the **Library of Celsus**. The magnificent library is one of the most impressive ruins here; in the second century AD it belonged to Celsus, the ruler of the province of Asia. The marble exterior wall of the library is well preserved, including the decoration and statues. Next to the library is a building that served as the city's brothel.

From the library, turn left into the street of Curetes, named after the priests of the Temple of Artemis. Among the many interesting buildings along this street, of special mention are the **Temple of Hadrian**, from the second century AD, the **Baths of Scholastika**, which were renovated in the fourth century AD, the marvelous **Fountain of Trajan** and the **upper agora** with an **odeum**, built in the second century AD to hold 1,400 people. The **Temple of Domition**, further down the street, was built in the first century AD and now houses a small museum of engravings found in the city.

The Street of Curetes

The **Efes Festival** is held annually in early May.

Green pastures and fragments – the Arcadian Way

During the festival performances are presented in the old city, including concerts, Turkish folklore and folk dancing in the huge amphitheater. In mid-January there are colorful camel competitions in the village of Selçuk.

After the tour of Efes, you can wind up the day at **Meryem Ana**, the home of the Holy Virgin Mary. It is said that Jesus' mother came here with John the Apostle, and lived here for 11 years until her death, in the year 48 AD. Historically, this legend could be based on real fact, and might explain why there was a Christian community in Efes even before St. Paul arrived. In Efes there was evidently an ancient synagogue, as the New Testament tells us that here Paul met with the Jews and baptized them (*Acts of the Apostles* 19:18). Ruins of the synagogue were not found in the excavations.

The site was not known until the nineteenth century. A German woman named Catherine Emmerich wrote that the Virgin Mary had appeared before her and described the location of her home and her grave. A team of religious archeologists left for İzmir in 1891, following the description in Emmerich's book, and found the ruins of a house amazingly similar to the description of her visions. Incredibly, it turned out that a memorial service for the Blessed Virgin was held here every year on August 15, for many years. Catherine Emmerich, incidentally, was disabled and never visited Turkey.

Over the years, the place was renovated and made into a focus of pilgrimage, and it became known for

The Sacred Way

its curative powers. Pope Paul VI visited here in 1967 and gave religious legitimation to the importance of the place.

Meryem Ana church, located some 4.5 miles (7km) from Efes, can be reached by taxi from the parking lot at the entrance to Efes or from Selçuk. There are a few restaurants and stores here for tourists.

From the Aegean Coast to Pamukkale

The busy road from Kuşadası on the Aegean Coast to Pamukkale passes through the valley of the large Menderes river along an ancient trade route to Anatolia and the Taurus mountains. This fertile valley was settled by the Carians, ancient Greek immigrants who set up the Carian kingdom in this area, in the first millennium BC.

The city of **Aydın**, about half an hour's ride east of Kuşadası, is a large farming city, close to the ancient city of Tralles. There is no reason to stop here, because a special entry permit must be obtained to see the ancient ruins which are located in a military zone. Further east on the road is the village **Sultanhisar**, and next to it the ruins of the ancient city **Nyssa**.

Ancient Nyssa is located next to a lovely stream in tranquil natural surroundings. The ancient city was established by the Seleucids in the third century BC, and prospered during the Roman era. Among the ruins in the city are an amphitheater, which has been grow over by natural vegetation, a well-preserved library building and a water canal alongside the river.

Aphrodisias

Almost seven-and-a half miles (12km) east of Sultanhisar is the city of Nazilli, where a road leads south to Karacasu and to the capital of the Carian kingdom, Aphrodisias. This city was the largest and most important in the kingdom. A Greek-style temple was built here in the sixth century BC. The temple was constructed in honor of the Goddess of beauty and love, Aphrodite (Venus), daughter of Zeus. The Roman emperors renovated the temple in the first century AD, and in the fifth century, the temple was converted into a Byzantine church. Among the things worth seeing here are the Hadrian baths, a well-preserved odeum and a stadium in the northern part of the site, which can seat some 30,000 spectators.

Next to the ruins is the only local hotel, *Chez Mestan*. There are simple restaurants in this hotel and in the nearby villages Karacasu and Geyre. From these villages you can get by bus or *dolmuş* to İzmir, Selçuk and Denizli, near Pamukkale. In Karacasu there are several taxis, which charge about $7 for the ride from the village to Aphrodisias.

Denizli

Denizli, a large grey farming city, 44 miles (70km)

east of Nazilli, would probably not be included in a travel guide were it not for its proximity to Pamukkale. The **tourist information office** in the city is located at the train station, Tel. 265-3393. You can get here by the slow train from İzmir, or in sleeping cars on the express train from İstanbul. The train station is near the bus station, where buses arrive from throughout Anatolia – Ankara, Marmaris, Antalya, Konya and more. The best links with the city are, of course, with İzmir and Kuşadasi, which are some 4 hours' drive away. From the Denizli bus station you can get a bus or *dolmuş* to Pamukkale, some 12 miles (20km) north of here. The last bus leaves at 10pm.

The best hotel in the city is the moderately priced *Altuntur*, located on Kaymakaçı Cad., Tel. 265-1114. The *Kuyumcu Hotel*, Tel. 265-13750 and the *Park Hotel*, Tel. 265-0849 are less expensive. Inexpensive hotels can be found near the bus station and along the streets leading to the city center. It is advisable to stay overnight in Pamukkale; try Denizli only if all the rooms near the site of the Pamukkale baths are taken.

Area code: 258

Pamukkale

The unique natural phenomenon of Pamukkale is one of the highlights of a visit to Turkey. The name means "the cotton castle". Imagine a huge white wall installed with various sizes of basins. Hot water cascades from the top of the wall into the basins. When a basin fills up, the water flows into the basin beneath it and fills it, and so on and so forth. Add to the picture white cotton-like stalactites, decorating the basins and the landscape of the fertile valley. That's Pamukkale.

Nature has invested in Pamukkale over 15,000 years of endless "work." Calcium-rich water falls from the thermal springs to the foot of Mount Çal. The water comes from the earth at a temperature of 36°C, and collects on the plain that reaches the top of the cliff, 328ft. (100m) high. Over the years, large quantities of calcium have sunken into the wall and created pools in which the water flows very slowly. In time, the flowing water changed the shape of the pools and colored them glaring white.

Area code: 258

Accommodation and Dining

The better hotels are located on the upper plain above the wall of the pools, and the simple hotels are located in the village of Pamukkale, at the foot of this wondrous sight. The good hotels offer pools and baths with thermal spring water. The best is the *Colossea Hotel Termal*, Tel. 271-4156, which also has a private pool. Other fine hotels are *Tusan*, Tel. 272-2010, *Koru*, Tel. 272-2430, whose prices are not low, but are still much less than the *Colossea*.

Simple and inexpensive hotels can be found in the

The extraordinary phenomena of the cotton-like stalactites in Pamukkale

village of Pamukkale. Most of them have do not adjacent bathrooms, but you can use the hot showers in the swimming pools of the fine hotels. At *Ali's Pension*, mattresses are placed on *kilim* spread on the floor, and this has become a favorite for young travelers. Hotel rooms with adjacent bathrooms can be found at the *Anatolia Pension.*

Sites to See
You can walk and splash through the water in the small pools that comprise the large wall, but for a real dip, you should go to one of the good hotels. The hot water contains natural minerals – sulphur, calcium and others, which are considered to be a cure for heart disease, high blood pressure and other ailments.

On the plateau above the site are situated the ruins of an ancient city of health baths, **Hierapolis**. The city was founded as a health resort by the king of Pergamon in the second century BC, and was cultivated by the Roman and Byzantine rulers, who attributed wondrous curative powers to the place. At the site there are ruins of a magnificent necropolis, churches, temples, an amphitheater, a museum and, of course, many baths.

According to the *New Testament*, there was a large Jewish community here. The site is not particularly interesting, and the high point is to bathe in the ancient bath located in the *Pamukkale Hotel* next to the ruins.

Those interested in health springs can continue 3 miles (5km) north to the village of **Karahayıt** where there are hot springs and red iron-rich mud, thought to enhance the skin and bring eternal youth.

İzmir

İzmir, the capital of the Aegean Coast, is the third largest city in Turkey, after İstanbul and Ankara. Some 2 million people live here, and it is the second largest commercial and industrial center in the country. The local industries focus mainly on the processing of agricultural products, and the city is one of the world's centers for dried fruit export. In contrast to other Turkish cities, İzmir is modern in appearance, and most of its buildings were constructed after the Turkish War of Independence, a war in which İzmir suffered greatly. Many tourists choose to skip this busy city on their way north (or south), and this is somewhat justified, although there are a number of worthwhile sights in its environs.

History of the City

The convenient mooring and the fertile bay attracted Greek settlers as early as the third millennium BC, and the settlement here was founded by the Aeolians and later taken over by the Ionians. In the first millennium BC the blind Greek poet, Homer, lived here; it is said that he wrote *The Iliad* in a cave near the river.

Alexander the Great, who passed through, was commanded in a dream by the Goddess Nemesis to build a great city here, called Smyrna. Alexander began the work, and it was continued by Antigones and Lysimachus. The city continued to develop under Rızmiroman and Byzantine rule, but was destroyed by Tamerlane the Mongol in 1402. Under Ottoman rule, the city again flourished as a large trade port.

After World War I, Greece sought to annex the coastal area; the Allies agreed, and in the Sevres Pact of 1920 Symrna, or İzmir in Turkish, was awarded to the Greeks. To strengthen their hold, the Greeks invaded İzmir under protection of British, American and French battleships. The conquest of Smyrna was seen as a national insult and humiliation in Turkey, and it accelerated the rebellion led by Atatürk against the Sultan. In 1922, the Turks attacked the city, and the very cruel battle was fought from house to house. As a result, a great fire broke out in the city destroying most of its wooden houses. The Lausanne Treaty in 1923 returned İzmir to Turkish sovereignty, and 1,300,000 Greeks, most of them from the İzmir area, were exchanged for 400,000 Turks who lived in Greece.

The Layout of the City

İzmir lies on a bay bearing the same name. The city center is located along the coast, south of the harbor, the beaches are not very clean and therefore not recommended. The Ottoman clock that has become the symbol of the city stands in Konak Square, the central square of the city. Two parallel boulevards lead from Konak to the harbour: Atatürk Cad. on the sea and the wide Cumhuriyet Boulevard.

How to Get There

By air: The Çigli Airport is located 15 miles (25 km) north of the city. Many international lines fly here from European cities and there are daily flights from İstanbul and Ankara, which is about an hour away. Turkish Airlines operate a bus and minibus service from the airport to the city center, near the *Büyük Efes Hotel.*

By sea: The Turkish ship company, *D.Y.* (Denizcilik Yolları), operates trips from Venice and from Ancona

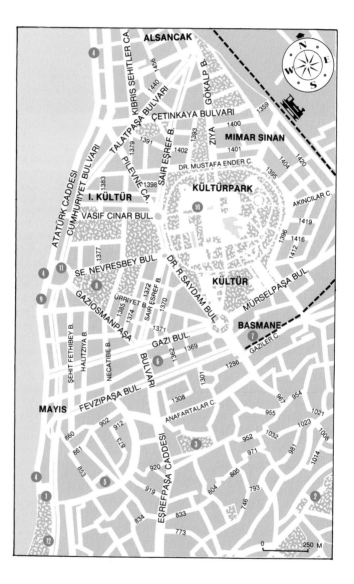

to İzmir once a week during the tourist season. The trip takes three days and fares start at about $220 for a chair on deck. The boats have modern cabins and room for cars. Other boats arrive in İzmir port from Marseilles, Genoa and Athens. Information on these routes is available from the travel agencies throughout the world as well as in İzmir. The coastal boat trip from İstanbul to Alanya stops in İzmir once a week in the tourist season. Another popular ferry links İstanbul to İzmir throughout the year. The international port is located north of the city center. Next to it is the train station of the Alsancak district, where you can get a bus, dolmuş or taxi to the center.

Yellow hues on residential buildings in İzmir

By train: There is excellent express train service between İzmir and Ankara. The night train, *İzmir Ekspresi*, with comfortable sleeping cars, is particularly recommended. Other trains leave for Selçuk, Kuşadasi and Denizli. The Basmane train station is located in the large Cultural Park along the centrally located Fevzipaşa boulevard. The Alsancak train station in the north serves the lines to the city's suburbs.

By bus: As one might expect in such a central city, lines to cities throughout the country, such as Çanakkale, Bursa, Kuşadasi, Pamukkale and others, operate from the city's large bus station. The station is located near the local stadium, some 2.5 miles (4km) from the city center. Outside the station is a taxi service, dolmuşes and bus number 50 to the city center. The

stop for passengers to the Çeşme peninsula is located near Fahrettin Altay Square. Passengers to Efes can catch the bus at Konak Square. Tickets can be purchased at the station and in the ticket offices near the train station.

Getting around Town

Bus lines and *dolmuşes* cover the city map efficiently. Despite the size of İzmir, the tourist sights are concentrated in a single area and can all be reached on foot or by short taxi rides. Another form of city transportation is the ferry that operates between Konak, the Alsancak district and the Karşıyaka district on the northern side of İzmir Bay. The trip is a tour in its own right. If you have the time, is worth taking a short boat trip to get to know İzmir Bay from a different angle.

Area code: 232

Tourist Services

The city has four **tourist informa-**

tion offices. One is located at 418 Atatürk Cad., Tel. 422-0207. The other is located next to the large *Büyük Efes Hotel*, at 10 Gazi Osman Paşa boulevard, Tel. 484-2147. The third is at the harbor, Tel. 463-1600, and the fourth, at the airport, Tel. 251-2626. At these offices one can obtain all the information required about tours of the city, as well as detailed maps. The post office is near Cumhuriyet Square, and it is open 24 hours a day.

Accommodation and Dining

Luxury Hotels

The *Grand Efes*, Tel. 484-4300 is located in the central Cumhuriyet Square. It overlooks the sea and has a private garden, tennis courts and a nightclub.

İzmir Hilton, Tel. 441-6060.

Expensive Hotels

Pullman Etap İzmir, which is located at 138 Cumhuriyet Boulevard, near Cumhuriyet Square, Tel. 489-4090, and the *İzmir Palas*, Tel. 421-5583 on Atatürk Boulevard, north of the same square, offer excellent rooms.

Well-established Hotels

There are numerous hotels in İzmir. The modern *Karaca*, Tel. 489-1940 is excellent but fairly expensive. It is located between Cumhuriyet Square and the Cultural Park. The *Anba Hotel*, at 124 Cumhuriyet Boulevard, Tel. 484-4380, gives full value to its guests. The *Babadan* at 50 Gazi Osman Paşa Boulevard, Tel. 483-9640, the *Billur*, next to the train station, Tel. 483-9732 and the *Kilim*, Tel. 484-5340 are good and relatively inexpensive.

Inexpensive Hotels

Those looking for an inexpensive double room with adjacent bathroom will find such accommodation on Fevzi Paşa Boulevard, near the train station, for instance at the *Oba Hotel*, at 1369 Sokak. Less expensive rooms, generally without adjacent bathrooms, can be found on Anafartalar Cad., on the other side of the train station. The International House Pension offers $5 rooms for the budget traveller. It is located at 435 Mithat Paşa Cad. The nearest camping ground is located 2.5 miles (4km) west of the city, along the road to Çeşme.

A monument on the promenade at İzmir

A view of İzmir from the Velvet Fortress

The city of İzmir offers a large selection of good restaurants in the exclusive hotels and along the sea shore, north of Cumhuriyet Square, such as the *Bergama* for seafood lovers and the excellent *Deniz* restaurant. For an especially festive meal, try the rooftop restaurant at the *Büyük Efes Hotel*. Simpler restaurants can be found in the vicinity of the train station and the large Cultural Park. A popular restaurant is *Mangal* in Atatürk St.

Sites to See

The war of 1922, which destroyed large parts of the city, also damaged the tourist sites. Today, little remains of İzmir's past, but **Velvet Fortress** (Kadifekale), located on the historic Mount Pagos stands out as one of the city's prominent sights. The climb is a difficult but fascinating one through authentic neighborhoods. The acropolis, constructed by the successors of Alexander the Great, particularly Lysimachus, is located in the Hellenistic city. The fortress was built at the end of the Byzantine period and was renovated several times by the Ottomans. From the fortress there is a breathtaking view of the city, particularly the *agora*, the old market square, northeast of the foot of the fortress.

Weaving fabrics at the Velvet Fortress in İzmir

According to local legend, in the third century BC the inhabitants of the island of Eos surrounded Smyrna. To the surprise of the conquerors, they found the *agora* completely deserted: the inhabitants were on Mount Pagos, celebrating the Dionysus festival, with much wine drinking and wild dancing. When the people of Smyrna noticed that the troops had reached their city, they ran down excitedly, and scared away the shocked invaders. After this glorious victory, the people of Smyrna returned to their festivities, which became especially wild. You can reach the fortress by *dolmuş* from Konak. The *agora*, which was destroyed by an earthquake in the second century, is open to visitors daily from 8:30am-5:30pm.

Among the modern sights in the city are the **NATO Command Base**, north of Cumhuriyet Square and the large green **Cultural Park** (Kültür Parkı), which is a suitable spot for a tranquil break from the bustle of the city. The **Archeological Museum** and the **Ethnographic Museum** are located in the Turgut Reis Parkı, south of Konak. Open daily 9am-noon and 1:30-5pm, closed Mon. Perhaps the most enjoyable way to become acquainted with İzmir is to take a carriage tour along the central street between Konak Square and the Alsancak district.

Special Events

The major event in İzmir is the International Trade and Industry Fair, held in the Cultural Park every year from Aug. 20-Sept 20. During the fair the city is full of merchants and buyers, and tourists may have difficulty in finding a vacant room. The Mediterranean Crafts Festival is held in İzmir in the first week of June.

September 9 is the anniversary of the 1922 liberation of İzmir from the Greeks, it is celebrated with parades down the city's streets. An interesting festival is held in Manisa, 25 miles (40km) northeast of İzmir, in the last week of April. The festival centers around taking a medicine made of gunpowder, which is said to bestow eternal youth and increase virility.

The lively market by Konak Square

Night Life
The large hotels offer tourists entertainment, including belly dancing and Turkish vocalists. Alternatively, you can dance at certain clubs in the city, such as the *Bonjour Club*, on Cumhuriyet Boulevard.

Another form of recreation is a visit to the baths, a highly recommended experience after a tiring day of touring. The *Hoşgör* baths are at Mithat Paşa Cad., south of Turgut Reis Parkı, and the *Karantina* baths are on the same street, opposite Mithat Paşa College.

Shopping
The large market of İzmir overflows with merchandise of all colors and aromas. Access to the lively market is from Konak Square, and it is especially bustling on the centrally located Anafartalar Cad. The flea market is at the intersection of Gazi Osman Paşa and Fevzi Paşa Boulevards in the city center. For more exclusive and expensive shops, visit the prestigious shopping district along Atatürk Cad., located between Cumhuriyet Square and Alsancak district.

Around İzmir

Sardis
In the first millennium BC, the Lycian kingdom ruled the region between the Ionian cities on the Aegean coast and the powerful Phrygian kingdom in the Anatolian plateau. Sardis, 55 miles (90km) east of İzmir, was the capital of Lycia. In the sixth century BC, Croesus, King of Lycia, captured the Ionian

Ruins from the Roman city at Sardis, that was destroyed in an earthquake

confederation along the coast, with the exception of Miletus. These triumphs brought him wealth and power, but Croesus then attempted to expand his kingdom to the Persian borders, an endeavour which ended in failure, and in 546 BC he was defeated by Cyrus, and his Lycian kingdom fell under Persian rule. Around the time of the birth of Christianity, the city was destroyed in an earthquake and most of the ruins we see today are from the Roman city that was rebuilt by Tiberius.

The most impressive ruins are of the **Temple of Artemis**, built during the time of Alexander the Great, a magnificent **gymnasium** dating from the Roman period and a large **synagogue.**

The synagogue in Sardis was discovered in 1962 by an American team of archeologists, and is considered to be one of the largest and most splendid in the ancient world, its area exceeding 10,750sq./ft (1,000m^2). Its construction began after the earthquake in 17 BC, and continued intermittently for 500 years. Apparently, it was built as a large public hall, and was given to the Jewish community in the second century AD. As is the Jewish custom, the building faces east, toward Jerusalem. The synagogue was destroyed, evidently during a Persian invasion, in the seventh century AD.

You can reach Sardis by an organized tour from İzmir or on the bus to Salihli from the central bus station in İzmir. The journey takes about an hour. Slow trains link the Basmane station and Sart, the Turkish name for Sardis.

Çeşme Peninsula

Lovely beaches and five Ionian cities are all that constitute the Çeşme Peninsula. Most visitors going west from İzmir cross this bit of land to reach the ferry on their way to the Greek island of Eos.

The most fascinating city of the five is **Teos**, located next to the village of Sığacık, 35 miles (56km) from İzmir. Teos was established in the ninth century BC, and was the site of the ritual to Dionysus, also known as Bacchus, god of wine, a ritual based on ecstasy and cruelty. The city was chosen as the home of groups of professional actors who were under patronage of Dionysus. Today, the site includes the temple of Dionysus, an odeum and an amphitheater. You can reach Sığacık from İzmir either directly, by *dolmuş* or through the town of Güzelbahçe. In the village itself there is a Genoan fortress as well as good bathing beaches.

Çeşme Village

Çeşme is a pleasant seaside resort, known by the many who come here from Greece as a point of entry to Turkey. The village is located 50 miles (80km) west of İzmir, and is linked by a frequent bus and *dolmuş* service to İzmir.

Remains from the Roman city at Sardis

The ferry dock and passport control are located next to the bus station. The ferry to Eos departs every Thursday in the winter and daily in the summer. The boats leave in the morning and return in the afternoon, so you can make a day trip to Eos and return the same evening to İzmir. The trip takes about an hour and costs about $30 per person and $70 per car.

Those who stay in Çeşme can visit the Italian fortress which was built by the Genoans in the fourteenth century and later renovated by the Ottomans in the fifteenth century. In the fortress there is a local museum, open 10am-noon and 1-5:30pm. The village is famous for a sea battle between the Turks and Russians, which took place in July 1770 opposite the village, and in which most of the Turkish fleet was destroyed. You can also enjoy a swim at the local beach.

In and around the village there are hotels and restaurants of all standards. The unique *Çeşme Kervansaray Hotel*, Tel. (232)712-7177, is located in a khan built in the sixteenth century, in the days of Sulayman the Magnificent. The khan was converted into a beautiful, slightly expensive hotel. It is worth eating here even if you are not a guest of the hotel.

Area code: 232

Turkish artifacts for sale at Bergama

Bergama

62 miles (100km) north of İzmir lies the farming city Bergama, near the ruins of Pergamon, one of the most ancient and most impressive cities in Turkey. You should try to reach Bergama in the morning in order to see all the sights by evening and then continue on, as the hotels here are not satisfactory. The best hotel in the city is the noisy *Tusan* next to the main road. It is low to moderate standard and is fairly expensive. The other hotels here are simple pensions without adjacent bathrooms, and they fill up quickly in the course of the day.

There is a **tourist information office** at the entrance to the city, at the intersection of the roads to Asklepios, before the bus station, Tel. 632-3368. The city spreads out between the bus station and the Selinus river. The Cumhuriyet Cad., the central street, leads from the bus station through the city to the acropolis of the ancient city. The other historical sites are to the east of the city center.

Area code: 232

Remains of the city
Pergamon

Pergamon

Ancient Pergamon was settled as early as the second millennium BC. It reached the height of its prosperity in the days of Lysimachus, a successor of Alexander the Macedonian. Lysimachus deposited the treasures he had acquired in his conquest of the city, and appointed the eunuch Philitarus as its ruler. After the fall of Lysimachus, Philitarus became an independent king. The eunuch king adopted Eumenes I as a son, and thus founded a powerful dynasty which at its peak extended to the Marmara Sea. Pergamon, the capital, became a wealthy and important city, one of the most prominent cities of the Hellenistic world. The Pergamon kingdom was an ally of the Roman Empire, from whom it received, extensive territories in Anatolia after the Romans' victory over Antiochus of Syria, in the early second century AD.

When Attalus III, King of Pergamon, died in 133 BC he had no descendants to inherit the throne, and he bequeathed his large kingdom to Rome. The Romans, although they had previously not wanted to rule Anatolia, did not hesitate to accept the gift. Pergamon was made capital of the Roman province "Asia," which quickly came to encompass most of

Fishermen at work in the coastal town Ayvalık

Anatolia. Thus, the Romans almost without intending it, came to rule this part of the world, a reign that paved the way for the rise of the eastern Roman or Byzantine Empire.

It is recommended to start a tour of the old city with a visit to the **Archeological Museum**. Located on the main street, near the bus station, the museum houses a splendid exhibit of *objets d'art* that were found in the area. The museum is open daily 9am-noon and 1-5:30pm. From the museum, continue to the Selinus river, where the **Red Court** (Kızıl Avlu) is situated. The basilica, which gets its name from the red bricks from which it is built, was constructed over an ancient second-century temple to the god Serapis. The Byzantines renovated the building and converted it into a Christian holy site. Next to the basilica, note the lovely Roman bridge of arches spanning the river.

From the Red Court, the road goes up to the **acropolis**. The site is open at the same hours as the local museum. The impressive acropolis includes many interesting buildings, including a **Temple of Athena**, built in the third century BC, and the famous **Library of Eumenes II**, which included 200,000 written works. The various sights in the acropolis include an **amphitheater** that had seating for 10,000 people and was built on an extremely steep slope, and a Temple of Trajan. Complete your visit to the acropolis by going up to the fortress and enjoy the spectacular view of Asklepios and the breathtaking scenery.

Asklepion

A splendid road led from the ancient city to Asklepion, via the stadium and theaters. Asklepion is open daily 9am-noon and 1-5:30pm. It is located in a military zone, and therefore taking photographs is forbidden.

The Asklepion was a sort of ancient hospital, where mainly natural medicine was practiced, such as physical and spiritual exercise, combined with mud baths and the like. It was a ritualistic and mystical center, devoted to the Greek God of medicine, Asklepios. The Asklepion was built by Archeas of Pergamon, who cured himself at a similar center in Greece. Pergamon is where Galen, the famous second-century BC healer practiced. His medical achievements served as a basis for western medicine for the next thousand years.

The road leading to the site is on an incline, and cynics attribute the high success rate in curing patients here to the fact that only those who were already fit enough to make the climb could be treated at the health center.

At the site are some interesting ruins of ancient medical devices and a round temple devoted to Asklepios, whose symbol is a snake shedding its skin and according to the belief, receiving a new life.

Ayvalık

Many visitors to Pergamon prefer to stay in the coastal town of Ayvalık, about an hour's ride northwest of Bergama. Ayvalık is a quiet fishing village, around which a vacation and tourist center has developed. Over 20 small islands dot the shores of this lovely bay. Trips between the islands and the bathing beaches is the main recreation here. There is a **tourist information office** along the bay, opposite the marina, south of the city center, Tel. 312-2122.

The bus station is located at a walking distance of about 20 minutes from the center of the town. A local bus runs between the station, the center and the resorts. You can also purchase tickets for the bus in the central square. Not all buses from Çanakkale to İzmir go through Ayvalık; it is advisable to check before boarding.

At Ayvalık – when there are no bread-trucks, one can always use a donkey

Boat trips from Ayvalık to the Greek island **Lesbos** leave the Turkish side twice a day, in the morning and in the afternoon. A similar schedule serves those coming from Lesbos. The price of the trip is about $20 each way. Boats from Ayvalık to the nearby island of Ali Bey travel back and forth throughout the day and evening. The evening journey can be very pleasurable and romantic. Another pleasant trip is to the observation point at Şeytan Sofrasi, the "Devil's Table," located atop a hill, south of the city, which can be reached by private car or taxi.

The hotels in the city are simple and inexpensive, such as the *El* and *Canlı Balık* Hotels, on Gümrük Cad. Higher-class hotels are located along Sarmısaklı Mevkii, 5 miles (8km) south of the town. Among the beach hotels are: *Ankara*, Tel. 312-1195, *Billurcu*, Tel. 324-1189 and *Büyük Berk*, Tel. 312-2311. These are moderately priced and have balconies overlooking the sea. On the nearby beaches there are more hotels, such as *Murat Reis*, Tel. 312-1680 or *Ortunaç* on Ali Bey island. These hotels are most suitable for a quiet vacation of sun and sea. Other hotel rooms can be found near the village Dikili, between Ayvalık and Bergama. A recommended seafood restaurant in Ayvalık is *Cale*. Ali Bey is the place for good restaurants and pensions.

Area code: 266

Edremit Körfezi

The road from Ayvalık continues along the beautiful Edremit Bay (*Edremit Körfezi*). The old city of **Adramyttium** did not survive, despite its rich past. The *Turban* resort, Tel. 384-1204, in Akçay, siyuated west of Edremit, is one of the country's most inviting vacation spots, offering guests beach houses, a swimming pool, a restaurant and tennis courts at the reasonable price of a moderate standard hotel. Four less expensive hotels, such as the comfortable *Öge*, can be found next to the resort village.

A few miles before the town of Edremit, the road

from the south turns east. This is the turn off to take for those who want to go directly to Bursa. The road we continue on, along the coast to the west, eventually gets to Çanakkale and to the Marmara Sea.

From Akçay, the road continues west to the ancient city of **Assos**. The city was established in the eighth century AD by settlers who crossed the bay from the Greek island of Lesbos, and it served as a storage station for cargo on its way inland. In the fourth century BC, a branch of Plato's academy was set up here, and Aristotle lived here for three years. Today, you can see the acropolis, with a spectacular view of Edremit Bay, which compensates for the sparseness of ruins here. Assos is located next to the village Behramkale, 12 miles (20km) from Ayvacık on E24, the express road to Çanakkale and the Sea of Marmara.

The acropolis at the ancient city of Assos

THE BLACK SEA

The region of the Black Sea and the Pontus mountains is completely different from the western part of the country. The forested slopes of the Pontus go down to the coast, while the narrow strip of coast and the hill slopes are used for growing tea, tobacco and various nuts. The area is rural and tribal, and its inhabitants have subsisted on agriculture for centuries.

Settlement on the Black Sea coast began in the eighth century BC with settlers from the Greek polis Miletus, who set up their base in Sinop. During the Byzantine era, Trabzon was annexed to the empire, a situation which continued even after the fall of Constantinople to the Crusades in the thirteenth century. It was in Samsun that the seeds of the Turkish Republic began to sprout, when Atatürk took refuge here when fleeing from İstanbul.

The climate in the region is very rainy, particularly in the winter. The temperatures along the coast are moderate, while on the mountain tops they are extreme. Most of the beaches are not suitable for bathing because the mountainous slopes extend right down to the water.

From Ankara to Samsun

The road from Ankara to the Black Sea coast goes through the large Hittite cities. After a visit to Hattuşaş (see "Ankara"), we continue on road 41 to the modern city of **Çorum**, where the Hittite festival is held in mid-September. The city is not particularly special, but it is a convenient place to stay after touring the Hattian kingdom. The **tourist information office** is located at 1/5 Şehir Isan, Tel. (364)384-7717.

Amasya

55 miles (88km) east of Çorum lies Amasya, on the banks of the Yeşilırmak, "the scarlet" river. The quiet town, now capital of the district, was once a large city, and in the first century BC, served as the capital of the Pontic kingdom. According to legend, the city was founded by Amaesis, Queen of the Amazons. The city possesses great charm, owing to its location along the river, but there are no special ruins here, evidently because of flooding and earthquakes. Strabo, the well-known geographer, was born in Amasya in 64BC, and he describes it as a beautiful city in the river valley, with magnificent palaces and royal tombs.

Fleecy white sheep – a common sight in Turkey

A tour of Amasya begins on the main street, along the river, to the **Ethnographic Museum**. The museum is open daily 8:30am-noon and 1:30-5:30pm, closed Mon. It is located in a lovely nineteenth-century wooden house, which also has an interesting archeological exhibit. Other handsome Ottoman wooden houses can be found along the river, where they are reflected in the water. From the museum, the road climbs up to Kızlar Sarayı, the "Palace of the Maidens," where the kings of Pontus lived. The maidens appeared in the Ottoman period, when the place served as the royal residence for Ottoman nobility on their visits to the area. On the ruins of the palace we find graves of the Pontic kings cut into rock. There are also impressive tunnels, which were apparently dug for protection and refuge in times of emergency. The view of the city from here is breathtaking.

Continuing along the river to the north brings us to mosques from the Seljuk and Ottoman periods. The **Beyazıt Mosque**, at the end of the road and the **Büyük Ağa Theological College**, opposite it, were built in the fifteenth century by Sultan Beyazıt II, and are among the most outstanding sights in the city. The **citadel** (*hisar*) is located about one mile along the direct road outside of the city. It is almost completely destroyed, but the spectacular view is worth the effort of climbing up.

Area code: 358

There is no tourist information office in the city, but

NORTH EASTERN TURKEY

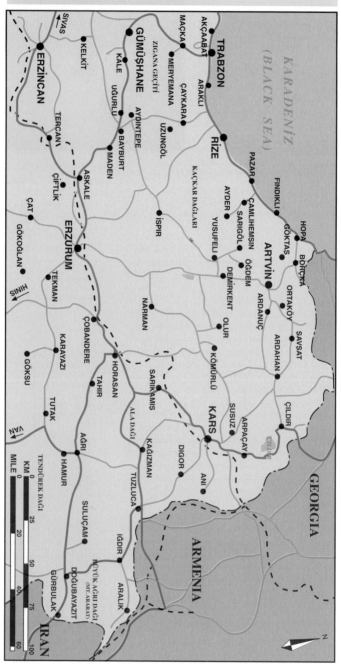

you can get an information sheet at the local museum or at the *Turban* Hotel, Tel. 211-4054. This is the best hotel in the city, and it is fairly inexpensive. Along the main street are a number of inexpensive pensions. There is a good restaurant in the *Turban*, and others along the river.

Samsun

Samsun is the largest city on the Black Sea coast. This port city is inhabited by some 280,000 residents, who make there living primarily from agriculture and agricultural industries, such as tobacco and tea. The city originated as Amisos in the seventh century BC, as a colony of the polis Miletus on the Aegean Sea.

Samsun became the birthplace of the Republican Revolution, when Atatürk and his troops sailed from İstanbul right under the nose of the furious Sultan. The young general reached Samsun on May 19, 1919, and here he began his private war of independence, which swept through the Turkish nation. Samsun is famous for its Folk Dance Festival, held here in July.

Area Code: 362

No interesting sights have remained in the city. The **tourist information office** is located at 19 Mayis Mah street, Tel. 431-1228. A number of weekly flights link Samsun to İstanbul and Ankara. A bus line, coordinated with the flight schedule, runs between the airport and the airline offices in the city on Kâzim Paşa Cad. The bus station is about a 15-minute walk from the city center. Many buses arrive here from the large cities of the country and from other locations along the Black Sea coast. The train to the city is extremely slow and inadequate for Western tourists. The Black Sea ferry leaves İstanbul on Monday and arrives in Samsun on Tuesday. From Samsun, the ferry sails for Trabzon the same day and returns to İstanbul every Thursday.

The hotels in the city range from the fine *Turban* to inexpensive pensions in the vicinity of the bus station. The *Turban*, Tel. 431-0750, boasts a swimming pool, and is located in the city center, along the coast. The *Burç*, Tel. 431-5480, is considerably less expensive.

Sinop

About a two-hour drive west separates Samsun and Sinop. The road crosses large tobacco fields and the wide delta of the Kızılırmak river. This is the location of the legendary land of the Amazons, ruled by the Virgin Queen Sinopa. Sinop is a natural harbor, which was first settled during the Hittite period. The harbor here served Hattaşuş and prospered when the people of Miletus established the base of their Black Sea coast colonies here. In 1853, the Russian navy sunk the entire Turkish fleet, and its 3,000 sailors, here.

The philosopher Diogenes was born in Sinop in the fifth century BC. Alexander the Great said of him that if he were not Alexander he would want to be Diogenes. The ruins of the city's past include a Byzantine fortress, a Seljuk mosque and a theological college, built in the thirteenth century by Alaeddin Keykûbad. The theological college now houses the local museum.

The moderate-priced hotel *Melia Kasım*, Tel. 61-4210 and the simple, inexpensive *117* hotel, both located on the coast, serve visitors to the city. The *Liman* is a good, reasonably priced restaurant in the harbor. The ferry between Istanbul and Trabzon stops at the local port.

Area code: 368

From Samsun to Trabzon

The road from Samsun east crosses the delta of the Yeşilırmak river and returns to the coast at the town of **Terme**. Legend tells us that this town was the center of the Amazons, the warrior women. According to early evidence, the Amazon women worked in agriculture and hunting for ten months of the year. For two months, in the spring, they would go to the mountains and meet with the mountain men. The matings were anonymous and arbitrary as they were intended solely for the purpose of reproduction. The male infants who were born were returned to the residents of the mountains and the girls were raised by the Amazons, after their right breast was shrivelled by burning in order to prevent its development from interfering in hunting and fighting.

From Terme the coastal road continues to Ünye. The town is located on the shore of a beautiful bay, and it is a good spot for a quiet seaside vacation.

The coastal road continues passed rock caves where seals live. The road continues east 43 miles (70km), until **Ordu**. In this friendly fishing village there are a number of simple hotels for travelers who want to spend a night in the city.

Giresun

32 miles (52km) east of Ordu is the town of Giresun. The Turkish name is a distortion of the name of the ancient city of Cerasus, established by settlers from Miletus. From the city fortress there is a beautiful view of the agricultural region along the coast. According to legend, the first cherries were brought to Europe from this city by the Roman General Lucullus, who conquered the area in the year 69 BC. It is from the name of the city that the word *cherry* is taken.

Opposite the city beaches, a short boat ride away, is a small island with another fortress. According to tradition, it was on this island, that Jason and his friends were attacked by huge birds on their quest for the golden fleece. In the city one can find a few simple and inexpensive pensions. The best of them is the *Giresun Hotel*, Tel. 212-3017, on Atatürk Boulevard. You can reach the city by bus, private car or ferry from İstanbul to Trabzon.

How to Get There

By air: Daily flights reach the airport, located east of the city, from Ankara and İstanbul.

A city bus operates between the Turkish Airlines office, near Taksim Square, and the airport, coordinated with flight times.

By sea: Trabzon is the last stop on the Black Sea ferry from İstanbul. The ferry leaves İstanbul on Monday and arrives in Trabzon on Wednesday morning, and leaves Trabzon for İstanbul the same evening.

By land: The bus station is located in the eastern part of the city, on the road to the Black Sea and the airport.

The *dolmuş* to Maçka, leaves from

this station; the *dolmuş* to Sümela is arranged and departs from the tourist information office, at 31 Taksim Cad., Tel. 321-4659.

Accommodation and Dining

The tourist office will assist you in finding accommodation.

The city has two moderate-standard hotels; the *Özgür*, Tel. 321-1319, next to the central Taksim Square and the nearby modern *Usta*, Tel. 321-2195. *The Horon Hotel*, Tel. 321-1199, across the street, offers less expensive rooms. You will find a good restaurant in the *Özgür Hotel*.

Area code: 462

Trabzon

A view towards Sümela Park from the Sümela Monastery

A row of fortress ruins lines the road to Trabzon, a reminder of the battles for control over the area. 62 miles (100km) before Trabzon, you can stop at Tirebolu and enjoy a visit to the Fortress of St. John and the nearby restaurant.

Trabzon lies on the slopes of Mount Pontus that dip down to the sea, and it has served as a port since the first millennium BC. The importance of Trabzon harbor lies in the city's position on the only convenient passageway through the Pontic mountains from the Black Sea to the Armenian and Persian plateau. Today, Trabzon is in the center of an farming region that excels in growing tea, tobacco and nuts. The city is suitable for walks and as a base for visiting the sights in the area.

History of the City

The ancient name of the city, Trapezos, was given it by settlers from Miletus, who founded the city in the eighth century BC. Hadrian set up the capital of the province Pontus here and built a large port, a temple to Apollo and other public buildings.

The city's prosperity continued in the Byzantine period. In 1204, when the knights of the Fourth Crusade conquered the capital Constantinople, Emperor Alexius Comnenus and his court fled here and set up the Byzantine kingdom of Trabzon. The kingdom lasted over 250 years, until the Ottoman conquest in 1461.

The city is concentrated between the fortress and the city wall in the west and the port in the east. Above the port is the central Taksim square.

Sites to See

There are more than 10 ancient churches in Trabzon, a reminder of the golden era of the Byzantine Empire of Trebizond, from the 13th to the 15th century. Some of the churches were converted into mosques during the Ottoman period. The most impressive church of that period is **Ayasofia Church**, located on the plateau overlooking the sea, some two miles west of the city center. The church, built in the mid-thirteenth century, is enhanced by its perfect proportions and its frescoes depicting scenes from the creation. You can reach the church by bus or *dolmuş*, which serve the residents of the western part of the city.

Atatürk Museum is located in Atatürk Köşkü. The white villa was built by the residents of the city and presented to their adored leader as a summer house. Atatürk only visited here a few times, but the place serves as a tourist attraction, visited by many Turks. The museum houses household items and clothing that belonged to Atatürk, as well as a few documents that have been preserved. Located 2.5 miles (4km) outside of the city in a pine forest, it can be reached by city bus or *dolmuş*.

The Trabzon Vicinity

In the beautiful mountainous area around Trabzon, you will find small picturesque villages and Armenian monasteries that have been abandoned over the centuries, such as the Kaymaklı and Kızlar monasteries. You can reach these remote places on the narrow roads and dirt paths leading southeast from the city. The monasteries now serve the surrounding villages for agricultural purposes. A trip through this area serves more as an introduction to a remote culture than a guided tour of a reconstructed and renovated site.

Sümela Monastery

The most amazing sight in the area, and a "must," is the Sümela Monastery (Sümela Meryem Ana). The winding road from Trabzon leads south to the village of Maçka, and from there to **Sümela Park**, consisting of 10 miles (17km) of spectacular, lush green scenery. Sümela Park is a marvelous forest crossed by a stream running between towering hills. The path up to the monastery ascends from the parking lot, and the climb is accompanied by a breathtaking view of the park.

Upon completing the ascent, the monastery of the Blessed Mary appears before you, seemingly planted in the cliff wall. Inside the building are the ruins of a monastery that was built in the Byzantine period, in the sixth century AD, and dedicated to the Blessed Virgin Mary. The monastery was abandoned in 1923, after the population exchange between Greece and Turkey.

The monastery is open 8:30am-noon and 2-5pm, and the climb takes about 45 minutes. You can reach Sumela from Trabzon by *dolmuş* to Maçka and from there hitch a ride to Sumela, or by *dolmuş* from the **tourist information office** in Taksim Square directly to the monastery. In the Sumela area there are other monasteries as well, such as the Vazelon and Kuştul monasteries, but they are less impressive.

The Sümela Monastery – a spectacular sight

From Trabzon to Hopa

The road from Trabzon east passes through the tea country, with its center **Rize**. The first tea plantation in the area was planted at the time of World War II and tea quickly became the most popular drink in the country. The city serves as a local vacation center. Next to it is the Araklı beach, one of the only bathing beaches in this region. During your stay in the city you should visit the botanical gardens, and enjoy the spectacular view of the bay. The **tourist information office** is located in Müftü Square, Tel. 213-0406. The city's *Fındıkli Turistik Otel 1*, Tel. 511-3368 is a simple, friendly establishment with an excellent restaurant.

Kaçkar

The road from Rize to Hopa brings us into a wild mountainous area, that has only recently been opened to tourists. Hikers are attracted to this region due to the fabulous mountain landscape between the eastern shore and the district capital of Artvin inland. The tourist services in the area are less than minimal, and most visitors sleep and eat in the homes of the villagers, something which enhances the uniquity of the experience.

You can reach this mountainous area from the village of **Pazar**, 25 miles (40km) east of Rize. A few miles past Pazar, a narrow road turns off toward Ayder Kaplıcaları, the hot springs near the village of Çemlihemsin.

From Pazar a *dolmuş* leaves for the village Ayder at 1pm. The village has one hotel, the *Maçka*, and next to it are the hot springs. There are also several stores and a bakery. From the village, a dirt road goes up to Kavron, about a three-hour walk.

Kavron is the summer village of the local shepherds, *Yayla* in Turkish. In Kavron you can leave your equipment, rest and hire a guide to take you to the top of **Mount Kaçkar** (Kaçkar Dağı),whose peak reaches 12,897ft. (3,932m) high. After resting on the spectacular peak, you can return to Kavron and from there go on to one of the villages in the area from which you can get a *dolmuş* to the village of **Yusufeli** and the town **Artvin**. From Artvin you can return to Hopa, or continue along the Georgian border to Kars or Erzurum in Eastern Turkey.

Travelers coming from the Kars area in the east should begin the trip at Yusufeli and end off in **Ayder**. It is extremely important to take food for the way and to hire a local guide from among the Turkish shepherds on this walk. When the sun goes down, the temperature in the high areas drops and you should find a roof for the night.

Hopa

The road along the Black Sea coast ends at the town of Hopa, some 19 miles (30km) before the Georgian border. The remote Hopa does not offer any attractions to the tourist, and with the exception of a single comfortable hotel, *Papila Oteli*, Tel. 351-3641, there are no tourist services here.

Area code: 466

EASTERN TURKEY

A tour of Eastern Turkey is completely different in nature from a visit to the western part of the country and the Anatolian plateau. The physical and human landscape here change entirely: The climate is extreme, from cold and frost in the Eastern Anatolia mountains to blazing heat on the Mesopotamian plains between the Tigris and the Euphrates; the only time to possibly tour here is during the summer. The tourist services, such as public transportation, hotels, restaurants and such are deficient in Eastern Turkey, and tourists to this area must take these difficulties into account when planning their trip.

Traveling through the barren countryside

Eastern Turkey is problematic for the national domestic policy. The area is inhabited by Armenian and Kurdish minorities, who are vehemently opposed to the central Turkish regime, and who have still not relinquished their aspirations for autonomy. It appears that the Turkish government does not want to encourage tourism here, so as not to develop close contact between the minorities and Westerners. The Turkish Ministry of Tourism prefers to invest the meagre means at its disposal in promoting tourism to the classical sites in the western part of the country and to the beaches.

On a more positive note, it is clear that the distance of the east from the bustle of industry and modern development has preserved the pristine character of this land, which attracts those tourists who are prepared to undertake the difficulties involved.

A tour of the east takes the traveler to tranquil villages, where farmers work the land with long-forgotten tools, and to palaces and temples that evoke the magnificent cultures of the past, dating back to the dawn of history. Eastern Turkey also offers marvelous mountain treks, lost cities and remote monasteries.

To cope with the hardships of the trip the traveler should be properly equipped and will need a sleeping bag, a coat and warm clothes for trips to the mountain and the Eastern Anatolian plateau, as well as mosquito repellent, a water canteen and a hat as protection against the oppressive sun in the southeast of the country. In addition, the visitor to the mountain areas must take food for the way because of the sparseness of places to eat once outside of the central cities. The pace of touring the east is slower, and tourists who do not have a car will find it difficult to get to each and every sight. The possibilities for accommodation in the east range from well-established hotels of a fairly low standard to the floors of farmers' houses when no other choice is available.

Visitors to the mountains have a choice of a number of mountain ranges to climb. Mount Ararat can only be climbed in an organized group (see "Mount Ararat"); the Hakkari range, which was a national mountain climbing center has been closed to hikers since the increase in Kurdish guerrilla warfare in 1985. The ranges where you can trek are: Ala Dağları, east of Niğde in the Cappadocian region (the height of the peak is 12,247ft. (3,734m); hikes leave from the town of Çamardı); the Kaçkar range between Kars and the Black Sea coast – the highest peak is 12,913ft. (3,937m); the central city – Yusufeli; the Manzur range between the cities Erzincan and Tunceli – its highest peak is 11,313ft. (3,449m); the main city – Ovacık. Details regarding these mountains and hikes can be obtained from the Turkish Mountaineer Club, Ulus Işhanı A-Blok, Ulus Ankara, Tel. (312) 310-8566, ext. 356 or from the Ministry of Tourism in Ankara, Tel. (312)488-7007 (or Ankara Free Phone "i", Tel. 900-447-090).

The Minorities in Eastern Turkey

The Armenians
The Armenians belong to a people that were found in Eastern Asia prior to the invasion of the Indo-European tribes who came from the plains north of the Black Sea, to which the Georgian tribes also belonged. The Armenian people were the first to accept Christianity as the state religion, a source of pride to them unto this day. Because of their early conversion to Christianity, the Armenian church maintains special rituals, unlike anything else in orthodox Christianity. The patriarch who heads the church sees himself as the heir of Jacob, brother of Jesus, who led the original community of believers in Jerusalem.

Turkish women traditionally dressed

The Armenian history has known a number of periods of prosperity. The first began in the first century BC, under the rule of Tigranes, in which it won full or partial independence. This independence was maintained until the Arab conquest in the seventh century. A period of prosperity came much later during the ninth century AD, under the Bagtarid dynasty, which chose Anı as its capital for two hundred years. The third and last period of glory was when,

between the eleventh and fourteenth centuries, the Armenians left Anı for the area of Kilike on the Mediterranean coast.

Since the Moslem rise to power, the Armenians have suffered persecution. An estimated million Armenians were either murdered by the Ottoman forces in 1915-1916 or died seeking refuge in neighboring countries. In addition to the man-made suffering, frequent earthquakes in the region have taken the lives of many of these people. Today, there are less than one million Armenians in the territory of Armenia which is divided between Turkey, Armenia, Georgia and Azerbijan.

The Kurds

More than half of the Kurdish nation, numbering some 16 million people, live in Turkey, while the rest live in Iran and Iraq. The Kurdish tribes accepted Islam at the time of the Arab conquest in the seventh century AD, but even after their conversion they maintained their Indo-European language and customs of the mountain nomads, which have been part of their culture since the beginning of time. One aspect of this culture was that the Kurds did not establish any large and fortified cities against conquerors, but rather packed their belongings and moved on when battles broke out. Therefore, with the exception of a few local princedoms, no strong Kurdish kingdoms emerged. Most of the foreign conquerors overlooked the unique character of the Kurds.

In the twentieth century the Kurdish minority rebelled a number of times against the central Turkish rule. These uprisings ended in the massacre of the Kurds and their subsequent exile to remote areas. The last outbreak of violence began in 1984, and continuous guerrilla warfare has caused the death of many Kurds throughout the country. The Kurd minority has often been persecuted, and whole villages were destroyed by the army toward the end of the 80's and the beginning of the 90's. In 1991, after the Gulf War, thousands were killed; the survivors fled to their Kurdish brethren, across the border from Iraq to Turkey. Several refugee camps were set up in Eastern Anatolia – and these people have not yet been resettled.

From Kayseri to Erzurum

Most travelers to Eastern Turkey choose to fly from İstanbul to Erzurum, one of the major cities of the east, where they begin their tour. This is the route described below, but for the benefit of land travelers, let's first describe the road that leads to Erzurum through Sivas, from Kayseri in Cappadocia.

Twelve miles (20km) northeast of Kayseri is a famous archeological site dating from the second millennium BC. There is evidence of an Assyrian trade colony that was established here 4,000 years ago, in the nineteenth century BC. This type of colony settlement, set up by Assyrian merchants for commercial reasons on major roads, were called *karum*. This colony, **Kaneş**, was the commercial center of the Assyrians in Anatolia. You can see an Assyrian trade archives in cuneiform, which contain the most ancient documents ever found in Turkey in this form of writing. Many of the findings that were discovered on this site, now called **Kültepe**, are on display in the large museum in Ankara. The site itself was destroyed, and a visit is only of interest to archeologists.

Further on, the road turns in the direction of Malatya. Those continuing toward Sivas will reach **Sultanhanı** 19 miles, (30km) on. This khan was built in 1236 by the Seljuk Sultan Alaeddin Keykûbad I. The khan, which served as a station for the merchant convoys, was cleverly renovated, and it is worth stopping here for a short visit. About 2 hours further northeast on the road, we come to Sivas.

Sivas

This is a distortion of the name of the Roman city, Sebastia. The city was founded in 65 BC by the Roman ruler Pompeius, and throughout history it served as a center of local rule for the kingdoms that conquered the area. Under Seljuk rule, Sivas was one of the most important cities in the Rum Sultanate.

Here, in September 1919, Atatürk convened the Congress for Liberation of the Homeland from its foreign conquerors. Thus, Sivas entered Turkey's political history as one of the first centers of support for Atatürk's republic.

Area code: 346

The **tourist information office**, Tel. 221-3535, is located on Vilayet Konağı, in the central Konak Square, near the post office. Near the square, at 11 Atatürk Cad., is the best hotel in the city, the *Köşk*, Tel. 211-1150, which is not very expensive. The *Sarırvan* restaurant next to the hotel is highly recommended. Simple, inexpensive hotels are located further down the Atatürk Cad., such as the *Evin* at No. 160.

The Seljuks built three theological seminaries in the city in 1271, which are the main attraction for visitors. **Muzaffer Bürücirde Medresesi** is located near Konak Square, and houses the city museum. **Çifte Minare Medresesi** is located southwest of Konak Square, behind the Ottoman Kale Mosque. Only the front of the impressive building of this seminary remains. The third seminary, **Gök Medrese** is the most impressive and most important of the three. You can reach it from the Cumhuriyet Cad., east of the large mosque, **Ulu Cami**. This splendid building was built by Fahrettin Sahipata, who built a similar theological center in Konya.

You can also reach Sivas by air. Flights arrive at the small airport a few times a week from İstanbul and Ankara. A bus leaves for the airport 105 minutes before each flight, from the Turkish Airlines office in the center of the city, Tel. 221-3687. The bus station is located on the main street, Larzingan, and from there you can take a *dolmuş* or taxi to the city center. Direct buses go from the station to Ankara, Kayseri and the eastern cities. Sivas is an important

train junction, but the train service to the city is slow and uncomfortable.

A good road links Sivas and **Erzincan**. Visitors with an interest in the art of Islamic construction should deviate from the main road to reach the town of **Divriği**. Here there is a large mosque (Ulu Cami) and a hospital (Darüşşifa), built in the early thirteenth century. The wonderful Seljuk buildings are some of the most beautiful of their type in all of Turkey. The town is far off the regular tourist route, and with the exception of these buildings it is not particularly interesting. The hotels here are of a very low standard. The road leading to and from the town is hard on cars and drivers. It is best to get here by train (on the line between Sivas and Erzurum).

In 1243, a great battle took place, next to the city of Erzincan, in which the Mongols defeated the Seljuk rulers of the area. The city was considered one of the most beautiful, with many mosques. In December 1939 a powerful earthquake destroyed the city, killing 40,000 people. The city was rebuilt but without any of the grandeur of the past. The well-established *Urarto Hotel* is its best.

Twenty miles (33km) east is **Altıntepe**, the "golden hill." Here we find the ruins of a major settlement of the Urartian kingdom, which was established in the early part of the first millennium BC, in Eastern Anatolia. Graves discovered at the site contained jewelry and beautiful bronze objects, which now decorate the museum in Ankara. You can see the ruins of a palace and of temples over 3,000 years old, and enjoy the breathtaking view of the valley and the snow-capped mountains. In the village of **Tercan**, east of the site, is the impressive twelfth-century tomb of Mana Hatun, which was built in Seljuk style by the rulers of Erzurum. The tomb and the khan alongside it are worth a visit.

Erzurum

Erzurum, the largest city in Eastern Turkey, is situated in a valley surrounded by towering mountains exceeding a height of 9,840ft. (3,000m). The city has more than 300,000 residents, who are forced to cope with the difficult climate

– terrible cold in the winter and burning heat in the summer. In this area a record temperature of -44°C was recorded. The extreme weather conditions are due to the city's elevation, 6,396ft. (1,950m) above sea level.

The importance of Erzurum stems from its location on the trade routes between Europe and the East – from Trabzon on the Black Sea coast to Syria, and from the Aegean coast and the Anatolian plateau to Persia and the Far East. Today, the trade in the city has ceased, but because of its central position and excellent transportation connections, many tourists pass through here on their way to the East.

History of the City

Erzurum was an ancient settlement called Camacha, which belonged to the Armenian kingdom. Toward the end of the fourth century AD, a fortified Byzantine city was established here, named Theodoseopolis, for the Byzantine Emperor, Theodosius. The city was apparently given the name Erzurum by the Seljuk conquerors in the early twelfth century. It means "Roman land," a name that was used by the Turkish tribes for areas under Byzantine rule.

Because of the city's centrality and importance, many armies fought to control it, including the Russian army, which conquered it for a short period in 1882 and again in 1916. Wars and violent earthquakes in the area have destroyed most remnants of the city's rich past, and not many interesting sights remain here. Erzurum maintains a special position in the history of the Turkish Republic: it was here that Atatürk convened the first Turkish National Assembly, in 1919.

An Important Note

Many travelers who stop by the city for a few hours are disappointed by the

Erzurum – the largest city in the East

TURKEY

grey faded look of the Erzurum. The local residents, who have earned a reputation of being stern and silent, are not always friendly to the tourists. Erzurum, however, is the gateway to the East, and here the tourist first gets the sensation of having arrived in a new land, so different from western and central Anatolia. It is a good idea to stay here for a day or two, to visit the ruins that remain and to adjust to the atmosphere of the East.

How to Get There

By air: Erzurum Airport is located 6 miles (10km) west of the city. Daily flights arrive here from İstanbul, via Ankara. The airport is served by a bus from the Turkish Airlines office in the city, *THY*, Tel. 218-1904, which runs in coordination with the flight schedule. A taxi to the city from the airport costs about $5.

By train: The train station is located about a 20-minute walk from the city center, at the northern end of Istasyon Cad. Like other trains in the eastern part of the country, the line to

Traditional carpets in an Oriental setting

Erzurum is slow and not very comfortable, and therefore the bus service is recommended.

By bus: There are good connections between Erzurum and the large Turkish cities, as well as all cities in the east. The trip to İstanbul takes 22 hours, and it is very tiring; the ride to Kars takes 4 hours. The central bus station is located on the road to the airport, outside the city center. It is a short ride to the station, by bus No. 2 or taxi. Those who wish to travel through the Kaçkar mountains (see "The Black Sea") should take a *dolmuş* from Erzurum to the village of **Yusufeli**. The minibus station to Yusufeli is located in northeastern Erzurum, near the *Çoruh Hotel*. Leave early in the morning and return to Erzurum after dark, or stay the night in Yusufeli in one of the village's simple hotels.

Accommodation and Dining

The well-established *Oràl*, 3 Terminal Street, Tel. 218-9740, is the city's highest-standard hotel, and its restaurant is excellent. The hotel is situated far from the city center, on the noisy road to the bus station. More simple and central hotels are *Sefer*, on Istasyon Cad., Tel. 218-6714, and *Büyük Erzurum*, 5 Ali Revi Cad., Tel. 218-6528, which also has a good restaurant. The *Tufan Restaurant* next to the *Kral Hotel*, Tel. 218-7783 is also recommended, particularly for their *pastırma*, a dish of beef dried in the sun and seasoned.

Area code: 442

Tourist Services

The **tourist information office** is located at 9/A Cemal Gürsel Cad., Tel. 218-5697, near Havuzbaşı Square. The post office is located on Cumhuriyet Cad., on the other side of the square. This street leads to the center of the old city, where a number of ruins await the tourist, all within walking distance of each another.

Sites to See

You should start your tour of the city at the **Çifte Minareli Theological College**, with its twin prayer minarets. The thirteenth-century building is similar to the Gök Theological College in Sivas, and it is obvious that the two were inspired by the same Seljuk source. Opposite the lovely college you will find the **Great Mosque** (Ulu Cami), built in 1179 by the local ruler, Abdul Fath Muhammad. With the exception of its size, there is nothing particularly special about this mosque. The builder was a member of the Saltuks, the Seljuk tribe that conquered Erzurum in the early twelfth century and controlled the city until the Mongol conquest in the mid-thirteenth century. The interesting tombs, where the rulers and their families are buried are worth a visit. The site of the **Three Tombs** (Uç Kümbet), including the octagonal tomb of the Sultan Emir, is located 165 yards (150m) south of the Great Mosque.

The **city fortress** (*Erzurum Kalesi*) was built by the Byzantines and renovated several times by the Seljuks and Ottomans. At the western end of the fortress is a Seljuk prayer minaret, **Tepsi Minare**, which in time became a decorative clock tower, and the symbol of the city. The original clock, according to the residents, was taken by Russian conquerors in the nineteenth century. The fortress is located in the center of the city, opposite Çifte Minareli and the Great Mosque.

You can complete your tour of the city at the **City Museum**, where there is the usual archeological exhibit and a nice collection of folk handicrafts. The museum, open daily 8:30am-noon and 1:30-5:30pm, closed Mon., is located about a ten-minute walk down Paşalar Cad., south of Havuzbaşıı Square. In the local bazaar, between the citadel and the train station, you will find many traditional objects, such as the thick woollen shepherd's hats that are still worn today by the local people. Next to the large market is **Rüstem Paşa Çarşısı**, a small and interesting market where you can purchase, among other things, chains of black prayer beads.

From Erzurum to Trabzon

A long, ancient road leads from Erzurum to the village of Aşkale in the mountains above the ruins of the large Byzantine fortress. From Aşkale the road continues to **Bayburt**, where you will find one of the most beautiful and striking fortresses in Turkey, built in the thirteenth century by the Seljuk rulers of the area. From Bayburt the road continues to Gümüşhane and to the **Zigana Pass** on the way to Trabzon. Zigana Pass is the only natural passage in the Pontic Mountains, and follows the ancient caravan route from the Black Sea to Persia and the Far East. It was the most important pass in the ancient world, and was used by Xenophon and his Ten Thousand, by Marco Polo on his way to China and by many others who changed the course of history. The importance of the mountain pass, over 6,560ft. (2,000m) above sea level, explains the many fortresses found along the way.

After Zigana Pass, the road descends toward Maçka and the Sümela Monastery next to it. From Sümela it is a short way to Trabzon and from there to Kars via Artvin.

From Erzurum to Kars

Two roads lead from Erzurum to Kars. The shorter one, used by the bus from Erzurum, is 131 miles (211km) long.

Many travelers prefer to travel from Erzurum to Artvin via the Tortum waterfalls and the village of Yusufeli at the foot of the Kaçkar range. From Artvin they continue to Kars by way of Ardahan (see "The Black Sea"). The length of this route is about 310 miles (500km), all of it on narrow, winding roads. It presents the visitor with marvelous, pristine country, where the peaceful villages have maintained a life style remote from twentieth-century Turkey.

Between Kars and Artvin wide plains stretch out, offering genuinely wonderful views of mud villages with shepherdesses, and flocks of sheep and geese. The plains end at the huge Yalnızçam range, which climbs to a height of over 9,840ft. (3,000m), and the road passes along splendid rivers and streams. The beautiful view compensates for the long and difficult trip.

Kars

Chilly Kars can make even the happiest of visitors feel miserable. The wide muddy streets, organized in a grid, the dusty houses and the silent residents chill the enthusiasm of visitors, who hurry on to the charming Armenian city of Anı.

You can reach Kars by train from Erzurum, but the ride takes twice as long as by bus. During your stay in the city until you go on to Anı, you can visit the interesting museum, where there is a fine exhibit of carpets. The museum is open daily 8am-noon and 1:30-5:30pm, closed Mon. The Kars Fortress houses a military base which is closed to the public.

The hotels in the city are very disappointing. Kars was chosen in a survey of British backpackers, as the city with the worst tourist facilities in the world. If you have no choice, you can try the *Yılmaz Hotel*, Tel. 223-1074, near the bus station, where you can get a room and alcoholic beverages, which may somewhat improve the look of the city...

Area code: 474

Anı

The trip to Anı should be organized in Kars, as the ancient city is located along the Armenian border.

The ticket seller at the entrance to the local museum can help you organize the trip, and will give you updated details. He has application forms for

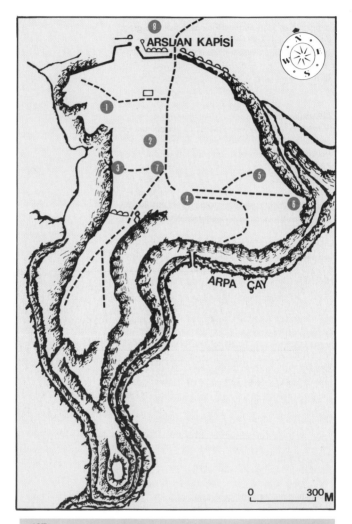

ANI

1. Church of St. Gregory (built by Gagik I)
2. Church of the Apostles
3. Church of St. Gregory (built by Pahlavuni)
4. Cathedral
5. Church of the Redemption
6. Church of St. Gregory (built by Tigran Honents)
7. Prayer minaret
8. Gate of the Lions (Arslan Kapisi)

visitors' permits to Anı, and will introduce you to a taxi driver, who will take you to the site for about $12. The taxi driver will take you to the local police station, where you will receive the permit. From there you continue on to an army camp, where you will have to leave your cameras, and then to another camp, where a Turkish soldier will join the group. At all points, documents and permits are examined, but the local residents are used to performing their tasks, and in the end you will reach your destination.

Sites to See

The tragedy of the Armenian people, which one can feel with any visit to the Armenian plateau, becomes most tangible in Anı, "The City of a Thousand and One Churches." The lovely city, once a capital populated by more than 100,000 people, is now a ghost town, so well preserved that at times it creates the impression that at any moment the king and his subjects will return from a short vacation of 500 years.

The name Anı apparently originated from a distortion of the name of the Persian Goddess Anahis. This goddess was one of the main gods in the Armenian pantheon before the nation's Christianization. After the death of Alexander the Great and the disintegration of his kingdom, the city was established as an important station on the famous Silk Route. The golden era of Anı began in the mid-tenth century AD, when the Bagtarid kings chose it as the capital of Armenia. The royal dynasty claimed that they were descendants of David of Jerusalem, and under their rule, the city flourished to become one of the four major cities of the world in the eleventh century – together with Constantinople, Cairo and Baghdad.

During its years of prosperity, the city's architecture developed greatly. The major invention in this area was the development of the dome over the central point in a structure. The modern observer may take the domes in the Armenian churches for granted, but this invention and its development made a crucial contribution to the transition from the ancient temple, with its single, horizontal story, to magnificent buildings with splendid niches and domes, in which several structures are actually combined. From Armenia this type of construction, known as the "Romanesque style," spread to Byzantium and Europe.

The tour of the city begins at one of the four gates in the city wall, the **Gate of the Lions** (*Arslanı Kapısı*), which leads to the main street. The most beautiful building seen from this special view is undoubtedly the **cathedral**. Its construction was begun in 989 by King Sembat II, and was completed in 1001 by Gagik I. The cathedral was built by the famous architect Tırdat, who renovated the Ayasofia in İstanbul after it was damaged in an earthquake in the tenth century. In addition to the cathedral, there are many beautiful churches in the city, such as the two dedicated to St. Gregory.

The death of Gagik I in 1020 marks the beginning of the disintegration of the city and the kingdom. The Seljuks captured the city in 1064, the rest of the kingdom followed in 1071. In the early fourteenth century the city suffered a strong earthquake. This, and the invasion by the cruel Mongol Tamerlane, drove the inhabitants out of the city, and there is no evidence of the existence of a settlement here after the mid-fourteenth century.

On from Kars

The road from Kars to the foot of Mount Ararat passes through the town of Tuzluco, famous for its salt mines, and continues near the Russian border to Iğdir. This town has several simple hotels, among them the *Kral*. The road from Iğdir north goes around Mount Ararat for 35 miles (55km), passing through the basalt plateau at a height of 6,560ft. (2,000m) until reaching Doğubeyazıt.

Doğubeyazıt

Doğubeyazıt is located only 21 miles (35km) west of the Iranian border. Before Khomeini's rise to power, which closed the doors to Iran, and prior to the Russian invasion of Afghanistan, the little city was one of the stops on the route from Europe to the Far East. Since the land traffic has ceased, Doğubeyazıt has again become a sleepy town.

In the town itself there are no special sights, but the interesting sights in the area justify a stay of at least one day. Four miles (6km) east of the city is the impressive **Işak Paşa Palace**, built over a period of 100 years, and completed in 1784 by the Kurdish ruler Ishak. The extraordinary beauty of the splendid castle overlooking Mt. Ararat makes a visit to it a "must" for any visitor to Eastern Turkey. From the city you can reach the palace by taxi or *dolmuş*, but the best way is on foot, weather permitting. Other sights near Doğubayazıt, although less impressive, include an Ottoman mosque and the ruins of a Urartian city from the early part of the first millennium BC. There is nothing particularly special about these sights, and you won't miss much if you decide not to visit them.

Some 25 miles (40km) east of Doğubeyazıt, along the road leading to the Iranian border, you will find two natural sights. One is a large **crater** about which there is some controversy as to how it was formed, one theory suggests by a meteor and another by natural geological forces. The other is an **ice cave** that penetrates deep into the mountain,

The Işak Paşa Palace

where the low temperatures, which are maintained all year round, freeze the water flowing there, and give it its name. Do not enter the dark cave without a flashlight. To get there, hire a *dolmuş* in Doğubeyazıt.

The hotels in the city are surprisingly pleasant, especially the *Isfehan*, located outside the city center, at 26 Emniyet Cad., Tel. 215-5139. It is also known by its former name, the *Ararat Hotel*. The friendly hotel, which is not inexpensive, has an excellent restaurant and a Turkish bath, which will help you get rid of the dust that is so plentiful in this part of the country. Another good hotel, *Simer*, Tel. 215-5601, is located on the road to the Iranian border, 3 miles (5km) from the city. Simpler hotels, with inexpensive rooms or beds in large communal dormitories, can be found on the main street of the city.

Area code: 472

Mount Ararat (Agrı Dağı)

The residents of Turkey object to the use of the name Ararat, which is derived from the ancient Urartian kingdom. The high mountain, with its peak 16,940ft. (5,165m) high, is called Büyük Ağrı Dağı, the Great Ağrı Mountain, in Turkish, after the Ağrı region in which it is located.

The fame of the mountain is derived from the story of the Creation. The Armenians see the mountain as the center of the world, and believe that they originated from this mountain. According to tradition, this mountain is the roof of the world, and the Tigris and Euphrates rivers come down through it from the Garden of Eden to fertilize the Mesopotamian plains.

The Işak Paşa Palace took 100 years to build

"And the ark rested in the seventh month, on the seventeenth day of the month, upon the mountains of Ararat. And the waters decreased continually until the tenth month: in the tenth month, on the first day of the month, were the tops of the mountains seen." (Genesis 6:4-5). Recently the mountain has attracted several groups who have tried to find Noah's lost ark. A

famous team, which failed in its search in 1982, was led by the American astronaut James Irwin. Reports, as yet unproven, reported a structure or large rock in the image of the ark on one of the peaks of the mountain.

Tourism to the mountain is still in its infancy. The Ministry of Tourism is in the process of opening a tourist center at the bottom of the mountain, to facilitate visits, but in the meantime, the possibilities for touring the Ararat are very limited. Because of its proximity to the Iranian border it is considered a military zone and you must have written permission obtained in Ankara in order to visit here. The hike itself is extremely dangerous because of the weather, the ruthless sheep dogs and the many smugglers who use various routes on the mountain to escape the law.

The only existing way to see the mountain is to join an organized group. The route climbs up the southern slope, where there are two camps for hikers. The ascent up the mountain beyond these camps requires special mountaineering equipment. The agencies in İstanbul that organize treks to the mountain are *Trektravel* in Taksim Square, Tel. 255-1624, and *Metro Turism* on İnönü Cad., Tel. 243-2438.

In Doğubayazit, *Ahmet Ağa* organizes similar hikes. Additional details about hiking on the mountain are available from the Turkish Mountaineer Club (see the introduction to this chapter).

From Doğubayazıt to Van

A direct road from Doğubayazıt to the city of Van passes through the village of Çaldıran and along the Bendimahi river. This road is snowed-in from September to May, and in the summer, is open to traffic in the daytime only, but even then road conditions are fairly poor making driving difficult. This is the road taken by the *dolmuş* connecting the two cities. The Muradiye waterfalls and the ancient bridge over the river may be reason enough to make this difficult, but scenic, trip.

Blue and tranquil – Lake Van

The main road, 155 miles (250km), longer than the direct road is well-paved. From Doğubayazıt it goes back west to the city of **Ağrı**, the capital of the district. There is nothing of particular interest in this town and it is mainly used by travelers as a transit point to change buses to Van or to rest for the night in one of the simple hotels, such as the *Divan*. From Ağrı the road winds south to Erciş on the shores of Lake Van.

Van

The modern city of Van is a trade and transportation center, which attempts to prosper in the face of the many errors made in the city plan since its establishment, after the First World War. Among these mistakes, the 100,000 residents of the city would include: building the city some 3 miles (5km) from the shore of the lake, establishing the major university of Eastern Turkey in Erzurum rather than Van and other urban problems. Van is developing as the bridgehead of progress in the east. The city offers good tourist facilities and transportation. It is the easternmost station of the train service and of the Turkish Airlines, and buses, *dolmuşes* and ferries link the city to important cities in Turkey in general, and to the east especially.

Alongside the modern city is the old city of Van, which has a rich history. The old city of Van whose origins are the ancient city of Tuhspa, capital of the Urartian kingdom. The Urartians conquered the city in the ninth century BC, evidently after the disintegration of the kingdom of Hurria, of which historic Van had been the capital since the second millennium BC. The new rulers named their capital Tuhspa after the god of the storm. The ancient city flourished in the ninth to eight centuries BC, particularly during the reign of King Menua, under whose leadership the city and the kingdom became the most central force in this part of the world. When Urartu weakened, the city fell first to Medes, then to Persia and finally to Alexander the Great, and was all but destroyed. Valashav, King of Armenia, renewed the settlement of the city during the mid-second century BC, and from that time the majority of the city's population was Armenian until the terrible massacre of 1915-16.

Accommodation and Dining

The best hotel in the city, *Akdamar*, located at 22 Kazim Cad., west of the local Ministry of Tourism, Tel. 216-8100, has an excellent restaurant. Next to the ministry is another well-established hotel, *Büyük Urartu Oteli*, at 16 Cumhuriyet Cad., Tel. 212-0660. The quiet *Tekin Hotel*, Tel. 216-1366, completes the city's leading trio. There are a number of simpler hotels in the city, and they are more comfortable and modern than is usual for non-luxury hotels in Eastern Turkey. Of these the *Bayram* *Hotel*, 1 Cumhuriyet Cad., offers guests hot baths and is recommended.

Area code: 432

Tourist Services

The *tourist information office* in Van is located at 37 Cumhuriyet Cad, Tel. 216-2018. The city bus station and *dolmuşes* are located at the northern end of this street, and the post office is situated between the information office and the *dolmuş* station.

Sites to See

The only tourist attraction in the city is the **museum**, located opposite the post office on Cumhuriyet Cad. The museum is open daily 9am-noon and 1-5:30pm, closed Mon. In the archeological exhibit you should note the Urartian jewellry, and in the ethnographic exhibit, the Kurdish weaving is particularly noteworthy.

The **Rock Fortress** (*Van Kalesi*) is an impressive sight despite the damage it has suffered at the hands of man and the ravages of time. The Rock of Van, some 2 miles from the city, towers 328ft. (100m)

Crossroads in Van

high, with the ancient city located around it. It is worth going up to the top of the fortress, to capture a view of the region and the city, which was one of the largest in Anatolia during the first millennium AD, and which was finally destroyed in the Russian invasion during the First World War. You can get to the fortress from the *dolmuş* station in Van, opposite the *Bayram Hotel*. The *dolmuş* takes passengers to the parking lot at the foot of the rock. Upon completing the visit, you can get back to the city with the *dolmuş*, which collects passengers at the same spot where you began. The view from the fortress is particularly magnificent here at dusk.

There are other remains of the Urartian kingdom two miles northeast of Van. **Toprakkale**, the "Fortress," was one of Urartu's most important cities. The ancient site is located in an army camp, and you must have a permit from the governor of Van to visit. True archeology buffs will not want to miss it, but most other tourists will suffice with a visit to the Rock Fortress in Van.

From Van you can fly to Ankara. The bus to the airport leaves the Turkish Airlines office in the city (Tel. 216-1241), an hour and half before take-off time. The city train station is located in the north of the city. There is another station on the shore of the lake, where the train boards the ferry on its way to İstanbul. In the tourism information office you can find out what time the ferry from Teheran that carries the train leaves. The train schedule is "flexible," and loading it onto the ferry takes quite a while. The trip across the lake to Tatvan takes about five hours. Tickets are purchased on board the ferry. The new bus station is located in the north-western part of the city, and bus lines reach other cities in the east, such as Diyarbakır, Malatya and Erzurum.

Before leaving the city you should visit the stores that sell Kurdish handicrafts such as *kilim*, clothing, belts and saddlebags. Van serves as the showcase of the Kurdish region around it. The charming and unusual handicrafts, produced by methods that are hardly used anywhere today, are displayed by the different merchants. They are worth seeing and even purchasing – if possible.

From Van to Hakkâri

Many travelers use the convenient tourist facilities in Van, and set out from there on day trips around the area. The most interesting trip is to Hakkari, 124 miles (200km) southeast of Van, in the heart of the Kurdish region. The trip to **Hakkari** presents the visitor with splendid mountain scenery and the ruins of a glorious past. The area was once a major spot for mountain climbing, especially on the Cilo-Sat mountains. Today hikes in these mountains are often forbidden because of the Kurdish guerrilla activity. You are advised to enquire on arrival.

Fourteen miles (22km) southeast of Van is the royal fortress **Çavuştepe**. The palace and its temples served the kings of Urartu as a place of residence and for rituals. The lower temple is better preserved than the other buildings here, and it includes polished basalt plaques inscribed in cuneiform.

Further south on the road 28 miles (45km) on is a

Lake Van is the largest lake in Turkey

striking Kurdish castle, **Hoşap Fortress**, built in the sixteenth century and renovated in the mid-seventeenth century by the Kurdish ruler, Sarı Süleyman. A visit to the impressive castle begins at the lovely ancient bridge near the village of Güzelsu, and from there a dirt path leads up the cliff to the massive entrance gate. It is worth visiting the fortress, which contained more than 300 rooms, baths, mosques and more.

During your visit here you might ponder on the disadvantages of genius: it is said that the Kurdish ruler was so pleased with the impressive fortress that he ordered the hands of the talented architect to be cut off, so that he could never built a similar castle...

From Hoşap fortress, the road goes up to Başkale and ascends mountain passes at a height of over 8,200ft. (2,500m) above sea level, before coming to Hakkâri, a town of 20,000 residents. The view is breathtaking. In Hakkâri and its environs you can see the nomadic Kurdish tribes setting up black tents on the hills and in the valley, in search of good grazing land for their herds. Mount Cilo, opposite the town, looms 13,671ft. (4,168m) over the Iraqi border, and it is one of the highest peaks in the country. Simple hotels serve the tourists who remain in town after dark. Because of tension between the Kurdish minorities and the authorities, no traffic is allowed in the area except on the main roads during the day. Evening travel is forbidden and you must check with the tourist office in Van as to what time the buses leave. Most travelers leave Van early in the morning by bus and return by the late afternoon, after a full day of mountain roads and Kurdish villages.

Around Lake Van

Lake Van is the largest lake in Turkey; it covers 1,485sq./miles (3,765 sq./km). Located 5,576ft. (1,700m) above sea level, it was formed when lava from the volcanic eruptions blocked up the valley of Mount Nemrut, which today is west of the lake. The lake water contains many minerals; it is oily to the touch and not fit for drinking, swimming in the lake is also unpleasant. The residents of the area use the water for cleaning clothes without having to add soap.

Akdamar

The road from Van west passes through the shores of the lovely lake. About a mile after Gevaş is the mooring for the boats, that sail to the small island of Akdamar, in the middle of the lake. The trip to the island and to the famous church there is a "must" for any visitor to the area, and only takes about 15 minutes. The Armenian King Gagik built a splendid church and monastery on the island, between 915-921 AD. The thousand-year-old *Church of the Holy Cross* (*Akdamar Kilisesi*) has been preserved in good condition. Particularly interesting here are the

The Church of the Holy Cross on Akdamar Island

wall reliefs, in which you can see depictions of biblical stories: such as Adam and Eve, Abraham and Isaac, David and Goliath, Jonah and the whale. The inside of the church is less interesting than its exterior.

The boats leave the platform in the morning and afternoon, (whenever enough passengers have assembled there). It is a good idea to take things with you to the island to have a picnic in the sun. At the end of the visit you can return to Van, about a half-hour ride from the mooring, or go on to Tatvan, on the western side of the lake.

Tatvan

Tatvan is not particularly interesting, and serves tourists as a transit point on their way to and from Van, by bus or ferry. The ferry trip takes four hours, twice as long as the bus ride along the shores of the lake. The boats leave several times a day.

In Tatvan there are a few simple hotels, the best of them the *Van Gölü Hotel* on the shore of the lake, outside the city center. *Karaman* is a simple and inexpensive hotel in the center of town, and opposite it is a simple, good restaurant.

Mount Nemrut

From Tatvan you can take an interesting trip to the top of Mount Nemrut (*Nemrut Dağı*), 10,004ft. (3,050m) high (this mountain should not be confused with the mountain of the same name that has an ancient temple with large stone statues). In

A shepherd and his herd on Mount Nemrut

the crater of the volcano there are several lakes and hot springs. You can bathe in a boiling spring and then go into a cave where water gushes out of the earth – a genuine natural bath house. The pumice stone found here is extremely lightweight.

The last eruption of the volcano, whose crater is over 4 miles (7km) in diameter, was in the mid-fifteenth century. There are no permanent settlements on the mountain and except for seasonal shepherds, who bring their herds here at the end of the snowy period, no one lives here.

It is only possible to visit in the summer. You can reach the summit by private car or by hiring a taxi or *dolmuş* in Tatvan, depending on the number of passengers. There is a camping area on the mountain. It is not advised to rely on the small restaurant here – bring food and water for the time you intend to stay.

Ahlat

From Tatvan you can continue by *dolmuş* from the center of town northeast around the large lake, making the first stop in **Ahlat**. The city, originally Armenian, prospered in the period prior to the Ottoman conquest, and you can see many tombs and mausoleums here. The most handsome and famous tomb was built in 1273 for the Seljuk ruler of the city, and is known today as **Ulu Türbe**, the great tomb. A sixteenth-century citadel on the shore of the lake is a remnant from the Ottoman period. North of Ahlat is the ancient Menzikert, where, in 1071, the Seljuk armies, led by Sultan Alp Arslan, defeated the Byzantine army, thereby opening the way to central Anatolia for the Turkish tribes. This eventually led to the establishment of the Ottoman Empire. Today, the city is called Malazgirt, but except for its historical significance, there is little here that is likely to attract the traveler.

Area code: 434

Some 18 miles (30km) east of Ahlat, the road comes to the large village of **Adilcevaz**. The village is located on an ancient site of the Urartian kingdom, next to which are the ruins of a Seljuk citadel. The village is located at the foot of Mount Süphan, which is the second highest mountain in Turkey, 14,543ft. (4,434m) above sea level. From this village you can climb to the citadel which is built in a marvelous location, 7,216ft. (2,200m) high. Hire a local guide from the village to show you around Mount Süphan for a trip of two days or longer. This is possible only in July and August.

From Adilcevaz the road around the lake continues to Erciş, where our trip around the large lake ends.

Bitlis

A short trip west from Tatvan brings the traveler to Bitlis. This picturesque town, inhabited by Kurds and Armenians who make their living from agriculture, particularly tobacco and honey, is located on a historically important trade route. The beautiful **Şerefiye Mosque** was built by a local Kurdish leader in the early sixteenth century. Another interesting mosque is the twelfth-century **Great Mosque** (Ulu Cami). In addition to these mosques, both located on the main street, it is worth going up to the splendid observation point in the Byzantine citadel, overlooking the city. Bitlis river, which is one of the tributaries of the Tigris, flows through Bitlis, making it a green area in the midst of a dry plain.

Area code: 434

The *Turist Hotel*, superb in its simplicity and cleanliness, is located in the city center.

From Bitlis you can take an interesting trip to **Siirt**, a Kurdish town not generally included in tour routes. The ancient city knew prosperous times under the Babylonians and Assyrians, and the interesting buildings in the city include the Seljuk Great Mosque (Ulu Cami), built in the early twelfth century, and a Seljuk bath house from the same century.

Important: Siirt is considered one of the eastern strongholds of the Kurdish guerrillas; in recent years there were even some violent clashes between government forces and the Kurdish fighters near here. You should inquire about the current political situation before visiting.

Silvan

The road from Bitlis to Diyarbakır goes through the town of Silvan, which was apparently founded in the first century BC as the capital of Armenia. It was fortified by the Byzantine Emperor Justinian, and thereafter served as a fortified border town between Byzantium and Persia. No interesting sites from its magnificent past remain in the town and with the exception of the large twelfth-century mosque, there is nothing to detain you before continuing another 62 miles (100km) to Diyarbakır.

Diyarbakır

If the Kurdish minority ever achieve their aspirations for autonomy and found their own state – Diyarbakır is the first candidate for its capital. As you pass through the gates of this romantic city and walk among the black basalt buildings to the market, populated with farmers in baggy sack pants and women dressed in black, you pass through a barrier of time and culture, something which happens from time to time in Eastern Turkey.

Diyarbakır is situated on the banks of the Tigris. The ancient city, surrounded by a wall, is located between the river on the east and the new city on the west. Istasyon Cad. connects the train station and the old city through one of the four original gates of the city. The gates were named for the destinations to which they led: Urfa Gate, Mardin Gate, and so on. Recently, additional entrances were opened in the wall in order to relieve the city's traffic problem.

History of the City

Evidence indicates that there was a settlement here as far back as the Bronze Age, in the third millennium BC. The city has been witness to the rise and fall of empires: Hurri, Urartu, Assyria, Persia, Greece and Rome were the most prominent of the conquering nations, but the history of the city includes many others. The character of the city today is a result of its conquest in 640 by Arab tribes. The tribe that settled in the city was called Beni Bakır, and it was they who changed its Roman name, Amida, to Diyar Bakır, "the land of the Bakırs." After the Arab conquest, the city had Moslem rulers from different nations, until the Ottoman conquest in the early sixteenth century. In the course of these years, the city maintained its Moslem-Kurdish character.

How to Get There

By air: Daily flights arrive here from Ankara. The flight takes some 80 minutes and arrives at the airport located slightly west of the city. Those flying to İstanbul can use Ankara as a transit point or take a direct flight (only once a week). From the airport you can reach the city center by bus or taxi.

By train: You can reach Diyarbakır by train from İstanbul, Ankara and Erzurum, but it is preferable to travel by bus, which is quicker and operates according to schedule. The *Kurtalan Ekspresi* train may be convenient for passengers returning directly to İstanbul from Diyarbakır – the sleeping car is quite comfortable, and the journey takes 19 hours. The train station is located at the end of Istasyon Cad., west of the old city.

By bus: The bus station, *otogar*, is located 2.5 miles (4km) north of the city. Buses arrive here from other cities in the east, such as Van,

Erzurum, Kâhta and Urfa. Others leave for Anda on the Mediterranean coast and other major cities in the country. From the bus station you can get a *dolmuş* or taxi to the northern gate (*Dağ Kapısı*) of the old city

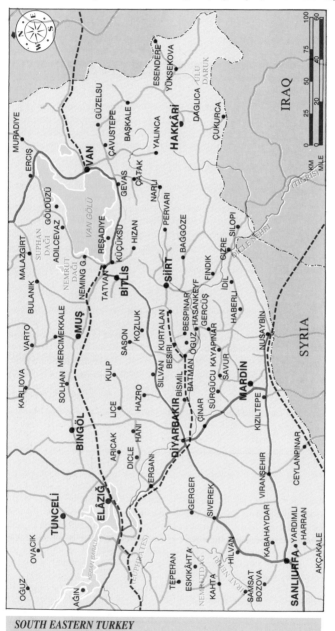

SOUTH EASTERN TURKEY

wall. The bus to Mardin leaves from the southern Mardin Gate once an hour.

Area code: 412

Tourist Services

The **tourist information office** is located at 24/A Lise Cad., Tel. 221-2173, in the new city, between Cumhuriyet Square and Ziya Gökalp Cad. The central post office is located in the old city, near the north-eastern entrance gate (*Hindi Baba Kapısı*). Another branch is located in the center of the old city, near the intersection of Gazi and Yenikapı Streets.

Accommodation and Dining

The *Büyük Hotel*, at 4 Inönü Cad., Tel. 221-5833 is the best in the city.

Another hotel that is not inexpensive is the nearby *Demir*, Tel. 221-2315. Both are located within the old city walls, offering easy access for a tour of the city. In the area between Inönü Cad. and the northern gate (*Dağ Kapısı*) there are simple and inexpensive hotels such as the *Derya*, Tel. 221-4966 and *Aslan*, Tel. 221-3971, close to the *Büyük*. The least expensive hotels are located near the *Demir*, among them is the *Surkent* at 19 Izzet Paşa Cad.

As in most of Turkey, the possibilities for eating in the city are varied, from grilled meat stands (*Kebapçı*) to fine restaurants. Among the latter we note those in the two good hotels, as well as the *Hacibabe* near the northern gate and the *Beş Kardeş*. Here it is worth trying the lamb dishes and having watermelon, the symbol of the city, for dessert.

Sites to See

The impressive **city wall** is 4 miles (5.5km) long. It was erected by the Byzantines at the end of the third century AD, evidently on the foundations of an older Roman wall. The wall had four gates, one in each direction.

A colorful collection of Turkish artifacts

The tour along the wall can be made in a *fayton* – a horse-driven carriage – or on foot. Carriages await tourists near the citadel at the northeastern corner of the wall. In certain parts you can also climb the wall and walk on it. Try to explain to the carriage driver that you want to go up and walk along on the wall and that he should wait for you at the end of the route.

An especially nice walk along the wall is up to the observation point over the Tigris from the **New Gate** (*Yenikapı*) in the eastern part of the city, and from there to the southern **Mardin Gate** (*Mardin Kapısı*). It is easier to walk on the wall between Mardin Gate and the western **Urfa Gate** (*Urfa Kapısı*), and at dusk this is a particularly beautiful walk.

The **Northern Gate** (*Dağ Kapısı*) is the best preserved and most impressive. From here, turn toward the citadel at the northeast corner, and go through the handsome **Palace Gate** (*Saray Kapısı*). The palace, which today is used as an army camp, was the home of the Turkish-Artukid rulers between the eleventh and fifteenth centuries.

There are several mosques in the old city. From the Northern Gate, Gazi Cad. follows the ancient Roman road to the southern Mardin Gate. A walk along the street takes us to a lovely sixteenth-century khan, **Hasan Paşa Hanı**, and opposite it the Great Mosque, **Ulu Cami**, the most impressive mosque in the city. It was built in the late eleventh century, just a few years after the Seljuk Sultan Malik Şah conquered the city. This is the largest ancient Seljuk mosque in Anatolia, and was built in Arab style, according to the model of the great mosque in Damascus. This represents the beginning of the style in which the Anatolian mosques were built, a style which was developed and perfected by Sinan. You should not miss out on a visit to this mosque when visiting the city.

From the Great Mosque, continue north to Ziya Gökalp Cad. and the **museum** housed in an ancient theological college bearing the name of the street. The lively **market** of Diyarbakır is opposite the eastern side of the Great Mosque. It is considered the cheapest market in the country for carpets and Kurdish handicrafts. Even if you don't intend to buy anything, take a walk through the market alleys, which may well include sharing a hand-rolled cigarette and some light conversation over a cup of *çay* with a merchant, with a lot of time on his hands.

You probably won't leave the market without at least one package.

Special Events

Toward the end of September the Watermelon Festival is held here, with a watermelon-growing competition as the main event. In the past, the local farmers will tell you, the watermelons grew to a weight of 154lbs (70kg) and more, but watermelons are not what they used to be, and the winner of the contest usually weighs "only" 110lbs (50kg). In addition to the competitions there is a large, joyful agricultural festival.

On from Diyarbakır

From Diyarbakır you can continue your trip in two directions. One is west, toward Cappadocia and western Turkey, with a visit to the wonderful summit of Mount Nemrut on the way. The other is south, to Mardin, and from there west toward the Iskenderun Bay and the Mediterranean coast.

Mount Nemrut (Nemrut Dağı)

Between Diyarbakır and **Adıyaman**, 111 miles (180km) to the west, lies Mount Nemrut and the temple on its peak, a definite must. As your base, you can choose **Kâhta**, at the foot of the mountain, or Adıyaman, some 25 miles (40km) from Kâhta.

The **Temple of Antiochus** was built during the Commagene realm, which was founded at the beginning of the first century BC by the local ruler, Mithradates, whose small kingdom lay between Adiyaman and Gaziantep. Mithradates's son, Antiochus, saw himself as a great ruler, a successor of Darius the Persian and Alexander the Great. In order to glorify his name, Antiochus built this magnificent temple, and inside he placed statues of himself, next to those of famous gods, such as Zeus and Hercules. The amazing location of the temple on top of Mount Nemrut, at a height of 6,888ft. (2,100m) above sea level, makes this site an eternal monument to the vanity of man. Ironically the temple never had any historical or cultural significance and had been completely forgotten, until it was discovered by chance in a geological study in the 1880's.

The Romans overthrew King Antiochus in the year 38 BC, and thus put an end to the tiny kingdom, which was eventually annexed to the Roman Empire and disappeared from history.

Those staying in Kâhta can find accommodation for the night in the simple Merhaba hotel, which is the best available. The *Nemrut Tur*, which has a good restaurant, or the *Euphrat* are other options. The *Zeus Hotel* is close to the temple. The windswept town also has a number of inexpensive pensions, such as the *Kommagene*, and a few neglected camping grounds. The hotel and pension owners here take advantage of the fact that visitors only stay for one night, and treat them accordingly.

For those who do not have their own transportation, the hotel owners offer two tours, both leaving the town about two hours before sunrise. The shorter and less expensive tour is from Kâhta to the temple at the top of Mount Nemrut; the visit to the site and back to Kâhta costs about $35. The longer trip goes on from the peak to Eski Kale, the capital of the ancient Commagene kingdom, where there is a nice statue of Mithradates, the father of Antiochus. From Eski Kale, the minibus continues to a fourteenth-century fortress (*Yeni Kale*), where there is a good view of the valley, and returns to Kâhta via the tombs of the nobility of the Commagene kingdom in Karakuş. The price of the longer tour is about $45. The other sights on the long tour are not particularly interesting, especially for visitors who wish to recover from lack of sleep and the freezing cold that accompany sunrise on Mount Nemrut.

The temple and the way leading to it are very impressive and they justify the effort and cost of a visit. The hotel owners put their visitors on the *dolmuş* that leaves at 2am and gets to the peak before sunrise, in freezing cold and wind. The trip to the mountain temple is relatively expensive in terms of Turkish transportation. As the sun rises, an unusual and special sight emerges, the exposed mountain with the ruins of the temple and huge stone statues, some of them only heads.

After the tour of the expansive site you can enjoy a cup of hot *çay* at the restaurant at the entrance to the site. As for food, you should bring your own. The *dolmuş* waits at the entrance and returns to the town via an extremely impressive **Roman bridge** over one of the tributaries of the Euphrates.

From Kâhta you can continue to Adiyaman for a rest from the busy night, or continue to tour to **Maraş** on your way to western Turkey and the Mediterranean coast.

Important: Visitors to Kâhta are exposed to terrible pressure from the moment they get off the bus. Characters speaking a little of every language pressure tourists to stay at hotels and go on tours that they organize, making empty promises. It is best to ignore them and plan the kind of trip you want yourself.

Another way to get to the temple is on a hike from the other side of the mountain. Go from **Malatya** to the village of Büyüköz, where the only accommodation is in farmers' homes, on a mattress on the floor. From the tiny village a direct road leads up the mountain, about a three-hour walk. If you plan to see the sunrise over the mountain, you must wear very warm clothing against the freezing cold, during all seasons of the year.

After your visit to Mount Nemrut, those interested

Remains from the Temple of Antiochus on Mt. Nemrut

in returning to Cappadocia in the Anatolian plateau should take the short route to Kayseri through the cities Elâzig and Malatya. This route is suitable for visitors who want to end their tour of Eastern Turkey with Mount Nemrut.

Mardin

At about a two-hour ride south of Diyarbakır lies Mardin, on a mountainside near the Syrian border. Because there are few visitors to the city, it has not developed such services as a tourist information office or reasonable hotels. The only hotel that is suitable for Western tourists is the 4 star *Nezirhan Hotel*, Tel. 415-1425. There are hourly minibuses to the city from Diyarbakır, and buses go on from Mardin to Urfa.

Mardin is an ancient city which, like all settlements in the Mesopotamian plain between the Tigris and the Euphrates, dates back to the roots of human civilization. The most important sight in the city is **Isa Bey Medresesi**, built in the late fourteenth century as a center for Islamic studies, and today houses a local museum. The museum is interesting both for its exhibits and because of the beautiful building and its ornate entrance.

The museum is located under the **City Citadel** (*Kale*), which was built on Roman foundations, when the city was still called Marida. The building itself is rather disappointing, but the view of the Syrian plains is ample compensation. The border crossing to Syria is located in the town of Masuaybin, about an hour east of the city.

The Monastery Region

East of Mardin is the **Türabdin** region, the "plain of the servants of God." The area is a center of orthodox Syrian monasteries. This Christian sect developed under Theodora, the wife of Emperor Justinian, in the fifth century AD. At its height, there were some 200 monasteries and churches in the area. Tourists can visit the **Zafaran Monastery** (*Deyrul Zafaran*), some 4 miles (6km) east of Mardin, or take a day tour (or longer) to the ancient and active monasteries, such as Mar Yakoub and Mar Malki. The central monastery in the area is **Mar Gabriel**, located approximately 12 miles (20km) east of Midyat, it is the most populated, being the residence of the bishop and just under 20 monks and nuns. Mar Gabriel was founded in the fifth century AD, and housed some 5,000 people at its peak, more than a thousand years ago.

In all the active monasteries mentioned you can spend a Spartan-type night and eat with the monks. The only payment requested is to observe the prayer service. There is little public transportation to the area. **Important:** The plateau is scorching in the summer, and you should not go out without a hat and water.

Area Code: 482

Şanlıurfa

Şanlıurfa, also known as Urfa, is a true pearl; it shows itself only to the most patient of tourists. Visitors who visit the scorching city for a few hours will probably be disappointed with the appearance of the city and its tranquil sights. The heat in the summer and the slow pace of the city dictate a different kind of tourist behavior. If you cannot remain in Urfa and the area at least two days, it may be better to forego a visit to the city, which has been in existence for more than 5,000 years. In Urfa, you should look for a hotel where the air conditioning works (you should check!) and rest from the tiring trip in a cool room; after a rest you can spend the evening roaming the streets of the ancient city.

History of the City

When the Hittites arrived here in the fourteenth century BC they found a flourishing farming city more than 1,000 years old. Among the great conquerors who ruled the city was Alexander the Great, who called it Edessa, after the Macedonian capital. The Hellenistic, Roman and Byzantine city of Edessa prospered as a religious and spiritual center. Its most important role was the introduction of Christianity to the area and the translation of religious and scientific works from Aramaic and Greek into Syrian, thereby enabling their dissemination in Syria and Anatolia.

The location of the city at the outskirts of the Byzantine Empire attracted neighboring rulers who tried to capture this religious center, and there were many battles in the city and its environs. The Arab forces conquered the city in 637 AD and controlled it for 400 years, until it was conquered in the early eleventh century by the Byzantines. Fifty-five years later it was again taken, this time by the Seljuks. The constant change of rulers continued, and in the late eleventh century a Crusader Latin colony was established in the city and its environs under the rule of Baldwin, who arrived during the First Crusade. The

Latin princedom did not last long, and in the mid-twelfth century the Seljuks again took the city, killing many Christians. The massacre and the humiliation in Edessa gave rise in Europe for a call for another Crusade, but despite the Christian threat, the Moslem rule in the city continued.

In the early seventeenth century, the city was conquered by the Ottomans, and they changed its name to Urfa. The title Şunlı, "praised," was given the city in honor of its endurance against the invasion of the French army, which tried to take control of the area in 1920 after the First World War. Like Urfa the Praised, the neighboring cities were also given impressive titles for their struggle against the French: "Fighting Antep" (*Gazi Antep*) and "Maraş the Hero" (*Kahraman Maraş*).

Tourist Services

The **tourist information office** in Şanlıurfa is located at 3 Asfalt Cad., Tel. 215-2467, near the intersection with Sarayönu Cad., near the *Turban Hotel*. The local post office is slightly south of the tourists information office.

Area code: 414

Accommodation and Dining

The hotels in Urfa are a pleasant surprise after Eastern Turkey. The *Harran*, Tel. 313-4743 and the *Turban*, Tel. 215-3530 are located in the city center and their standard is higher than that of most hotels in the east, the modern *Harran* is the better of the two. In a cheaper range we note the *Kapkalı* and the *Güven*, close to the tourist information office. Less expensive and simpler hotels can be found next to the good hotels, such as the *Ipek Palas* at 4 Köprubaşı Cad. As usual the good restaurants in the city are located in the good hotels, such as the excellent one in the *Harran*.

Sites to See

In the southern part of the city is ancient Urfa. It is best to start your tour with a climb to the **Citadel** (*Kale*) in the cooler morning hours. The citadel, which was rebuilt several times since the Hellenist period, as the central point of defense of the city, is open to the public from 8:30am-6:30pm. The pair of Corinthian columns in the citadel are known as Nimrod's Crown, as according to local tradition it was the biblical hunter who founded the city. From the citadel you can go down to Gölbaşı, location site of the famous **Pool of Abraham** (*Birket Ibrahim*).

The water in the Pool of Abraham and in the nearby Ayn-i-Zeliha pool come from a spring at the foot of the citadel. The enchanting Pool of Abraham is decorated with arches that are reflected in the water, and it is full of holy carp. There are many legends connecting the pool and the fish to Abraham. One of them tells us that Abraham was set alight by an Assyrian king, who was furious about Abraham's shattering of the gods and the idols. God created the pool here in order to put out the fire, and the fish guided him through the canals until he escaped the king.

Near the Pool of Abraham there are two interesting buildings: the seventh-century **Abdürahman Theological College**, north of the pool, and **Makham Al Kalil Theological College**, which was established in the early thirteenth century.

It is pleasant to have a short rest and lunch at one of the shady restaurants near the pool or in the nearby park. After the rest you can continue east to **Abraham's Cave** (Hz. Ibrahim), near Mevlidi Halil Mosque. According to local tradition, Abraham was born in this cave, and many Moslems come here on a pilgrimage. East of the cave are other, less interesting mosques, and the handsome Gümrük Khan, near the covered market (*Kapalı Çarsı*).

During your visit to the region, don't miss the market. This charming bazaar is perhaps the most colorful and least expensive in the country. You can wander slowing through the streets and stores for hours and drink a cup of tea offered by the store merchants. Don't forget your camera when you visit here. You are bound to return to the hotel laden with packages.

Harran

Abraham the patriarch lived in Harran some 4,000 years ago: "And Terah took Abram his son and Lot the son of Haran his son's son and Sarai his

The Pool of Abraham

daughter in law, his son Abram's wife; and they went forth with them from Ur of the Chaldees to go into the land of Canaan; and they came unto Haran, and dwelt there. And the days of Terah were two hundred and five years: and Terah died in Haran" (*Genesis* 11:31-32). People have lived in the ancient city consistently through many periods, and today, upon entering the town, it becomes clear that not much has changed since days bygone. The village, with its mud houses, resembles a beehive, with poor children running around asking the tourists for money and candy. Near the village there is also an eleventh-century citadel and the ruins of a large eighth-century mosque. What is unique here is the unspoilt atmosphere, that conveys the sense of the beginning of time, rather than any special sites or views.

Harran is located some 28 miles (45km) south of Urfa in the direction of the Syrian border. There is no regular public transportation; you can get here by private car or *dolmuş* from Urfa. Details are available from the tourist information office. After visiting Harran you have to return to Urfa to continue your trip.

Gaziantep

From Urfa there is a good road to Siverek, at the crossroads to Kâhta and Mount Nemrut (see "Mount Nemrut"). Another road continues west from Urfa to Gaziantep. This road goes over the Euphrates river at Birelik. The Hittite Carchemish, at the point where the Euphrates meets the Syrian border, was completely destroyed and is of interest only to archeologists, who need permission from the army to visit the area.

Gaziantep is a large industrial city on the way to the Mediterranean coast. It has some 1 million residents, and it is the country's sixth largest city. Gaziantep is famous as a center for bronze work and pistachio growing. Despite its glorious past (this is where the Hattian period, which preceded the Hittite Empire, began), not many sites are

Busy at work

left, with the exception of a sixth-century citadel built by Justinian. Most tourists passing through the city use its bus and train service and do not stay here overnight. Those who do, can try the well-established *Kaleli Hotel*, Tel. 230-9690 on the main Hürriyet Cad., opposite the post office. Other, simpler hotels, can be found on Atatürk Cad. at the corner of Hürriyet, such as the *Gap Güney*, Tel. 234-2101, and the *Çatuk Otel*, Tel. 231-9480. From Gaziantep you can continue directly to Adana or Antakya for a tour of the Hatay kingdom and Iskenderun Bay.

Area code: 342

The Hatay Kingdom – Iskenderun Bay

The Hatay kingdom, stretching from Adana to the Syrian border, is different in both geographic and human landscape from the other coastal areas of Turkey: east of Adana, the coastal plains between Alanya and Mersin turn to wooded hills, and the population clearly demonstrates strong Arab Syrian influence, with some French tones. Many of the inhabitants of the region speak Arabic as their native language.

This region was settled in ancient times, and it is here that the Seleucids set up the district capital, Antiochia. Hatay flourished under the rule of the Seleucids and the Romans, who followed them. Throughout history, the area changed hands many times, and at the end of World War I it was annexed to Syria as part of the French Mandate. Atatürk strove to restore Turkish rule in the border areas, and made many contacts with the Allies regarding this matter. In 1939, France returned the Hatay district to Turkey, apparently to assure its neutrality in World War II. To this day there are tensions between Turkey and Syria, which claims sovereignty over this land.

Antakya

After the death of Alexander the Great, most of Anatolia was controlled by Antigonus the One-Eyed. When Antigonus fell in the battle of Ephesus in 301 BC, Seleucus Nicator took control of the area, and in the year 300 he founded the city Antioch, named for his father Antiochus. Twenty years later, the city became the capital of the Seleucid Empire, which included Babylonia, Syria and Mesopotamia – today's Turkey, Syria, Iraq and Iran. As befitting the capital of such a tremendous kingdom, Antioch grew to an estimated population of some half a million – a huge number relative to other cities of that ancient period.

After the Roman conquest, in 64 AD, Antioch became the third most important city in the Western world, after Rome and Alexander, and it was here that the first Christian community outside of Palestine was founded, after Peter's journey to the city. It was also an important station on the Silk Route from the Far East to Europe. The

Romans and the Byzantines glorified the city with public buildings and churches, but after the many invasions and earthquakes, almost nothing of these remain. The city particularly suffered during the Mamaluke conquest in 1268. After World War I the French ruled the city for twenty years, until 1939. Today there are 200,000 residents in Antakya.

The city of Antakya is divided into two areas: the old city is located on the eastern bank of the **Asi River**, which is the ancient Orontes river. The city walls, 18 miles (30km) long, give you a sense of the former size of the city. Among the impressive ruins is a **Roman Bridge**, built by the Emperor Diocletian in the year 200 AD, which has now been replaced by a modern bridge, built in 1970, while the aqueduct was built by King Herod of Jerusalem. Most of the city's hotels, as well as the bus station, are located in the old city.

The new city is located on the western bank of the Asi. The central sight here is the **Hatay Museum**, located south of the bridge that connects the two parts of the city. The museum houses a collection of Roman mosaics considered to be one of the most beautiful in the world. Open daily 8:30am-noon and 1:30-5pm, closed Mon.

Area code: 326

The **tourist information office** is located at 41 Vali Urgen Alani Cad. the new city, Tel. 213-2636. The post office is opposite the new *Antakya Hotel*, Tel. 213-5860. The *Atahan Hotel*, which is less expensive, is at 28 Hürriyet Cad., Tel. 214-2140.

Near the bus station there is the usual selection of inexpensive pensions and hotels. The *Kent Hotel*, is located opposite the bridge, charges about $6 for a double room with a shower.

Outside of the city there are a number of historic sites. **Harbiye** is the location of the ancient **Daphne**, where a temple to Apollo, was built in honor of his meeting with the nymph Daphne. It was here that Mark Anthony and Cleopatra married, though today nothing remains but the gardens, laurel bushes and small waterfalls. The ancient cities Seleucia and Pieria were also completely destroyed.

Another interesting trip in the Antakya region is to

the **Church of St. Peter**, some 2 miles from the city. This church is thought to be the oldest in the world built outside of the Holy Land, although the building we see was built by the Crusaders in the thirteenth century. Every year on July 29, St. Peter's Day, a festive mass is held in the church. You can reach the church on foot from the city (it is a pleasant walk) or by taxi which will cost about $2.5 for a round trip.

From Antakya to Adana

From Antakya road E5 goes through the fertile Amik valley, with an artificial lake, Amik Gölü, in it center. This was created as a result of the dam built on the Asi River. Some 15 miles (25km) from Antakya, a side road leads to the **Bağras Citadel**. This impressive Byzantine citadel was built in the tenth century, but was captured by Crusaders in 1097.

Belen Pass (Belen Geçidi) is located 2,460ft. (750m) above sea level, further down road E5. This pass is known as "The Syrian Gates," as whoever controlled this point benefited from a considerable strategic advantage over the road to Syria. Today, it is a vacation town and health resort because of the water here, which is good for digestive and abdominal problems. In the friendly *Kamelya Hotel*, Tel. 03 there are 44 rooms and a restaurant. Some 6 miles (10km) southwest of Belen is a quiet mountain resort, Soğukoluk, where you will find the moderate-standard *Ayvazyan Hotel* and simpler hotels.

From Belen, the road goes on the coast as far as **Isk-enderun**. Alexander the Great founded this city after his famous victory over the Persians, in 333 BC, in the battle on the nearby Issos plains. As was customary at the time, Alexander named the city after himself, Alexandretta; Iskender is the Turkish name for Alexander the Great. Today, the city and the bay on which it lies are called Iskederun. Its former glory has passed, and today the city has 150,000 residents, a port and a few hotels. The best of these is the *Hataylı*, 2 Osman Gazi Cad., Tel. 613-1551. Another hotel, is the simple *Hitit* in Cumhuriyet Square. There is a **tourist information office** at 49 Atatürk Boulevard, Tel. 613-4286. A good restaurant on the same boulevard is the *Sara*.

Some twelve miles (20km) from Iskenderun is an impressive khan, built by Sulayman the Magnificent. In the past the khan was called Payas, and today its name is Yakacık. From here the road continues to the Issos plain and to **Toprakkale**. The Byzantine fortress, which was renovated and fortified by the Crusaders, is impressive today as well. 23 miles (37km) further down the road from Toprakkale is the **Castle of the Snake** (Yılan Kalesi), on the western bank of the Ceyhan River. The castle was built in the late twelfth century by Leo II, King of Armenia. According to an ancient Turkish legend, the king of the snakes lived, hence the name of the castle.

Dictionary

English	Turkish	English	Turkish
Good morning	Günaydın	Room	Oda
Good night	İyi geceler	Rest rooms	Tuvalet
Hello	Merhaba	Shower	Duş
Goodbye	Güle güle	Bath House	Hamam
Please	Lütfen		
Thank you	Teşekkür ederim	River	Nehir
		Mountain	Dağ
Much	Çok	Mountain range	Dağlar
What...?	Kaç	Port	Liman
When...?	Ne zaman...?	Mooring	İskele
Where...?	Nerede...?	Ferry	Feribot
Is there...?	Var mı?	Bus	Otobüs
How much does this cost?	Kaç para?	Bus Station	Otogar
		Train	Tren
I would like	İstiyorum	Train station	Gar/ İstasyon
I don't understand	Anlamıyorum	Airport	Hava alanı
There is no...	Yok	Ticket	Bilet
		Mini-bus	Dolmuş
		Taxi	Taksi
Yes	Evet		
No	Hayır	Restaurant	Lokanta/ Restoran
Big	Büyük		
Small	Küçük	Water	Su
New	Yeni	Bread	Ekmek
Old	Eski	Meat	Et
Open	Açik	Cheese	Peynir
Closed	Kapalı	Cold	Soğuk
Left	Sol	Hot	Sıcak
Right	Sağ		
Straight ahead	Doğru	1	Bir
		2	İki
Post Office	Postane	3	Üç
Boulevard	Bulvar	4	Dört
Street	Caddes	5	Beş
Lane	Sokak	6	Altı
Market	Çarşı Pazar	7	Yedi
		8	Sekiz
Mosque	Cami	9	Dokuz
Fortress	Hisar	10	On
Church	Kilise	14	On dört
Gate	Kapı	20	Yirmi
Hotel	Otel	26	Yirmi altı

30	*Otuz*	90	*Doksan*
40	*Kırk*	100	*Yüz*
50	*Elli*	133	*Yüz otuz üç*
60	*Altmış*	500	*Beş yüz*
70	*Yetmış*	1000	*Bin*
80	*Seksen*	One million	*Milyon*

INDEX

INDEX

INDEX

NOTES

NOTES

NOTES

NOTES

NOTES